RELUCTANT FAREWELL

RELUCTANT
FAREWELL

Andrew Nagorski

A NEW REPUBLIC BOOK
Holt, Rinehart and Winston / New York

Contents

Acknowledgments

Of the many people I feel indebted to for their friendship and help, three deserve special thanks. In Moscow, David Satter was unfailingly generous in sharing the fruits of his long Soviet experience when I arrived; he introduced me to his wide circle of contacts and offered his support at every opportunity. In Rome, Michael Mewshaw provided me with the encouragement, practical advice, and constructive criticism that enabled me to make the transition from writing articles to producing a book. And, wherever I was, my wife Christina was simply magnificent. Without her, I would have had neither the kinds of experiences I had in the Soviet Union nor the ability to convey them. Without her partnership, there quite literally would have been no book.

I also want to thank my editor, Steve Wasserman, for his invaluable suggestions. Finally, a special toast to my many good friends in Moscow who cannot be named here.

RELUCTANT FAREWELL

INTRODUCTION

A part of me reacted with complete calm, coolly recognizing the finality of it all, the impossibility of further discussion or appeal. Although no American reporter had been expelled from Moscow since 1977, the possibility of expulsion haunts every foreign correspondent in the Soviet Union. I had more reason than most to fear such action. But when I was summoned to the Foreign Ministry on August 2, 1982, and informed that I was being expelled for "impermissible methods of journalistic activities," my emotions rebelled. It could not be over so quickly, so abruptly; there had to be a way to fight back.

There wasn't.

When Christina and I, our three children, and our Russian collie boarded an Alitalia flight for Rome two and a half weeks later, we were physically and emotionally drained, our senses numbed by too many tearful farewells and the knowledge that this departure was unique. It was more a rupture than a parting—of friendships, of a part of our lives that was far more than just another foreign posting for *Newsweek*. I had an overwhelming sense of loss.

Moscow had been a personal odyssey for me. It began much earlier than our move from Hong Kong, my previous assignment, to Monterey, California, in January 1981 for an intensive three-month course in Russian. Russia had shaped the destiny of at least three generations of my family, and must have played a decisive role in the lives of earlier generations as well. Since my family comes from Poland, it could not have been otherwise.

At the beginning of the century when Poland was still partitioned among Russia, Prussia, and Austria, my grandfather presaged my own experience by angering the Russian authorities in Warsaw and St. Petersburg. He was expelled from the universities of both cities for involvement in Polish nationalist movements. (He was later expelled from Berlin University for the same reason, and he finally obtained his law degree in Heidelberg.) During the First World War, he was drafted into the Russian Army, as were other Poles living in the Russian-occupied part of Poland, and he served as a military prosecutor until Poland regained its independence in 1918. Between the wars, he became one of Warsaw's most prominent lawyers and participated in the codification of the country's legal system.

A short, distinguished gentleman, in the best sense of the word, my grandfather lived by a moral code that he could no more relax than he could his rigid sense of dress. The only proper way to come to breakfast was in a suit and tie, his chin and cheeks shaved smooth, his mustache neatly trimmed. After Marshal Josef Pilsudski's coup in 1926, he turned down an offer to become either the agriculture or justice minister; his misgivings about the new rulers were too great. An activist in the Peasant party, he was a defense counsel at the major political trial against leaders of the opposition parties in 1930. Along with other liberal and moderate Catholics, he denounced the increasing anti-Semitism of the far right.

My grandparents left Poland at the outbreak of the Second World War. They were joined by my father's new bride; her family had lived near Minsk until shortly after her birth in 1917, when the Bolshevik Revolution forced them and other Poles to abandon their farms and resettle in areas that would become part of the new Poland. My father, after fighting as a tank battalion officer in the doomed September 1939 defense against the German invaders, refused to turn himself in when Poland surrendered. He fled, most of the way on foot, to Hungary, and made his way to France to rejoin the Polish forces and his family there. When France fell, they escaped to England, where my father served in the Polish Army under British command and my grandfather was a member of the Polish government-in-exile. Stalin's imposition of a Communist regime in Warsaw at the end of the war meant that there was no going back. After I was born in Edinburgh in 1947, our entire family emigrated to the United States.

I grew up as an American instead of a Pole, but I always spoke Polish at home and early felt the tug of my roots. At seventeen, I visited Poland for the first time and a few years later, in 1968, during my senior year at college, I spent one semester as an exchange student at the University of Kraków, my father's alma mater. It was a politically explosive time. Soviet troops had just invaded Czechoslovakia and, within Poland itself, a protest movement of intellectuals and students had been brutally suppressed. I met and married Christina there. Like most of her fellow students, she had been swept up in those protests.

The fate of Poland and, therefore, its subservient relationship to the Soviet Union remained the passion of my grandfather's life even after he had settled in the United States. He was president of the Polish Institute of Arts and Sciences and founded the Polish Juridical Society in New York, and he wrote for émigré publications. The United States always remained a foreign land to him all during the quarter century he lived there until his death.

My father's career took a different turn. After starting off as a specialist in Eastern European and Soviet affairs, he broadened his range of interests to other foreign-policy areas and he plunged into American life in a determined effort to transform himself from the émigré outsider to the consummate insider. He served in the foreign service—which meant that I grew up in Cairo, Seoul, and Paris—and then entered the world of private foreign-policy institutions like the Council on Foreign Relations. In the process, his rather rigid view of the Soviet Union softened. He invested considerable hope in the emergence of détente in the 1970s and the expansion of East-West trade. My involvement in the anti-war movement of the 1960s initially provoked angry disputes between us, but later my father would also come to oppose American policies in Vietnam.

Curiously, despite our family history, I had few distinct impressions of the Soviet Union. I did not entertain many illusions about the nature of Soviet power and how that power was exercised in Eastern Europe, but Soviet society itself and as simple a matter as the appearance of its cities and its people were largely a mystery to me. I had no mental image; at most, I had a vague sense from travelers' tales that the Soviet Union must look like a grayer Poland. Although I had traveled to many parts of the world, I had never set foot there and, like many people in the West, assumed that it was somehow inaccessible. While studying in Poland, I had signed up for a Polish student trip to the Soviet Union, which would have given me a far different perspective than Western tourists get, but the complications of hastily arranging my marriage to Christina before my return to the United States forced me to cancel.

Despite the fact that I had always taken a natural interest in the Soviet Union, reading and studying what I could about developments there, I never felt that I really understood the dynamics of that society. Too much remained unexplained and distant. The first time that I became seriously interested in working abroad was when *Newsweek* was deciding to select a new Moscow bureau chief in 1976; I asked for the job but did not get it. Two years later, I did get a foreign assignment in Hong Kong. When Moscow was suggested as my next post, I eagerly agreed. Christina was swayed by my enthusiasm; later, as our transfer approached, she had serious misgivings.

That part of her reaction was typically Polish. Whatever their political inclinations, Polish relatives and friends were bewildered by my desire to go to Moscow. On a trip to Peking, I spent a long evening with a Polish correspondent who maintained that he would take any assignment anywhere, except Moscow. Christina's family in Poland was stunned: they could not comprehend someone voluntarily moving from the West to the Soviet Union. Even my father, who would certainly appreciate the career benefits of such a move, tried to dissuade me. When all other arguments failed, he maintained that there would be very few stories for me to cover there and that the assignment would amount to a form of journalistic exile. Intellectually, he could embrace a more flexible view of the Soviet Union; but when his son was suddenly about to go there, the visceral fear of Russia, ingrained in his family and in his country of origin, surfaced anew. There was an instinctive dread.

I was not completely immune from such feelings, but

my curiosity was stronger. I was also more nervous about whether the Soviets would grant me a visa. I could hardly have looked like an appealing prospect to a Soviet bureaucrat. Aside from my family background, I had written occasionally on Soviet affairs and had done some reporting for *Newsweek* in Eastern Europe in the mid-seventies. During my assignment in Hong Kong, I had reported on such events as the Soviet-backed Vietnamese invasion of Cambodia and the "boat people" exodus from Vietnam. A trip to Laos in 1980 produced a piece that provided a highly uncomplimentary picture of local attitudes toward Soviet advisers there, prompting an angry denunciation from Tass. Then, too, my application for a Soviet visa was submitted just when Soviet fears about events in Poland, the birth and blossoming of the independent trade union Solidarity, were escalating daily. That made me all the more eager to reach Moscow, but the idea that the authorities would accept a Polish-American correspondent at such a moment seemed doubtful.

During our intensive course in the Russian language at the Monterey Institute of International Studies in California, Christina and I frequently joked about the possibility that I might be refused a visa. But I could not really imagine that happening. The Monterey experience made me want to go more than ever. Despite her occasional jitters, Christina felt the same way. She had begun the grueling Russian lessons with me by noting the irony of her situation: in Poland, it had been a point of pride for her and her classmates that, during seven years of obligatory Russian instruction in school, they had learned as little of the language as possible. Now she was voluntarily studying Russian. But she quickly acquired a facility with the language and kept pulling my more halting efforts along.

Both the language training and, perhaps more important, the personalities of our Russian teachers and friends there nurtured the conviction that we were about to embark on a trip to a land and a people not totally foreign. But Russian and Polish are far apart in the Slavic languages, and much to my distress I soon learned that I could not get away with putting Polish endings on Russian verbs. There were other traps as well: a few words that sounded the same in both languages had different or exactly opposite meanings. *Zapomnieć*, the Polish word for forget, means to remember in Russian; *uroda* in Polish means beauty, while in Russian *urod* means a monster. During the first couple of lessons, I could not understand why our teachers kept telling us not to remember what they were explaining to us. But the roots of many words and grammatical concepts were similar. From the beginning, my accent in Russian was far more Polish than American, something that would later prove to be important in the Soviet Union.

Through our teachers and their friends, who were almost all recent émigrés, we caught our first glimpses of Soviet life and attitudes, and were exposed to their conflicting emotions about the country they had left behind. We also learned of the bitter quarrels that divided the émigré community. Vadim Kreydenkov, a gentle and perceptive teacher from Leningrad, was exceptionally adept at avoiding taking sides in the constant feuds and maintaining friendly relations with just about everyone. Others were far more doctrinaire, dividing into rival camps determined by their support or opposition to the controversial views on Russian nationalism espoused by Aleksandr Solzhenitsyn. Underlying this complex debate was the question of whether there was reason to hope that the Soviet Union could one day evolve from totalitarianism to a more open society.

Vladislav Krasnov, one of our teachers, firmly shared Solzhenitsyn's exalted belief in the "Russian spirit" that would one day prevail over a political system imposed, in his view, by outsiders. Sasha Sokholov, a gifted young novelist who also taught us, scornfully rejected that notion. "Solzhenitsyn has his fantasy of reviving czarist Russia and that the Communists, not the Russian people, are to blame for all that has happened. Others like [physicist Andrei] Sakharov believe in the possibility of establishing a liberal democracy," he said. "Many émigrés now believe neither. They believe that maybe the Russian people have the system they deserve and nothing can be done to change it. It is time to write Russia off."

Sasha's alienation from his family and from the Soviet system ran deep and were intertwined: his father had been a senior official of GRU, Soviet military intelligence. When Sasha married an Austrian woman and asked to emigrate, he staged a dramatic press conference in which he identified his father's profession. He had feared that his own parents might commit him to an insane asylum if he did not have the protection of international publicity. But Sasha's boyish face would suddenly light up when he talked of his life in Moscow and as a warden on a game preserve; he was nostalgic about his student days, the informal literary gatherings and the inevitable drinking bouts. In the evenings in California, he would still tune in to Radio Moscow's short-wave service.

Sasha was not alone in his intense, mixed emotions about the Soviet Union. Even the most outwardly cynical, embittered émigrés, who professed to see no hope whatsoever that anything could change for the better inside the Soviet Union, were swept up in the excitement of the "renewal" taking place in Poland. As we struggled over the intricacies of Russian grammar in Monterey, they wanted to know everything Christina and I could tell them about the Polish situation. They would endlessly speculate on the possible effect on the

Soviet Union. Kreydenkov was firmly convinced that the rise of Solidarity signaled "the beginning of the end" of the Soviet empire. He refused to predict its immediate collapse but, like a growing number of people in both East and West, he believed that the Polish crisis would one day be regarded as the first stage in the inevitable long-term disintegration of the Soviet system.

In their passionate friendships and bitter feuds, their sweeping predictions and alternate bouts of pessimism and optimism, the émigrés we met in Monterey touched something Slavic in both Christina and myself. In discussing the Soviet Union and Poland, we felt a kinship, whatever our disagreements or different backgrounds, an easy understanding that rendered personal reserve unnecessary. Their notion of friendship was different from that of their adopted country. Unlike Americans who seem to make friends easily but superficially, they were either more demanding or more rejecting; neutral ground was harder to find. With them, friendship sometimes seemed to be a form of politics. For Christina and, to a lesser extent, for me, that was familiar, reminiscent of our student days in Poland, where friends and enemies were also made more rapidly. We realized that in the Soviet Union itself friendships would probably be more difficult and dangerous to establish, but our Monterey experience gave us a sense of the potential that existed if we could break through the barriers imposed by the authorities. We were increasingly excited by that prospect, although uncertain as to just how great those barriers would prove to be.

In their different reactions to the United States the émigrés also offered clues to the prevailing attitudes in the country they had left behind. Lyona Khotin, a witty sociologist who joined our tutoring team in our final month in Monterey, was an unending source of observations and anecdotes about the assumptions, values, and behavior of his former friends and colleagues in Moscow and his fellow émigrés. "New émigrés are often surprised how people in the West generally obey the laws," he told us. "In the Soviet Union, everyone violates the law. Only dissidents try to live according to the law." Or, in explaining the workings of the pervasive and illegal Soviet underground economy, which provides countless millions with an additional income that makes life endurable, he would recall the famous Odessa curse: "May you live from one salary."

During a break in our Russian course, I traveled to the East Coast to talk with several of the Soviet specialists in universities and in Washington. As in California, the sense that Poland was only a symptom of underlying problems within the Soviet bloc was shared by many I spoke to. At Harvard, economist Marshall Goldman pointed to the Soviet Union's dismal agricultural performance and shaky industrial structure and concluded that his earlier more favorable assessments of the Soviet economy were wrong. "I have turned around and am now a pessimist," he said. Others talked about the uncertain leadership, the cost of the Afghanistan war, and the question of ethnic nationalities within the Soviet Union. Many agreed that such factors could contribute to future instability. Richard Pipes, at the time the Reagan administration's Soviet specialist on the National Security Council, told me: "I feel they are on the edge of some crisis."

I was fascinated, but the more such theories were bandied about the more I realized how little empirical evidence there was for all of this. Everyone was implicitly making assumptions about the attitudes of Soviet citizens, but were they correct? I did not know, and that made me all the more eager to go to the Soviet Union and to find out for myself. I returned to Monterey for my final month of classes—and to await the response to my visa request.

Our classes concluded at the end of April and still there was no word. We went to New York, where I was supposed to spend a week or two at *Newsweek* before going to Moscow. I kept hoping that the Soviet Foreign Ministry was merely sticking to its standard routine of keeping an applicant dangling until the last possible moment, but more pessimistic thoughts pestered my mind. On my application form, I had put May 20 as our planned day of arrival in Moscow; on the afternoon of May 19, with me suitably on edge, the Soviet embassy informed me that my visa had been approved and could be picked up. That little drama was deliberate, and I would see it played out with others later on. The purpose is to make the recipient of the visa feel inordinately grateful that he got it at all. Despite the irritation at the needless delays and the difficulties in arranging travel plans, this tactic usually works. I know it did in my case: I felt the elation of at last being permitted to see and report Soviet reality firsthand.

This book is about what I saw and experienced in the Soviet Union during the fourteen months I spent there before my expulsion in August 1982. It does not pretend to be an authoritative survey of the Soviet Union as a whole; other authors have done that far more systematically than I. While in the Soviet Union, I traveled extensively, deliberately seeking out ordinary Russians who would shed light on the issues that seemed most important to me and to Westerners in general trying to understand the nature of Soviet society in the 1980s. I reported as energetically as I could within Moscow itself, establishing as wide a spectrum of contacts as possible. There are obvious gaps in my experience, many geographical areas and subjects I never had the chance to explore since I was not allowed to complete my planned three-year stay in the Soviet Union.

I was fortunate, however, to arrive in Moscow at a time when certain internal and external forces were at work that demonstrated the strengths and weaknesses of the Soviet system more vividly than ever before, revealed the fundamental nature and uses of Soviet political power, and illustrated the problems the country will undoubtedly continue to face in the coming years. Those forces included the ongoing Polish crisis and its repercussions inside the Soviet Union, the leadership struggle that pitted Andropov against Chernenko, the growing failure of the economic and social structures to meet the basic needs of the Soviet people, and the war without end in Afghanistan.

My time in the Soviet Union, however brief, was a voyage of discovery that left as many questions unanswered as it answered, but it forged certain strong convictions about where we in the West have been most often wrong in our understanding and treatment of the Soviet state. I sought to be as honest as possible in discussing American weaknesses and misconceptions as I have been in presenting Soviet reality itself. This required some blunt words about the failings of my own profession because I felt that this issue could not be sidestepped. I have deliberately not used many names when discussing this issue; my purpose is not to single out any individual for criticism but to indicate a broader problem that the American media have not been willing to face. For a different reason—the protection of the many Soviet citizens I knew or simply talked to—I have had to respect the tacit agreement that most of them would remain anonymous when represented or quoted in print. As a matter of convenience, I have given some of them fictional first names in this book.

Throughout my stay in the Soviet Union, I always had a sense that perhaps nothing could be taken for granted, whether about larger issues such as the fate of the Polish experiment and the future of the Soviet leadership, or about my own stay in Moscow. Looking back, I realize that a strong subconscious suspicion that I was operating on borrowed time in the Soviet Union motivated me to try to get the most I could out of my experience as quickly as possible. From the beginning, I approached my assignment with the conviction that I would exercise my rights fully as a journalist as spelled out in the 1975 Helsinki Accords, which the Soviet Union had signed. While I would follow prescribed procedures and not try to sidestep any legal requirements, I saw no reason to assume that certain subjects, even the most delicate ones, were off-limits or that a reporter in the Soviet Union should not try to investigate stories there as vigorously as he would anywhere else. I knew that this attitude might anger the authorities. However, I could not allow that possibility to influence me; I was not about to engage in self-censorship. Otherwise, what was the purpose of taking the Moscow assignment?

And I was taking it on. A few days after five Soviet visas were issued to the Nagorski family, we were on Aeroflot Flight 242 from London to Moscow.

1

SUMMER

I may not have known what to expect from Moscow, but I thought I knew what not to expect: color, warmth, vivacity. I discovered all three shortly after our arrival in late May 1981.

We did have the advantage of arriving at the most attractive time of year. The trees had just blossomed, offering brief-lived splashes of green that softened the harsh and ponderous concrete and brick buildings that tend to darken Moscow's cityscape. Summer came early, with unusually comfortable June weather that turned into a prolonged heat wave in July and August. But the warmth was also distinctly human: we rapidly began making Russian friends, who surprised us with the openness of their reception, while other Russians we saw betrayed hints of independent thought where we least anticipated it.

The heat was withering in crowded apartments and offices; the buses and the subways reeked with the odor of human sweat mixed with cheap brands of eau de cologne that serve as the only local deodorant. At ice cream stands, women in white smocks did a brisk business selling *eskimos*—the Soviet equivalent of the Good Humor bar on a stick. People fled to grass, sand, and water, wherever they could find them. In the center of Moscow, Gorky Park provided a large expanse of shady paths, amusement-park rides, and rowboats on a small pond. The rolling Lenin Hills below Moscow University provided a quieter space for sunbathers, picnickers, and the occasional jogger. At Serebryany Bor (the Silver Forest), an island in the Moscow River connected to the center by local bus lines, and along the river's narrow sandy beaches and embankments farther out of the city, the crowds grew every weekend.

The mix of dress and behavior spanned continents and cultures. Teenagers sported Levi's and Wranglers, University of Michigan and Dallas Cowboys T-shirts, and played Abba tapes on their portable cassette recorders ("Money, Money, Money" seemed the summer favorite). Women casually stripped down to their panties and bras as their families sprawled out on blankets for a day in the sun. As they dug in the sand little boys wore white paper hats at the insistence of mothers convinced that the short season of strong sunlight would otherwise induce sunstroke or some other acute medical damage.

At an embankment that had to be reached by a perilous footbridge of ropes and flimsy boards, children would swing off a rope hooked over a large tree branch overhanging the river's edge and drop into the murky but clean water below. Their parents would watch from the shore—a father occasionally easing himself into the water to paddle around for a few minutes with his frolicking children. The scene evoked images of a simpler time in America, more out of the paintings of Norman Rockwell than of the high-tech 1980s. It quickly became one of our favorite spots.

In the city itself, the foliage could not completely hide the oppressive architecture, such stolid wedding-cake structures as the Foreign Ministry and Moscow University and the shoddy new apartment complexes set on otherwise desolate landscapes on the periphery. Main arteries like Kutuzovsky Prospekt, where we lived in the largest foreigners' compound, and the inner road that encircled the core of the city attempted to project an image of modernity, broadened to accommodate several lanes of traffic and outfitted with pedestrian underpasses. Sometimes I despaired of ever learning my way around the labyrinth of bleak avenues and monotonous buildings that revealed so few traces of individuality. The problem was made worse by the absence of readable street signs, the result perhaps of a policy aimed at frustrating foreign spies. Real spies were unlikely to be deterred by such an inconvenience, but it certainly made life complicated for the rest of us. Accurate and complete maps were also impossible to find. The most highly prized possession of even the officially assigned Russian drivers of foreign diplomats, journalists, and businessmen was the CIA-produced *Moscow Guide to Streets, Metro Stations, Public Buildings, Embassies, Hotels, Theaters.*

Other first impressions also strengthened rather than weakened the bundle of clichés about Soviet society that are a part of the baggage brought by almost every Western visitor. There was the omnipotent traffic cop, who needed only to incline his white baton slightly in the direction of a passing car to have the driver immediately pull over, get out, and contritely trudge up, documents in hand, often unaware of what his offense was but nonetheless ready for punishment. There were the special center lanes on main streets reserved for Zils and Chaikas, the limousines used to ferry top Communist Party leaders to and from the Kremlin. Long before such a vehicle approached, policemen at

16

every intersection would efficiently stop all traffic until the official roared by. Above all, there was the sense that Soviet society operated on the cardinal principle that if you have power, you flaunt it as blatantly as possible; any other behavior was a sign of weakness. Thus the leaders' black Zils and Chaikas force all less important vehicles off the road. Thus, the traffic cop, after saluting the oblivious official in the limousine, turns to the next motorist and often displays his authority by fining him or making him pay a bribe to avoid an official offense. So the driver of a large Volga will never yield to a small Soviet Fiat and the driver of the Fiat will never yield to a pedestrian, who is the most defenseless of all. Everyone seems to accept this as perfectly normal.

Uniforms abounded, not just of policemen but of the military. Officers, briefcases in hand, briskly walked to jobs in government ministries; from the back of army trucks waiting at red lights, young recruits, fresh from the countryside, could often be seen as they gawked at the capital, sometimes grimly, sometimes laughing and pointing to a pretty girl or a foreign car. A remarkable number of their faces bore Asiatic features, evidence of the demographic shifts in the Soviet population: the high birthrates in Central Asia and the declining birthrates among the European nationalities. All this is such a common sight that one of the first questions asked by Soviet émigrés arriving in Western cities is "Where are the soldiers?" They are perplexed by the absence of uniforms.

But then just as the clichés of Soviet life seemed to be confirmed, they would be confounded. The first lectures I attended at the Znaniye (Knowledge) Society, which were open to the public and intended to promulgate the party line, produced a picture of less submissiveness and acceptance to established authority than I had expected. The theme for the evening was "Man and the Law" sponsored by a monthly magazine with the same name. T. A. Kopylova, a woman of about forty, introduced as a "special correspondent," began the evening with a talk about widespread adolescent crime, which she blamed on conflicts in the home and the country's increasingly high divorce and alcoholism rates. She spoke about chronic alcoholism among teenage girls, observing that many girls began drinking at age twelve or thirteen. Her delivery was authoritative—and blunt.

While she was concerned with alcoholism, she maintained that many of the most serious crimes were committed by perfectly sober adolescents. She described the case of two sisters, fifteen and eighteen, who fell heavily into debt because of their love of the high life; they murdered a rich student so that they could take his jeans and other valuables. (Jeans on the black market can cost as much as $300, more than a month's salary for the average worker.) She blamed parental neglect for such behavior.

Kopylova questioned the mother of another fifteen-year-old girl involved in a murder, who shrugged off her daughter's activities with the response: "She was old enough to do what she wanted." The girl in question had seven pairs of jeans, Kopylova said. Her parents had bought her only one pair, but they never asked where she obtained the rest. Teachers were equally negligent, refusing to flunk many students in an effort to boost their proportion of passed students. "Many girls of fourteen can't read well," Kopylova concluded. "They watch TV and spend time in restaurants and bars with older men."

Dressed in a black leather jacket and a blue shirt and tie, police colonel V. N. Vinogrodov followed with a discussion of how investigators solve murder cases. He was both less specific and less sweeping than Kopylova, describing "the psychological duel" between the police and criminals. But he, too, spoke of violent crime as a commonplace in Soviet society, which is a far cry from the official line. And he described a uniquely Soviet crime: theft from communal apartments. About 20 percent of Moscow's 8 million inhabitants live in communal apartments; typically, a four-bedroom apartment houses four families, each squeezed into a single bedroom with everyone sharing the kitchen and bathroom. One burglar, who specialized in such dwellings, would walk in with a suitcase when several people were at home. He would either empty the hallway of coats and boots once the inhabitants went back into their rooms, seeing that the visitor was not for them, or enter any room that was empty, close the door, and proceed to fill up his suitcase.

Just as I was concluding that I was a witness to a remarkable evening, almost devoid of ideology and propaganda, the next speaker proved me wrong. *Man and the Law* editor G. V. Ryzhikov launched into a vigorous speech about international terrorism intended to refute Western charges that Moscow supported terrorist movements. The real contemporary terrorists were "Zionists," Ryzhikov maintained, including "that Zionist Gestapo" the Jewish Defense League, backed by Washington. The West had lost its colonies and the days of cheap oil and other natural resources were over, he declared. That had prompted the Western powers to fund terrorists who could destabilize Third World countries with the aim of taking them over again. The recent assassination attempt on President Reagan provided a good example of American terrorism at work: the would-be assassin was a friend of Bush's family; the vice-president along with former president Jimmy Carter were members of the Trilateral Commission; Carter had been defeated by Reagan, and Bush would become president if Reagan were killed. The connections were obvious.

How much of this the audience believed was hard to know. Composed of party activists who might be picking

up pointers for their own lectures and of the simply curious, they appeared impassive during Ryzhikov's tirade. But
their questions afterward, which were written on slips of
paper and passed up to the panel, suggested considerable
skepticism.

"Why isn't a serious battle conducted against anti-
Semitism?" one listener asked Ryzhikov, who had just spun
out the Zionist-imperialist theme.

"In our country, anti-Semitism has not existed for a long
time," he replied. "I have heard the word *katsap* [a derog-
atory term for Russians] used in Lithuania, but that doesn't
mean I consider those people anti-Russian." Even in the
West, he seemed to feel that anti-Semitism was a canard.
He described a recent synagogue bombing in Paris as an
attempt to embarrass then-president Giscard d'Estaing who,
he claimed, had tried "to stand up to the Zionists."

Colonel Vinogrodov was asked why the police did not
do something to eliminate prostitution in Moscow, since an
evening walk down Gorky Street suffices to demonstrate the
dimensions of the problem. He grinned and tugged at the
lapels of his leather jacket. "I haven't noticed this. When I
see a young woman walking in the evening I don't assume
she is a prostitute." The audience tittered.

It was a pattern I would see at other lectures. While the
political message would usually be more heavy-handed and
open discussions of sensitive issues such as crime rarer, members of the audience would still persist in asking embarrassing questions. "How does one explain the economic
development of Japan, since it lacks natural resources?"
someone asked at an evening devoted to Asian affairs. The
lecturer strained to produce the acceptable ideological explanation (exploitation of the work force, low wages), and
on such occasions no one expected anything more. However,
the anonymous questioner must have felt the satisfaction of

having asked something difficult and provocative, which others could think about and answer for themselves. No one would have asked such a question if they had to get up and speak, but it was precisely to avoid embarrassing silences after the lectures that questions were submitted in writing at most meetings. That method had other advantages as well: it offered party activists tips on how to handle difficult questions, and provided a chance for the panel to set aside quietly any query deemed too inflammatory.

In private, Russians were eager to volunteer their own answers to almost any question. Christina and I struck up new acquaintances faster than we had anticipated. Several Russian émigrés in California had asked us to pass along small parcels of clothing for their families and friends, and we contacted them upon arrival. Arrangements were often intricate, depending on the anxiety of the person contacted. In many cases, they had never met a foreigner before and they had jobs that could be jeopardized by such an encounter.

We would call, always from a pay phone instead of our own tapped lines. I had learned early to keep a good supply of 2-kopeck coins needed for pay phones in my pocket at all times. A few people had no qualms about seeing us openly; others would designate neutral ground for a quick encounter that they hoped to keep unobserved. Sometimes that meant a seemingly casual meeting in a park, on the street, or in a subway station; sometimes it meant stepping into a car that pulled up for a moment at a designated corner. I agreed to whatever arrangements the person felt were necessary, since the risk was his and he knew best how to minimize it. I followed the same principle with everyone I met: they set the ground rules for our encounters, indicating the degree of caution they wished to maintain.

With a number of people, I had only one contact. They

were grateful, but they were not about to complicate their lives by striking up a personal relationship with an American correspondent. Others were eager to get to know us, and we were only too happy to oblige. We made additional early acquaintances through the help of correspondents like David Satter of the *Financial Times* and Kevin Klose of *The Washington Post*, who had already spent several years in Moscow. Kevin, who was just winding up his tour when we arrived, graciously introduced us to several people, as did David until his own departure several months later. People we met introduced us to others, and our circle of acquaintances began to widen.

It also produced surprises. There was nothing astonishing about hearing a well-known dissident or refusenik, a Jew who has applied to emigrate but has been refused permission, berate the system for its brute inequities. However, it was a jolt to meet people who were quite successful by Soviet standards and who were similarly bitter and cynical.

Take Misha, a tall, stooped social scientist in his late fifties, with perpetually disheveled hair and a generally disoriented appearance that masked a sharp, penetrating mind. Because he held an important position and was widely respected in his field, he was one of those who took elaborate precautions to conceal our meetings from the authorities. Even when we were alone, he would switch on the radio or television, cranking up the volume in order to thwart any possible listening devices. But once he had instructed me on the joys of biting into a large pickle or salted bread after downing a shot of icy vodka, he would spin out iconoclastic theories on any contemporary Soviet subject.

At our first encounter, he ranged over the issues of shortages, the arms race, and the nature of the relationship between the leadership and the people. The common thread was alcoholism. "We can't pay for a new arms race, but the

Soviet people are used to suffering. They don't need food, only give them vodka and they will endure anything," he insisted.

"But what about the tremendous economic losses caused by heavy alcoholism?" I asked.

He waved his hand in a dismissive gesture and swept his hair back, a futile effort that only added to its disarray. "The government talks about an anti-alcoholism campaign, but no one wants to fight alcoholism here. A drunk person is better for the economy—he is drunk five days a week but for two days he works hard because he's making up for the other lost time. Other people don't work at all."

The most important asset of a drunk, Misha continued, is that he doesn't complain, at least not about any larger issues. In his view, that was also the dominant consideration in the structuring of the economy in a manner that ensured continual shortages. "If you had free enterprise in agriculture, this country would start producing at a fantastic rate— but in five years people would start asking about political freedom." He shook his finger at me, making sure his warning was understood. "Don't ever make the mistake of thinking the leadership is composed of a bunch of idiots. They know very well what they are doing."

He anticipated my next question about the degree of popular acceptance of such policies before I could ask it. "If there is less to eat, people will eat less. If the army is told to shoot Afghans or Poles, they will do that, too."

Like so many people I would come to know and see frequently during my stay in Moscow, Misha naturally assumed the role of my teacher about Soviet society, believing I would swallow whole his sweeping conclusions. I had no intention of doing that: I knew no single person could possibly possess the final word on Soviet reality. Still, Misha's iconoclasm raised new questions: Was his disparaging view of his own people justified? How many others shared his cynicism about the nature of the Soviet system? Even if there were many, did they matter? I had no answers yet.

Other people I met echoed Misha's pessimism. Pyotr, a Jewish writer from Leningrad, took me out for a long walk along the Moscow River, where he talked despairingly of the stagnation of the seemingly endless Brezhnev era. "Brezhnev has led us into a swamp where nothing moves. People may not really accept this, but they don't know how to express their disapproval. The Russians are the least revolutionary nationality in the world. The Revolution could only happen here because of the war and the fact that the Bolsheviks would stop at nothing," he said. We were turning up Kutuzovsky Prospekt, where an army officer in boots and baggy pants, his florid face straining with the effort, was running to catch a bus. Pyotr glanced at him and added, "The Russians are largely a rural people who are used to obeying."

Pyotr described a recent interrogation by the KGB following a search of his apartment that had revealed nothing incriminating. It was more a warning than a guarantee against future harassment, but he was reluctant to take the hint that he might be better off applying to emigrate. He smiled wanly. "My mother is old, and I have lost my urge to travel with middle age." That reluctance was not based on any optimism that Brezhnev's approaching death would lead to more liberal policies. "People ask who will come after Brezhnev," he said. "Another Brezhnev. The way people rise to the top here precludes anyone radically different from ever emerging."

A month later, Pyotr told me he had applied to emigrate. The KGB had summoned him again, warning that failure to do so would mean trouble.

Nowhere was the atmosphere freer than in the privacy

of Russian homes, where we began to be invited to dinners. The normal fare was heavy on salads or pastes made of cheese, eggs, cucumbers, and an occasional sausage mixed with sour cream, mayonnaise, vinegar, mustard, and herbs. This was the substitute for unobtainable cold cuts, which would have been the preferred evening meal, and allowed for disguising the poor quality of whatever sausage might have been bought. It also had the virtue of stretching the sausage's usefulness to the limit. Desserts were store-bought sweet cakes; homemade cakes were rare because both cream and yeast were in short supply. But the conversation, not the cuisine, was important. People recited poetry, argued, and denounced anyone and everything, shedding the inhibitions they carried like a shield in less private settings.

But this was only possible among small circles of friends who knew each other intimately. Christina and I soon learned that, while we could enter some of those circles, any attempt to mix them was an invitation to social disaster. When we asked Russians over for dinner who we thought would be compatible but had not previously met, the evening was invariably stiff and awkward. The distrust and suspicion were almost palpable. Afterward, several of the guests explained that we were foolish to have friends like the others at the party, warning that they could not be trusted: "They may not want to but they can get you in trouble. If they are squeezed by the KGB, who knows what they will say?" The other explanation was frankly elitist. One writer had been miffed by the presence of someone he considered beneath his stature. "As a correspondent in Moscow, you can have access to the best writers and artists here," he told me. "Why associate with a mediocre writer like him? As a correspondent, you are like a general. You should be with colonels." In other words, stick only with him and his circle. We learned our lesson and from then on avoided bringing our different groups of friends together. Everywhere in Soviet society, even among dissidents, a pecking order was rigidly followed.

My introduction to the theater was the Taganka, Moscow's avant-garde showcase. Tickets could be obtained only through "connections," and before each performance people in the subway stop across the street and outside the entrance pleaded to buy an extra seat. One of my first trips there was to attend a dress rehearsal for a tribute to Vladimir Vysotsky, a balladeer whose bittersweet lyrics discomforted the authorities and made him a national folk hero. When he died at the age of forty-two in July 1980, his funeral was attended by tens of thousands of ordinary citizens. I had first begun to apprehend the extent of the Vysotsky phenomenon from a friend who boasted he had found the perfect bribe for any traffic cop. Whenever he was pulled over or needed to park illegally, he slipped a picture of Vysotsky to the policeman; it worked every time. Similarly, a limited edition of Vysotsky's ballads and poems, which appeared on sale one afternoon only at the hard-currency bookstore for foreigners, was instantly sold out; anyone with Russian friends knew that this was a priceless gift or bribe. Now, a year after Vysotsky's death, Taganka director Yuri Lyubimov wanted to stage a special production about his former friend's life— but the authorities had agreed to allow only one formal performance. Thus, the dress rehearsals were the hottest ticket in town.

I had one, but I did not get in that day. The crowd of ticket-holders and those hoping to force their way in became so massive and unruly that I was trapped between the outer and inner doors of the theater as everyone pushed and shoved. Before I could fight my way to the inner door, the theater was forced to bolt it closed to prevent a riot. On the day of the formal performance, to which I was lucky enough to receive another ticket from a well-placed friend, the police had taken the precaution of sealing off the entire square outside the theater, only allowing ticket-holders to approach it.

Lyubimov's productions were impassioned to the point of bordering on melodrama, but they won the audience every time. One of my early favorites was *House on the Embankment*, based on the novel by Yuri Trifonov about the betrayal of neighbor by neighbor during the Stalinist era. The purges themselves were never specifically mentioned in the play, but they formed a backdrop that everyone recognized. I emerged from the theater stunned by the audacity of the performance and the electrifying response it elicited from the audience.

Igor agreed with my enthusiasm about the performance but simultaneously brought me back down to earth. An artist who has enjoyed great success and is frequently exhibited both in the Soviet Union and abroad, he was used to meeting foreigners in an official capacity and therefore was rarely frank with them. Most people thought he was happy with the recognition, money, and position he had achieved. He wore fashionably casual Western clothes and lived with his wife Nadia in a comfortable apartment in the heart of Moscow, stocked with Western music and posters from exhibits in London and Paris. We began to meet privately and soon the friendship that developed between Nadia and Christina put our relationship on a different footing. Discussions, like the one we had after I had seen *House on the Embankment*, bore no resemblance to the ones Igor normally had with foreigners.

"Today everything is freer," Igor said, alluding to the period portrayed by the play, "but the fact is that if the right conditions existed the same things would happen again. People would act no differently." He described his father's disappearance in Siberia at the end of the Second World

War after he returned from a German POW camp. Along with the Soviet citizens who served in the German Army, the Soviet POWs who found themselves in the hands of the Allies at the end of the war were forcibly repatriated. Between 1944 and 1947, the West sent back more than 2 million men to the Soviet Union. Stalin, who was convinced that anyone who had been captured was a traitor and a spy, dispatched them to the Gulag. Many, like Igor's father, never returned. Igor pointed out what hurt him the most. "Even now, one can't tell stories like this about your own family and be sure that it is safe to do so."

Christina and I had been in Moscow less than two months. In a letter sent through the diplomatic channel available to American correspondents, my parents asked if we did not find our personal life oppressive in Moscow. It was a question I could have anticipated but had not even thought about in those first hectic weeks. Thanks to the Russians we had met, the answer was different from what my parents expected. I had never felt as personally caught up in an assignment or as fascinated by the kaleidoscope of first impressions.

"This is Anna Mikhailovna from UPDK. I am to be your children's Russian teacher."

"Glad to hear from you. I'm anxious for my daughters to start taking lessons because they will probably be enrolling in a Russian school in September. When can you start?"

"I am afraid that I will be leaving Moscow shortly for my holiday, so we cannot begin until after the summer."

"Well then, I suppose they'll need to start with another teacher in July and August and they can continue with you once you return."

"No teachers will be available. You know this is the normal vacation time for everybody."

"But surely there must be someone in Moscow who can tutor them in the summer?"

"No, there isn't anyone. As I said, all of our teachers go on holiday in this period."

"My whole point is that my children need tutoring in Russian before school starts. If you can't provide anyone, we'll have to make other arrangements. I can't believe that there is not a single person in Moscow capable of teaching my children Russian over the summer."

"I have told you no one from UPDK is available, and it is against the law for you to hire anyone who does not work for UPDK."

The Administration for Servicing the Diplomatic Corps, or UPDK, is a government agency whose main task is to surround foreign residents with its choice of Russian employees—translators, drivers, maids, piano teachers, maintenance workers, and the like. As with our Russian teacher, a foreigner is not allowed to hire any Russian who is not sent by UPDK, and so we never did get a teacher that summer. A foreigner does not have to accept the candidate for a job sent to him by the agency, but there is no guarantee that another prospective employee will be sent soon or that the next candidate will be any better. If a foreigner fires a UPDK employee, there is a good chance that it will take a few months before anyone new is offered as a replacement.

This means that diplomats and correspondents in Moscow employ Russians whose first loyalty lies elsewhere: they remain UPDK employees, although they are paid from a foreigner's payroll. How many of these people also work for the KGB is not known. Some certainly do, but the others know that they must report on their employers whenever required; the obligation goes with the job.

Many UPDK employees do develop a genuine loyalty to their foreign employers and a personal rapport, but if they are to keep their jobs they must be careful never to make it appear that they have lost sight of their first loyalty. The UPDK can and does fire people working for foreigners, usually in cases where it believes that too close a relationship has developed between the Russian and the foreigner. However, most of the time an experienced employee will instinctively know just how far he can go, and it is in UPDK's interest to keep foreigners generally satisfied with the performance of their workers.

The *Newsweek* office I inherited came with two Russians, a driver and a translator, and an apartment with a maid. Pavel, the driver, was a virtuoso fixer, always knowing where to find a plumber or electrician, how to get tickets for the circus, or how to finesse the complex postal regulations so that we could send parcels to Christina's family in Poland. He would leave a bottle of vodka here, a box of chocolates there, and bureaucracy would be banished. By watching him operate, I learned my first lesson in the Byzantine workings of the Soviet economy. He was also a warm human being, whose death from a heart attack nearly a year after our arrival touched us all deeply.

Tamara, our maid, had helped bring up several *Newsweek* children and she immediately embraced Adam, our youngest who was a year and a half old when we went to Moscow. She soon had him responding to her in babytalk that was a loose mixture of the Polish Adam already knew and the Russian he was hearing from her.

Dima, the office translator, was the only one of the three who took a distinctly lackadaisical attitude toward the job. Since I found that I needed his services only occasionally to draft official letters in Russian and to provide me with direct translations for quotations of the Soviet press, he busied himself mostly with his own reading.

Good or bad, hardworking or lazy, friendly or indifferent, the Russian employees from UPDK contribute to the cocoon in which most foreigners live in Moscow. Their very presence was an inhibiting factor for other Russians considering a visit to our home or office. With a few exceptions, we only had Russians over in the evening or on weekends when Tamara was not working. I would generally ask those Russians who were bold enough to come to my office to visit during Dima's regular late lunch break, and I would make sure that Pavel was out on an errand during that time. Such visitors had no illusions that our contact would go unnoticed. They knew that my apartment and office were bugged and the phones were tapped; that was true for all correspondents. But knowing that a government employee was in the next room dramatically increased their discomfort.

The authorities did everything to encourage as cloistered a life for foreigners as possible. Housing was assigned: in our case, the *Newsweek* correspondent, no matter what the size of the family, had occupied the same small two-bedroom apartment in the largest foreigners' compound on Kutuzovsky Prospekt for more than a decade. By converting the dining room into a third bedroom, we lived there quite comfortably. From the outside, the complex—which houses several thousand diplomats and journalists of many nationalities—looked like a well-protected low-income housing project, except for the collection of posh cars in the parking lot. The entrances to the three enormous brick buildings consisted of crumbling concrete steps and dark passageways to antiquated, erratic elevators; the common playground featured rusty, broken slides and seesaws. Every June, for the entire month, the hot water was turned off, it was said, "to clean the pipes."

But those were minor inconveniences, and we appreciated the relative luxury of our existence. What was more irritating were the police guards stationed at a booth at the single driveway entrance to the compound and at another booth located in the middle of the parking lot. Ostensibly those guards were for the protection of the residents, but their real function was to check and prevent Russians from entering on their own. When we had guests, we would either drive or escort them in; otherwise, they would be stopped, and sometimes subjected to a lecture. After one of our neighbors, UPI correspondent Walter Wisniewski, had been attacked in *Sovetsky Sport* for a retrospective piece he had written about the Moscow Olympics, a Russian friend coming to visit him was questioned by the guard, who asked why he was visiting such "an anti-Soviet" person: "Didn't you see what they wrote about him?"

The guards were good at distinguishing foreigners from Russians, but sometimes they would make mistakes. Occasionally, a Russian guest, especially if he was dressed in Western clothes and strode purposefully by, would not be stopped. Just after we arrived, Christina and I met in front of another housing compound and hesitantly went in because we were not sure if we were at the right address. A guard, who had been watching us for some time, came rushing up to challenge us as soon as we stepped into the compound. *"Kuda vy?"* he demanded, using the sharp commandlike form of the question "Where are you going?" His manners improved when he realized we were foreigners, but it was not hard to imagine the chilling effect of such an encounter on a Russian trying to visit a foreigner for the first time.

One group of Russians had no problem contacting the residents of our housing compound and other foreign buildings. In the summer months when wives and children of foreign diplomats and correspondents often left their husbands behind and traveled home for visits, young women with long wavy hair, outfitted in short skirts and high heels, stood on the sidewalks and on Kutuzovsky Prospekt propositioning any foreign-looking driver who slowed down. When we returned home in the late evening, they would try to wave us down or approach our car as we slowed for the turn into our driveway, only backing off when they spotted Christina. Normally, any pedestrian stepping out on Kutuzovsky would be sternly reprimanded by a policeman because everyone was supposed to use underpasses to cross the broad avenue. But the young ladies of the night seemed to have no problems with the police and the agents in and around our compound. I would see them sitting in a police car a couple of blocks away having a smoke and a friendly chat. They, too, were in the service of the state, at the very least earning hard currency and, when necessary, providing blackmail opportunities for the authorities.

On only one occasion did Christina and I witness a prostitute in trouble. Driving home after a dinner with Russian friends, we were startled to see a woman in the middle of Kutuzovsky shouting angrily at a tipsy young man trying to cajole her into going with him. When she continued to refuse, he clumsily grabbed her by the arm and began pulling her. She yanked herself free and fled in disgust, letting loose a stream of abuse. Apparently, the problem was not that the man had had too much to drink; it was that he was Russian. The women who appeared on those summer evenings in front of our housing compound were for foreigners only; ordinary Russians had to settle for a lower class of prostitute.

Even among the prostitutes who were allowed to solicit foreigners, a hierarchy existed. The women outside our compound were often attractive and reasonably stylish, but they also tended to have the hardened look of veterans of their trade the world over. The true elite never waited on street corners. Instead, they sipped drinks at the bar in the lobby of the Mezhdunarodnaya (International) Hotel, a brand-new skyscraper complete with glass elevators that is part of the convention center constructed by American businessman Armand Hammer. These were the best of the lot, truly striking women who never wore a stitch of anything Russian, from their Finnish underwear to their Italian shoes. My informant on this group was Christina, who discovered that the beauty parlor she went to on Gorky Street was also the favorite of the women from the Mezhdunarodnaya. They would come in for manicures and pedicures, bringing their own Western nail polish and showing off their gifts from their customers. While Christina was there, one woman had all the staff and customers enthralled by a set of colorful pillowcases and sheets that looked like it could have come straight from Bloomingdale's. For the hairdressers and manicurists, the reward was not extra pay but an occasional foreign gift—a far more valuable bonus.

That summer I received a phone call from a woman asking for one of my predecessors. "He left many years ago," I said.

"That's too bad, we were such good friends." She paused and her voice grew huskier. "Perhaps we could meet. I would like that very much."

"Thank you, but unfortunately I have no time."

"That's too bad, really too bad. I would like so much to meet you."

I learned from other correspondents that such phone calls were not an infrequent occurrence, and they would take place as soon as someone's wife would leave town. When a correspondent was on a trip, his wife sometimes would be called by a man offering a flimsy excuse to arrange an encounter. The assumption seemed to be that bait should be cast in various directions to see who might bite.

But most of the authorities' energies were focused on routine surveillance rather than entrapment, and the monitoring of foreigners' movements in Moscow was less obtrusive than generally believed for the simple reason that it was efficiently organized. The bugs and phone taps were annoying because they forced us to wait until we were outside before engaging in certain conversations. It was not a question of censoring one's own views: the Soviet authorities could hardly convict a foreigner of anti-Soviet slander for curses uttered in his kitchen or bedroom. But any mention of Russian friends, of conversations with them or plans to get together with those who would be afraid to visit us in our goldfish bowl, had to take place elsewhere. For our daughters Eva and Sonia, who were eleven and nine when we arrived, the bugs were initially a source of fascination. When I began hammering picture hooks into the walls, Sonia asked with alarm, "Won't that damage the microphones?"

Soon the novelty wore off and the listening devices were largely forgotten, so long as certain rules were remembered. Going out to visit Russian friends, Christina and I would leave their phone number on a scrap of paper that I would destroy later, with the understanding that it was not to be discussed or used except in an emergency. We also used the children's "magic pads," which could be instantly erased by lifting the top sheet, for communicating when we did not want to take the trouble of going outside.

When we drove anywhere, our car was obvious evidence of who we were; it was about as subtle as a billboard. We had a blue Volvo station wagon imported from Helsinki, immediately marking us as foreigners. But all foreigners' cars have distinctive license plates. Ours, for example, was K-04-644, the "K" for correspondent, the "04" for American, and the "644" my registration number. When we visited friends who were nervous about our encounters, we never drove up to their buildings. One Russian who made a point of telling us that he did not care who knew about our visits encouraged us to park right in front of his apartment complex. He later received complaints from his neighbors. Why, they asked, was he placing them all under suspicion by allowing our car to be parked outside for several hours at a time?

Marked as he is, a foreigner can never hope to drive out of Moscow unobserved. A correspondent or diplomat cannot travel more than twenty-five miles outside of Moscow without giving two days' notice to the authorities, and police guards on all the roads leading from the city will stop any foreign vehicle exceeding that limit unless it has been properly cleared. Some exceptions are made: foreigners can drive to the "diplomatic beach" on the Moscow River, which is a bit farther. However, it is impossible to get lost and wander off on a "closed" road. Policemen stand at the intersections during the summer and direct foreigners only to that destination. Those restrictions apply not just to Westerners but also to diplomats and journalists from the "fraternal" Eastern European countries. All foreigners are not to be trusted.

Many foreigners are content to turn a blind eye to such constant surveillance and control. They have accepted the fact that they must lead an isolated, privileged existence in Moscow, only among other foreigners. They live in their compounds, entertain each other endlessly at cocktail parties and dinners, and shop at *beriozkas*, special hard-currency stores. While such stores lack fresh produce and offer nowhere near the variety obtainable in supermarkets in the West, they stock liquor, high-quality meats, butter, and other foodstuffs that are generally impossible to find in regular Moscow stores. Like everyone else, Christina and I liberally availed ourselves of those privileges as well. But we soon realized that only a distinct minority of the foreign community moved beyond that shuttered existence to spend a significant proportion of their time with Russians, or even knew more than a handful of select Russians on a social basis.

For American diplomats, that isolation will increase when the new embassy complex currently under construction is finally completed. Aside from the embassy itself, the complex will contain housing for much of the staff, the school, an enlarged commissary, and other facilities making it a little American colony in the heart of Moscow. Diplomats and their families, who now at least have to commute to work and school from scattered housing compounds, will have little incentive to move about. Soviet officials will be delighted. As one Russian friend told me, "They will have all the birds in one nest." Before we left New York to go abroad, the Soviets had put up a huge apartment building in the Riverdale section of the Bronx, where we lived. Its purpose was to keep the families of Soviet diplomats assigned to the United Nations as isolated from American life as possible. From the Soviet perspective, this makes perfect sense: they want to keep their personnel, in particular their children, far from the pernicious influences of American life. But American interests are hardly served by taking similar measures. The reasons for putting up the new U.S. embassy complex in Moscow may be different, but the effect will be the same.

After our arrival in late May, we took Eva and Sonia for a visit to the Anglo-American School sponsored by the British and American embassies. Our conversation with the American headmaster was perfectly pleasant until we mentioned that we were thinking about enrolling them in a Russian school in the fall, although we had still not made a final decision. He suddenly became curt and dismissive, his tone suggesting that we would practically be guilty of child abuse if we did so. We attempted to question him about what activities there were in his school to take advantage of the Soviet setting, but it was clear there were practically none: it was an island unto itself. We parted with the headmaster predicting that if we did send the children to a Russian school, it would be a disastrous experiment.

In fact, Eva was extremely unhappy in the neighborhood Russian school that fall because she made little effort to adjust, found making friends difficult, and yearned for more familiar surroundings. After less than two months of classes, she switched to the Anglo-American School. Sonia, who was younger, did quite well at the school and learned Russian quickly, but she tired of the rigid rote learning of the Soviet system and after one semester found the lure of the Anglo-American School irresistible as well. So the results were mixed at best. But what disturbed me was the assumption of the headmaster, and others in the foreign community, that any effort to involve their children or themselves in their Soviet surroundings was unnecessary. They wanted to live apart.

Correspondents, I discovered, were divided between those who shared such attitudes, thus comfortably slipping into the foreign community cocoon, and those who did not. The single most important factor in determining which group a correspondent belonged to was whether or not he spoke Russian, since a reporter without at least a rudimentary working knowledge of the language had no chance of truly understanding Soviet society. I had thought before coming to Moscow that almost all correspondents working there would have achieved at least a minimal level of competence in Russian, but within days of my arrival I learned otherwise.

The American press corps in Moscow was composed of about thirty people. That number is strictly determined by the Soviets themselves, who only allow major news agencies, newspapers, magazines, and the radio and television networks to maintain bureaus there. The Associated Press had five correspondents and United Press International had four; *The New York Times* had two people and other newspapers such as *The Washington Post*, the *Los Angeles Times*, the *Chicago Tribune*, and the *Baltimore Sun* had one each; *Newsweek*, *Time*, *U.S. News & World Report*, and McGraw-Hill publications had one each; and the three radio and television networks each had a correspondent and a small crew. There were a few additions made during and after my tenure in Moscow—the Cable News Network and the *Philadelphia Inquirer*—but most of the news organizations represented there had maintained a bureau in Moscow for a long time. That made it all the more surprising for me to learn just how casually they selected and sent correspondents to Moscow, often without searching for candidates who already had some background for the job or without giving them proper language training.

The news agencies had particularly large needs for a steady supply of Moscow correspondents, but neither AP nor UPI had any regular training program. Occasionally they sent someone who knew the language already, but generally they selected young correspondents who spoke no Russian and who often had never worked abroad before. They sometimes gave them a little time for language lessons before they arrived, but that was hardly enough to make them functional. During most of my stay in Moscow, only one of the five AP reporters had even a passable grasp of the language. This was in direct contrast to Reuters, the British news agency, which had similar staffing requirements for Moscow but did not allow anyone to go there without first demonstrating some proficiency in Russian. But even a prestigious British news organization like the BBC was represented by a correspondent who spoke no Russian. The American television networks generally sent people with minimal or no preparation.

On the whole, newspapers and magazines were better in this regard. But even among correspondents of that group, there were those who for all practical purposes did not speak Russian. Some, like the wire-service reporters, had been sent without any language training; others had been given time for study but either had chosen a poor program or had not applied themselves. Indeed, only about half of the total American press corps in Moscow spoke Russian well enough to communicate freely with Russians and to travel on their own.

This is in marked contrast to Soviet correspondents working in the United States, who all prepare themselves for years for such an assignment. They arrive with an excellent command of English and with at least a working knowledge of American affairs. Soviet correspondents receive the same thorough training as diplomats; that is hardly surprising since they, too, are government officials, not journalists in the Western sense of the term. But Western news organizations would do well to learn a lesson from their meticulous preparation.

Why haven't they? One reason is that correspondents who don't speak Russian like to convey the impression that this is a minor inconvenience instead of the crippling handicap it really is. Their editors, many of whom have no foreign reporting experience and no direct knowledge of the Soviet Union, are easily convinced. At one of the first cocktail parties I attended, I listened to a British correspondent, who did not speak Russian, declare that even a rudimentary knowledge of the language should not be a prerequisite for the job of Moscow correspondent. We stood there in a foreigner's apartment among other Western reporters and diplomats, and he won at least the nodding agreement of many of those around him. His advice for any editor was "to just get someone with good reporting instincts."

A more important reason is that the Soviet authorities are well versed in the practice of feeding correspondents government pronouncements and stories on the English-language Tass machine that they know will receive prominent play. The handout stories just keep coming, and most editors in home offices measure a correspondent's performance by the volume of his output and the news play they give his stories. They rarely stop to consider the degree to which they demonstrate a lack of original reporting.

There is also a bias in journalism against specialization in one area of foreign affairs. Editors invariably say that they would prefer to prepare a good reporter for a difficult assignment like Moscow than to take a Soviet specialist and train him to be a journalist. In fact, many good reporters with no prior expertise in Soviet affairs have done well in Moscow after they learned Russian and prepared themselves for the assignment. But the problem is that editors too often only pay lip service to the notion of investing time and money in serious training programs; they simply spare their organizations the expense. For news executives, the current haphazard approach has the added virtue of requiring little forward planning, something they avoid whenever possible. Instead, they can—and often do—appoint Moscow correspondents at the last possible moment.

In earlier Moscow days, like the ones Harrison Salisbury covered for *The New York Times* in the late 1940s and early 1950s, the notion of just sending a good reporter to Moscow without any special preparation could have been defensible—up to a point. Even if a foreign correspondent spoke the language, contacts with Russians of any kind that were not specifically authorized were extremely rare: Russians who engaged in them literally risked their lives. Censorship of outgoing dispatches ensured that most of what a correspondent picked up on his own would not appear in print anyway. But after the transition from Stalin to Khrushchev, the written and unwritten rules of reporting in Moscow began to change dramatically. The possibilities for contacts with official and ordinary Russians vastly increased and censorship of foreign correspondents' stories was lifted in 1961.

The opportunity to do independent reporting did not unfold without constant government repression and attempts to intimidate Soviet citizens who were eager to contact foreign correspondents and the reporters themselves. Censorship had formally disappeared, but correspondents could be punished for filing "hostile" stories or for behavior that did not meet with the authorities' approval. A reporter could be consistently denied permission to travel outside of Moscow, could be harassed or provoked and, as a last resort, expelled. The most serious incident in the period before my arrival involved Robin Knight of *U.S. News & World Report*. In 1979, he was drugged during a trip to Tashkent in an attempt to charge him with unruly behavior. The plan failed only because his wife refused to leave his side despite repeated attempts by the Soviets to separate them; thus she could vouch for him every moment.

Nevertheless, working conditions for journalists did improve, especially in the détente years of the 1970s. In 1975, the Soviet Union signed the Helsinki Accords which led to major changes in the lives of Western correspondents. For the first time, they were granted multiple-entry visas, allowing them to leave and reenter the Soviet Union during their tours without having to obtain new visas for each trip. This eliminated a major inconvenience that could also be used as a threat: the authorities had been able to keep a correspondent on edge because he never knew whether his next trip out of the Soviet Union might prove to be his last.

The Helsinki Accords also established new procedures for traveling within the Soviet Union. In the past, trips to areas ostensibly open to foreigners had to be authorized in advance. But correspondents frequently received no response at all to their travel requests, which amounted to a refusal. Under the new regulations, a foreign correspondent still had to notify the Foreign Ministry at least two working days in advance about any travel plans outside of Moscow, complete with dates, train or flight arrangements, or, if traveling by car, the license plate number and the roads he would use to get to his destination. Unless the Foreign Ministry then informed him that he could not go, he was free to make the trip. No written or oral authorization was necessary. While the broader provisions of the Helsinki Accords pledging freedom for correspondents to go about their jobs without government interference or monitoring were routinely ignored by the Soviets and ways were found around the loosening of specific rules, journalists were able to do their jobs better than before.

Many did just that. Hedrick Smith of *The New York Times* and Robert Kaiser of *The Washington Post* took full advantage of the relaxed atmosphere of the early détente era to travel widely and meet Russians from many walks of life, including such dissidents as Aleksandr Solzhenitsyn and Andrei Sakharov. AP correspondent George Krimsky maintained extensive contacts in the dissident community, which was his particular beat, and Russians I met still remembered his willingness to meet virtually anyone, anywhere, anytime. That produced good reporting, but it also led to his expulsion in 1977 when the crackdown on the dissident movement began to intensify. Among my contemporaries in Moscow, ABC's Anne Garrels, who was the only network correspondent with a background in Soviet studies and who spoke Russian, proved that first-rate television coverage of the Soviet Union was possible, despite the particular hardships under which broadcast journalists work. David Satter, an American who worked for Britain's *Financial Times* in an office next to mine, traveled all over the Soviet Union and developed an impressive array of Soviet friends and contacts.

Unfortunately, my first weeks in Moscow convinced me that those correspondents who took full advantage of the reporting opportunities in the Soviet Union were a distinct minority. Most Western reporters did not. Those who did not speak Russian were totally dependent on three less-than-reliable sources of information: the English-language Tass news service and whatever was gleaned from the Soviet press by their Russian translators; English-speaking Russians, most of whom were likely to be Soviet journalists and officials who were the mainstays of the foreigners' social circuit; and Western diplomats, many of whom were as isolated from Soviet life as most correspondents themselves. Any non–English-speaking Russian trying to phone such a correspondent would find himself talking to his UPDK translator instead. If such correspondents traveled at all, it was on Foreign Ministry press trips, group excursions designed to produce as one-sided a picture as the authorities could get away with.

Successive correspondents of one newsmagazine, all of whom arrived speaking almost no Russian, relied heavily on a UPDK employee who was treated more like a reporter than a translator. He was not only consulted regularly about the significance of stories but actually was sent out to conduct some interviews himself, even on sensitive subjects. Ilya Glazunov, the controversial Russian nationalist painter who has been variously depicted as anything from a KGB agent to a dissident, told me of his astonishment when the UPDK employee showed up alone at his studio to interview him, introducing himself as the magazine's representative. The Soviet "reporter" traveled around town in a light green Soviet Fiat bought for him by the magazine and outfitted in the "K-04" license plates reserved for American correspondents.

Even among those correspondents who did speak Russian, I found that some were not particularly interested in either traveling around the country on their own or meeting many Russians, aside from officials and journalists. Shortly after I arrived, I invited a colleague to dinner, along with a Russian writer who had published his poetry in samizdat and émigré journals. The correspondent, who represented a major East Coast newspaper and spoke Russian well, fidgeted throughout the meal and left early. I attributed his behavior to a difference in personalities and left it at that. But not long afterward, the same correspondent and I went to see a dissident who had recently been released from an insane asylum. Neither of us had met him before and the three of us had a long, rambling conversation on a bench in Pushkin Square. After we parted, my colleague said, "If you look at the situation logically given the odds against him, anyone who becomes a dissident in this society must be at least a bit crazy." His voice turned irritable. "I keep getting calls from these crazy people."

That was the last time we ever went to see someone together. It was obvious that the correspondent intended to shun such contacts in the future. In varying degrees, several other colleagues appeared to share his attitude. Partly, it was a question of not wanting to be bothered with meeting and listening to people with grievances that are likely to receive little attention in the West. The Russian who takes the considerable risk of trying to contact a Western news organization directly is usually either a dissident or someone with a personal complaint, who feels that his only hope is for the outside world to know about his plight and thus pressure the authorities to respond. Partly, there was genuine uncertainty as to how much credence could be given to such "unofficial" contacts who offered information on a variety of subjects, not just their own individual cases. I was myself still weighing the reliability of what I was hearing from a steadily expanding circle of contacts. Finally, I also sensed an undercurrent of fear among many correspondents, often insinuated or expressed obliquely in our early conversations, that extensive ties with such Russians could prove dangerous. There was the ever-present fear of becoming the victim of a government provocation or of sparking retaliation by the authorities.

Those correspondents who were the most insulated also tended to be the ones who complained the loudest about the hardships of living in Moscow. Nevertheless, I met only one or two correspondents who appeared eager to end their tours early. Even if nothing about Soviet society interested them, they had powerful incentives to remain. Since Moscow is considered a particularly difficult journalistic assignment, the perks are considerable. Housing is provided free of charge by one's employer, usually along with a maid, and correspondents and their families receive frequent paid vacations almost anywhere they choose outside of the Soviet Union. In addition, a tour of duty in Moscow gives a correspondent strong leverage to get a choice post afterward, invitations to lecture, and often a book contract. Few journalists resist such temptations. However much I wanted to go for other reasons, I was not indifferent to the concrete and potential perks.

I could not help but believe that the widespread fear of jeopardizing one's job by vigorously pursuing one's profession was somehow linked to the desire to retain the prestigious career advantages that an assignment in Moscow conferred. I had always taken a great deal of interest in stories from the Soviet Union, but it was only in Moscow that I began to read as a matter of course the full output of most Western news organizations. What struck me was the curious set of criteria that determined what was deemed reliable information. When sources loosely identified as dissidents asserted something, it was often dismissed out-of-hand as unreliable. But whenever something clattered over the Tass machine, most journalists had no hesitation about immediately reporting it. The easiest possible reporting consisted of recycling what the Soviet authorities wanted to put out. A correspondent like David Satter, who based many of his reports on unofficial sources of information, was resented by others who relied on established channels. He produced independent stories they simply could not match.

The vast majority of copy produced by Western correspondents amounted to a rewriting of dispatches and articles issued by Tass and the Soviet press. An AP reporter told me that about 90 percent of the copy from his bureau fell into that category; most other news organizations could not claim a significantly lower percentage. Of course none of us could ignore the official speeches, statements, and information disseminated in this fashion and a careful reading of the Soviet press was necessary and often productive. But it was only when I encountered the skepticism among my colleagues about different sources of information that I began to ponder the other forces that were affecting their news judgment.

I had met the same correspondent who had branded dissidents "crazy" shortly before he was scheduled to begin his Moscow tour. He had worked in the Soviet Union in an earlier period, and he already had set ideas about how such an assignment should be approached. The correspondent he was replacing had antagonized the authorities and encountered harassment, he told me, because he did not understand "that you can't keep hitting them over the head." He added: "You have to know how to deal with these people." It was only after observing him in Moscow that I understood fully how he intended to put these ideas into practice. While largely shunning contacts with dissidents and other "unofficial" Russians, he relied primarily on the Soviet press and Soviet officials and journalists. His reporting, even when critical of certain aspects of Soviet life and policy, remained within what the authorities considered acceptable bounds.

This particular correspondent may have been more deliberately calculating than most, but he was hardly unique in weighing the risks of reporting and writing freely. David Shipler, a former *New York Times* correspondent in Moscow, wrote in his book *Russia: Broken Idols, Solemn Dreams*: "Despite the pressures, I never knew a journalist stationed there who pulled any punches." What I was seeing convinced me that the truth, at the very least, was not that clear-cut.

It is often less a matter of a conscious decision that a particular story is too risky than a general attitude that keeps certain reporters, including some of those who speak Russian well, away from anything that may have a high risk potential. Michael Binyon, who was the *London Times* correspondent during most of my tour, wrote in his book *Life in Russia* that one reason he based his reporting largely on the Soviet press was "because it is far wiser and more tactful to let the Russians make their own criticisms of their society than to judge them and pontificate as an outsider with different assumptions and outlook." Many correspondents, who would not accept such a rationalization for continually echoing a government-controlled press elsewhere, shared Binyon's view that this was perfectly acceptable in Moscow.

What about official sources other than those gleaned from the Soviet press? Like other new correspondents in Moscow, I entertained vague hopes that some worthwhile cooperation might be extended to me by those Russians charged with our handling, despite their mistrust of our motives and their inability to understand our role. ("Of course we know that you take your orders from the State Department," a Novosti press agency editor told me when I made a call on his office to introduce myself.) My first visit to the Foreign Ministry press department, and my only one except for my considerably less pleasant visit fourteen months later, gave me a good sense of the prevailing attitude toward correspondents.

I was picking up my press card, which turned out to be an occasion for meeting Yuri Chernyakov, the director of the department. I already knew Yevgeny Petrusevich, a thin, nervous official responsible for dealing with the American press corps. He led me into Chernyakov's office, where we sat down in big, overstuffed armchairs and were served tea. Chernyakov, a former ambassador in the Middle East, languidly stirred sugar into his cup and gradually shifted the conversation from small talk to my job.

"Working as a correspondent in the Soviet Union is not really much different than working as a correspondent anywhere else. But there are certain rules to observe, on trips for example." He indicated that Petrusevich could fill me in on any details of rules I might not be aware of. "And while people in your government are perhaps too talkative, here they are perhaps too silent," he observed.

Working from what I thought might be a tiny opening, I responded to his question about what they could do for me with a shot in the dark. Could they, I inquired, help me obtain interviews with officials on occasion?

Chernyakov looked pained, and he launched into a story that he claimed had happened some years back. The press department had arranged an interview for two American correspondents with the oil minister, and the journalists had "somewhat distorted" what he had said. As a result, the oil minister had to answer a lot of questions from the government and in the end committed suicide. Since then, he said, the Oil Ministry slams down the phone anytime anyone from his department calls.

"An extreme example, perhaps," he sighed, "but you see the difficulties that can arise." Whatever the truth of that story, I did.

A Russian I met later told me a similar story. Because accurate information is usually hidden in the Soviet Union, rumors abound—and they are often worse than the truth that is so carefully concealed. A few years earlier, for example, there were rumors of a killer on the loose in Moscow. There had been several brutal murders, it seemed, but as usual not a word about them had appeared in the press. Crime statistics are a tightly guarded secret. Soon the rumor mill had created a virtual panic, with stories of an entire trainload of deranged criminals escaping and stalking their victims across the capital. After some other wild tale began making the rounds, the Russian told me, a friend of his decided to get to someone who could tell him the truth. He tried long and hard, finally managing to get through on the phone to the Central Committee's information department. Triumphant, he demanded to know what was really happening. The frosty response from the voice at the other end: "This is the information department. We collect information—we do not give it out."

I decided early that I would seek to develop my own channels of information and not spend much time trying to set up the rarely granted interviews with officials. Nor would I nurture contacts with the small group of officials and journalists who were specifically authorized to maintain such ties with foreigners. Naturally I was willing to interview or meet such people when the opportunity arose, but it seemed clear that such contacts had limited value and should not be allowed to become a major preoccupation. There had to be a more productive use of a reporter's time and energies.

There was. Christina and I were meeting as many people as we could, discovering that the problem was not a lack of people willing to see us but a lack of time to see everyone as often as they wanted. If we did not see someone for a week or two and then I made the trek to a pay phone to call, I would be inevitably asked: *"Kuda ty propal?"* (Where did you disappear?) The conventions of Russian hospitality demanded that friends see each other often, for long evenings and to keep in constant touch. As foreigners, we were also sought after by some Russians because we represented at least a small window on the outside world. Many Russians who were not dissidents, who held responsible but not top-level positions, were among those who were anxious to open such a window.

Those with political or personal grievances who tried to contact me and other correspondents in the hope of publicizing their cases, underscored the fact that I was on an assignment unlike any other I had previously held. The very act of contacting a foreign correspondent signaled defiance, and how I or my colleagues responded could directly affect people and events more than they would in most other countries. In the Soviet Union, normal journalistic judgments did not suffice: a correspondent had to recognize that his role went beyond his purely professional responsibilities. There was a moral dimension as well.

One of my earliest drives to a remote section of Moscow was to see Valery, an intense man in his thirties who had proclaimed a solitary hunger strike in the apartment of a friend. The trip had the feel of a major expedition because it involved three other correspondents and we kept losing our way among streets and apartment buildings that looked depressingly similar. The reasons for Valery's hunger strike, which had stretched to nearly a month, were complex—so much so that as a newcomer on the scene I had difficulty understanding them. The gist seemed to be that Valery had been denied a residence permit in Moscow, where he felt he was entitled to live. Vague suggestions that this was motivated by political considerations, black marks in his past, did little to enlighten me. But the four of us had not gone that afternoon to try to unravel the details of his case. His friend, whose tiny apartment we finally found, had called to tell us about Valery's deteriorating health and to urge us to do something, anything that might help.

We went, but not with any message of encouragement. We told Valery, whose face was gaunt and whose body looked skeletal under the thin sheet of the cot where he was lying, that, as much as we sympathized, his case was not receiving any attention in the world press. Our visit, we continued, did not mean this would change, since even if we wrote about his case our editors would be unlikely to print anything. Therefore, we urged him to call off his hunger strike. It was all that we could do. We were relieved to hear a couple of days later that Valery had taken our advice.

I left other such encounters with a sense of sadness and inadequacy. On a visit to Moscow from a provincial city, a woman arranged for a hurried meeting in front of the toy store near my office. We passed each other twice before either of us was certain that we had identified the other; she had said she would be wearing a patterned shawl and I was dressed in jeans and a jacket, but neither qualified as distinctive garb on a Moscow street. We fell into step and she explained that years ago her husband had disappeared into the camps and that her son had recently been convicted on trumped-up charges, making her fear that she would lose him forever also. Everything, she said, was chronicled in a thirty-five-page, single-spaced story of her life that she had written. Now, she wanted the whole story to be published, every word exactly as she wrote it.

I told her that I would be happy to take a look at what she had written to see if there was any way I could make use of the information, but that it would be impossible for a magazine like *Newsweek* to do what she wanted.

She looked at me suspiciously. "I understand, you're afraid of them, too." Nothing I could have said would have changed her mind.

Such misunderstandings occurred frequently. That was hardly surprising. Having no direct knowledge of the Western world or its press, Soviet citizens who summon the courage to contact a foreign correspondent often have exaggerated notions of what can be accomplished or what is of sufficient interest to the outside world to be published. Like the woman clutching her thirty-five-page manuscript, they insist on telling their stories in painstaking detail, unable to believe that Western reporters would be happier with a brief summary.

But I felt that I should be willing to see anyone who sought to contact me, at least once, unless there was something so suspect in his approach that it suggested a provocation. Some meetings ended in frustration, while others proved quite useful. All of them, however, offered insights into Soviet society. They were one source of the human contacts I was seeking.

Another was travel. That Moscow or Leningrad is not the Soviet Union is as true as that Washington or New York is not the United States. Perhaps more so. With its mixture of nationalities, religions, and local customs, the Soviet Union does not lend itself to easy generalization about popular attitudes. Most generalizations apply more to the Russian majority than to the national minorities. But the non-Russian peoples, taken together, now make up almost half of the Soviet population. By the end of this century, given the high birthrates in the Central Asian Muslim republics, they will outnumber the Russians for the first time. But before I could explore the implications of this demographic shift, I needed to turn my attention westward. The rise of an independent trade union, Solidarity, in Poland, the Soviet Union's next-door neighbor, was not likely to go unnoticed by Soviet citizens just across the border, many of whom were members of minorities traditionally squeezed between the Russians and the Poles.

My first weeks in Moscow had left little doubt about what the government wanted its people to think about Poland. The daily barrage of official propaganda portrayed Poland in a steadily more negative light as Solidarity grew increasingly militant. Beneath the rhetoric about the unbreakable bonds of socialist friendship between Poland and the Soviet Union, the unmistakable message was that the Poles were lazy, insolent, and disgracefully rebellious—above all, that they were violently "anti-Soviet." Poland was painted as a society where everyone was continually striking, while hardworking Soviet citizens had to pay the price by providing massive aid to keep its economy afloat. (An officially inspired joke: Two Poles meet at work. End of joke.) Any act of vandalism against a Soviet war memorial in Poland received prominent, indignant treatment; war veterans appeared on television to denounce the desecration of the sacrifices of their comrades in liberating Poland from the Nazis.

The propaganda campaign seemed to be effective among many people. "We spill our blood for them and now we'll have to feed them," a Moscow taxi driver told me. "The Poles have more to eat than us anyway."

Driving across town one morning, I gave a lift to two factory workers who turned out to have already had several shots of vodka. Once they learned I was an American, they insisted on talking politics. "Why does the Reagan administration want war? Why does it want to put new missiles in Western Europe aimed at us?"

I spoke of mutual American and Soviet fears, and asked how they explained their government's SS-20 buildup. At the time, the Soviet press had yet to acknowledge the existence of the SS-20s, and this appeared to be news to them. But that did not prevent my passengers from responding.

"Our missiles are only defensive. The Soviet Union does not threaten anyone."

"That's what we say about our weapons."

As I made a wrong turn and found myself driving through an unfamiliar section of Moscow, they kept up a steady attack on the aggressiveness of the Reagan administration that amounted to a paraphrasing of the daily articles in *Pravda*. Frustrated by my inability to make a left turn— they are forbidden at most intersections in Moscow—I was growing irritated. "You talk about American aggression. What about Afghanistan—isn't that aggression?"

"We are fighting against the exploiters there and to prevent the Americans and the Chinese from coming in."

"So you believe whatever your newspapers say about this?"

"Everything our newspapers write is true."

I made a U-turn, which is legal in designated areas, hoping to find my way back to someplace I recognized. My passengers in the back seat, whose words were increasingly slurred, did not seem to know or care where we were. I asked about Soviet pressure on Poland.

"We are only trying to help."

"Maybe the Poles don't want that kind of help."

"Then they are idiots and don't know what to think."

A familiar landmark appeared followed by the ring road, and I was able to deposit my passengers a few blocks farther.

They urged me to join them for some more drinking and left convinced that I had only declined because I was afraid of continuing a losing argument.

Among Moscow intellectuals the party line on Poland was not parroted. Indeed, like the émigrés we met in California, they were fascinated by the revolution taking place in Polish society and dreamed that it might succeed. "At every party, the subject is always Poland," one woman told Christina. "In our hearts, we all feel Polish now." We drank too many "for Poland" toasts to remember, always proposed by our hosts or other guests, not by us. But such intellectuals knew their views were not held by the majority of Russians.

It took longer than I expected to make my way west to see whether other nationalities, nearer to Poland, felt differently. My editors in New York were worried that the events in Poland made it doubly important that I remain in Moscow to chart the Kremlin's every reaction. Other correspondents felt the same pressure, making it difficult for me to find someone to travel with. Traveling alone, I had been warned, was a risk no correspondent concerned about his job security could afford to take: he would have no witness if an "incident" was staged to get him into trouble. But in the middle of July, Robert Gillette of the *Los Angeles Times* and I finally went to Vilnius, the capital of the Baltic republic of Lithuania on Poland's border.

The Lithuanians have long been linked with the Poles. Poland dominated the two nations' union that spanned the fourteenth through the eighteenth centuries until Russia swallowed up both countries; Vilnius itself was grabbed by Poland when Lithuania briefly existed as an independent state between the two world wars. Lithuanian nationalists still recall some of that history with bitterness, but their shared heritage is stronger. Vilnius boasts such famous Polish native sons as nineteenth-century poet Adam Mickiewicz, whose verse was intensely nationalistic and anti-Russian, and Czeslaw Milosz, whose winning of the 1980 Nobel Prize for literature caused great private rejoicing in the land of his birth. Above all, the Poles and Lithuanians share a deep commitment to Roman Catholicism and an equally deep resentment of Russian, and now Soviet, domination. Lithuanian partisans resisted the 1940 seizure of their country well into the 1950s, and national antagonisms have never disappeared. I was interested to see if the Lithuanians had been touched by the events in Poland that summer of 1981 when Solidarity was at its height. If not, I reasoned, one could safely write off any potential spillover of the wave of Polish unrest into the Soviet Union.

Gillette and I flew in early on a Sunday morning and took a taxi to our hotel. We were in a good mood, glad to be on our way and relieved that we had not received a last-minute phone call from the Foreign Ministry telling us we could not make the trip, a frequent occurrence when correspondents attempted to travel to the Baltic republics. At the hotel, however, the Russian desk clerk sternly informed us that the management had sent a cable to the Moscow booking office denying our request for a room. We protested that we had not been informed of this, but that was of no interest to her. There were no rooms available, she claimed, and that was that. An appeal to her immediate superior was equally unproductive. Convinced that in the end they would not turn two American reporters out on the street, we left our bags and promised to check back in the evening. In the meantime, we set out to explore the city.

We walked up and down the cobblestone streets in the city's center, which retained more of a traditional European feel than any section of Moscow. They were lined with two-story beige and brown houses with red tile roofs, arched windows, and solid stone frames that could have stood in Kraków or Prague. The churches swept the eye upward to their simple but imposing steeples, topped with crosses, and the old city gate bore witness to centuries past. Known as the Ausros Vartai (Gate of Dawn), it is a graceful example of Renaissance architecture; the top of its arch forms the base of an intimate chapel housing a famous seventeenth-century painting of Our Lady of Vilnius. The goods in the shops were not of much better quality than those found in Moscow, but their windows boasted bright if modest displays, a sign that the city's entrepreneurial spirit had not completely disappeared. Young women were slimmer, better dressed, more attractive than in Moscow; a colorful blouse, nicely tailored skirt, swept-back long blond hair attested to their greater fashion consciousness. This, too, reflected Lithuania's proximity to Poland, where women have traditionally kept close tabs on Western fashions.

The old elegance was badly frayed, however, the houses showing considerable signs of wear and neglect. A gate leading to the courtyard of a dilapidated house bore the inscription that Mickiewicz had lived there; the walls were covered by a series of muddy brown splotches, and the courtyard was strung with laundry. While the authorities had restored few buildings and allowed the gradual deterioration of the old city to continue virtually unchecked, they had at least recognized the importance of preserving its character. The architecture of historic buildings clearly had influenced the design of newer buildings, like the central post office, built in a compatible modern style, low in height and subdued in tone. But from the top of the fourteenth-century Tower of Gediminas on Castle Hill, we could see where the postwar city planners had devoted their real energies: the familiar five- and nine-story housing projects, identical to those in Moscow, ringed the old town. We could also see, near the airport, a cluster of electronic towers, which we later learned were erected to jam foreign radio broadcasts.

But the Polish border is too close to be effectively sealed. Although local inhabitants complained to us about the jamming of Western broadcasts, they easily picked up Polish radio stations and, in many areas outside of Vilnius itself, Lithuanians had been able to watch everything on Polish television from Pope John Paul II's first visit to Poland in 1979 to Lech Walesa's emergence as Solidarity's leader. When I asked one man on the street directions in Polish, a language most Lithuanians still understand, he asked for news from Poland. "I live outside the city and I can watch Polish television because I have fixed up a special antenna, but I haven't heard the latest," he said, speaking a rough mixture of Polish and Russian. I filled him in as best I could, although I explained that I had not come from Poland. He shook my hand vigorously, evidently assuming nonetheless that I was Polish, saying, "I know things are difficult in Poland, but I wish you success."

That would not be the only time I would be mistaken for someone I was not. When Gillette and I reached St. Theresa's, a church near the center of the old town, worshippers of all ages were streaming in for virtually nonstop masses throughout the morning and early afternoon. They were alternately conducted in Lithuanian and Polish, since Vilnius still has a sizable Polish minority. On the steps, beggars pleaded for coins and, on the street, peasant women did a brisk business selling rosaries, imitation gold crosses, and holy cards. When Bob and I started taking pictures of the back of the crowd spilling out of the church, looks of alarm were exchanged and a middle-aged woman hissed: "Get out." Apparently, we had been taken for agents of the KGB.

The misapprehension was quickly cleared up. "We are

not afraid of Americans, only of our own," said one of the rosary sellers. The woman who had tried to get rid of us apologized profusely, explaining that the authorities were always trying to intimidate the faithful. "They are trying to prevent what is going on in Poland from happening here," she declared.

She and other parishioners we talked to described the changes that had taken place in Lithuania since the birth of Solidarity. Personal contacts between Lithuania and Poland had been drastically curtailed. Visas for family visits that had been routinely issued in the past were now being granted grudgingly, if at all. "I don't know what is happening with my family," said one elderly Polish woman who had not received a single letter since the Polish strikes had begun in 1980. Polish newspapers, once available at most Vilnius newsstands, were now limited to "safe" issues, and subscribers to Polish magazines had found their subscriptions canceled and their money refunded. The Polish press had attained an unprecedented degree of freedom in the Solidarity period, and it offered a steady diet of articles that openly discussed the country's shortcomings and popular discontent. From the Kremlin's perspective, such an outburst of honest reporting was dangerously inflammatory.

We were told that the Lithuanian KGB, which had always been extremely active, had stepped up its surveillance of the local Polish population and of anyone with links to Poland. Shortly before our arrival, we learned, regular Soviet Army units based in Lithuania along with local reservists had been called up for exercises in the Kaliningrad region near the Polish border. This seemed to fit in nicely with Moscow's strategy of constantly reminding the Poles of their armed might, but the people we met maintained that it was also aimed at the young Lithuanian reservists. During the exercises, the reservists were warned by political officers that anyone who had visited Poland could expect to be watched closely. In Lithuanian factories, political lecturers stressed the dangers of "counterrevolution" in Poland and claimed that the Poles had been "spoiled" because too many of them were allowed to travel to the West.

All day long we wandered about the city, meeting more local inhabitants, a mixture of ordinary citizens, priests, and even outspoken Lithuanian nationalists. Although Vilnius, like all capitals of Soviet republics, has a large Russian population, on that Sunday Lithuanians and Poles were out and about and Russians were hardly to be seen. (The one time I asked somebody who turned out to be a Russian a question in Polish, he brusquely dismissed me with a *"Nye panimayu"*—"I don't understand.") From our conversations, it seemed clear that the Polish events were having a considerable effect on many Lithuanians; no one we talked to— and we talked to dozens during the course of our stay in Vilnius—expressed anything but sympathy for the Poles. "Everyone talks about Poland all the time," said one woman of mixed Polish-Lithuanian background. "Some of the Russians here ask what those Poles want and say we should just partition them out of existence again. But the Lithuanians say that the Poles are smart and know what they are doing. If only it could be like that here."

But few Lithuanians hold such illusions. Numbers alone tell why the Polish example is unlikely to be followed in Lithuania: the republic's population is only 3.4 million, 80 percent of whom are listed as ethnic Lithuanians. The risks of dissent have always been much greater in tiny Lithuania, where the Soviet authorities can turn loose the full force of their security apparatus. Nevertheless, wherever we went in Vilnius, Bob and I found a willingness to express sentiments that would doubtless have been branded as "anti-Soviet" by the government. It was obvious that Poles and

Lithuanians shared many grievances. Once we identified ourselves as American correspondents, and in my case as someone with a Polish background, inhibitions disappeared and conversations were wonderfully candid.

A young priest, with a pudgy, innocent face and soft hands, quietly listened to me as I explained who we were to an even younger colleague and then led us into the sacristy of his small church. He spoke of Soviet efforts to suppress Catholicism in Lithuania, pointing to the failure of those policies but not minimizing the problems they created for the church. In Vilnius, which now has a population of 500,000, ten churches are permitted; in 1939, when the city had 200,000 inhabitants, there were thirty-three churches. Lithuania's only seminary, situated in Kaunus, barely survived the Stalin era when only a handful of priests were ordained, but now it graduates about a dozen priests a year. That is not enough, though, to replace the priests ordained before World War II who are now dying off. As a result, Lithuania is experiencing a priest shortage that grows more acute with each passing year.

The problem, unlike in the West, is not of declining vocations, the priest said. There are usually more candidates than spaces in the seminary. But the KGB must approve all candidates, and the priest described how he, like almost everyone else, was approached with offers to serve as an informer. Even when young men clear all the hurdles and are accepted, their families can be made to pay for their "ideological failings." The parents of one recent entrant lost their teaching jobs and his sister was expelled from the university. Priests are not permitted to teach religion to the young, and all church appointments must be approved by the authorities. But government propaganda is obvious and heavy-handed, as it rather ineptly tries to push atheism. We visited the Vilnius University church, for example, now a

"Museum of Science." It featured a telescope, rock samples, and pictures of scientists and doctors, but its most prominent exhibit displayed the speeches and books of Brezhnev and Lenin along with a history of the Lithuanian Communist Party.

Still, the priest was confident. "The faith is alive in Lithuania. Among the youth, there is a movement back to religion." Ways are found around government restrictions. Religious education takes place informally, and even some party members, we were told, have church weddings, quietly baptize their children, and send them to first communion. If a young man intent on priesthood is persistently denied entrance into the seminary by the authorities, he is trained in an underground seminary. All orders are banned, but many women belong to secret orders of nuns while working in such innocuous occupations as nursing.

As in Poland, the mere act of going to church has political significance: religion is inextricably bound up with nationalism. The election of a Polish pope and the potent mixture of religion and nationalism next door has strengthened the Lithuanian church. "The fact that the pope is from a socialist country has true meaning. He understands how things are in Poland and Lithuania," the priest said. "We thank God we have a pope who is giving new life to religion." He and others believe that Vilnius bishop Julijonas Steponavicius, who was removed from office in 1961 by the government and sent into internal exile to a small Lithuanian village, is the cardinal named by John Paul II *in pectore* (in the heart) in 1979. Popes can name a cardinal *in pectore* when they believe that announcing his name publicly could endanger him or his church.

The priest also discussed the recent wave of beatings and arrests of organizers of religious processions and voiced his suspicion that the KGB was responsible for the murder the previous year of a pastor of a local parish. At the end of our talk, he hesitated and answered a question we had not yet asked: Why should he be willing to say so much to two outsiders he had never met before? "It is important for the world to know what is happening here. If we make some noise when they try to repress us then they will think twice before trying again." He paused. "The worst thing from our point of view is for repression to take place here and no one knows about it."

Later in the day, we met an intense, tall woman with a strikingly angular face who invited us to her home. She told us of her commitment to Lithuanian nationalism over tea, bread, and homemade jams. Her brother was serving a seven-year sentence for his involvement in the underground samizdat journals that continue to circulate widely, despite sustained efforts by the authorities to stamp them out. Each time someone is arrested, another takes his place, she told us. Publications like *Chronicle of the Lithuanian Catholic Church* publicize the harassment of the church and, at the time of our visit, carried accounts of Solidarity activities in Poland, statements of opposition to the Soviet invasion of Afghanistan, and attacks on what the anonymous authors called a new "Russification" program. Such programs stressed the teaching of Russian language and culture in non-Russian areas, weakening other nationalities' identification with their own distinct history. When the Baltic republics first came under Soviet control, "Russification" policies were even less subtle: mass deportations of Lithuanians, Latvians, and Estonians to Siberia were followed by an influx of Russian settlers, altering the demographic picture.

What the woman had to tell us was delivered in tough, determined words. Russian was now taught to Lithuanian children starting in first grade, she pointed out, instead of from the fifth grade as had previously been the case. "To destroy a country, the most important thing is to destroy its language," she said. Soviet claims that Lithuania's national income has shown a fivefold increase since the war and the fact that Lithuanians live better than most Russians did nothing to dampen her resentment. "I know we live better than people in most parts of the Soviet Union, but that doesn't mean anything. Lithuania is an occupied country."

We met other men and women on the streets, at the market, and in stores who echoed similar sentiments. The evidence of recent bad harvests and the notorious ineptitude of Soviet agriculture was less visible in Lithuania than in other parts of the U.S.S.R. because the Soviet authorities try to keep the Baltic republics better supplied to avoid stirring greater discontent; nevertheless, residents complained of an erosion of their living standards. Butter disappeared altogether at times and state stores offered only abysmally low grade meat, obligating anyone who wanted better to pay more than double the official prices at the farmers' market, where collective farmers could sell the produce from their small private plots.

Throughout our conversations, Poland kept intruding. What was happening there seemed an impossible dream, a renewal that Lithuanians could only pray for but not realistically expect to emulate. So long as Solidarity survived, it provided hope that someday they could win a small measure of what the Poles had already achieved. But people voiced fears of a Soviet invasion of Poland. They knew that the anxious men in the Kremlin worried that the Polish "disease" might infect Lithuania, that hope for change, however fragile, might blossom on Soviet soil. The people we spoke to wanted to believe that the Poles could triumph, but they were almost holding their breath in anticipation of a confrontation they sensed was looming.

Late that evening, Bob and I returned to our hotel. All

day long we had been surprised by the willingness of people to speak openly with us; more surprising was the absence of any signs of surveillance. In a tightly policed republic where foreigners were routinely subjected to special scrutiny, we appeared to have been ignored. At the hotel, the desk clerk still refused to accommodate us and no other hotel would take us either. That was stranger than the lack of visible monitoring. We were both forced, and free, to look for a place to stay on our own, a highly unusual predicament for Western reporters in the Soviet Union.

We concluded that the local KGB must have thought that we had not yet arrived and so had not assigned any agents to tail us that Sunday. All the KGB knew was that we had been informed that we had no place to stay, which normally was an effective method of turning a correspondent away without formally refusing him permission for a trip. Taking the precaution of going a bit out of the center of town, we began knocking on doors and asking for a room for the night. An affable Pole in one courtyard began asking his neighbors to help us. "Someone here has to have a place for these Polish boys to spend the night," he announced loudly, disregarding my explanation that the description was not exactly accurate. We ended up staying with a friendly working-class family. In the Soviet Union, nothing like this is ever supposed to happen. I imagine that someone in the local security apparatus eventually paid for the fact that we sprang loose, even for a brief period, from a system designed to insulate correspondents as much as possible from such direct contact with Soviet life.

The next morning we thanked our hosts but refused their offer to put us up for the rest of our stay. We were convinced that we had not endangered them yet, but to stay any longer might do so. We returned to the hotel, where a room was suddenly available. I asked the maid on our floor whether the room had been occupied the previous night; it hadn't.

We also found ourselves back under the kind of "care" that we had expected in the first place. People were still willing to see us, but the risks were greater. One young woman we talked to was detained before a planned second meeting with us on the final day of our stay. "So you didn't meet with your friends," a police officer told her at the station where she was taken. She was held for several hours until we left Vilnius, but she called me later in Moscow to report what had happened. She told me the essentials, and the line went dead.

After my story about the trip appeared in *Newsweek*, at least two other Western correspondents filed travel plans for Lithuania that summer. The Foreign Ministry denied them permission "due to reasons of a temporary nature."

I had never seen a beach quite like it. A mass of human bodies, of all sizes and shapes, were jammed together on the long narrow stretch of seashore covered with fist-sized, dark gray rocks; not a speck of sand was to be seen. Those who lined up early enough in the morning to rent chaise longues and umbrellas situated themselves in relative comfort, while others had to fight for a few square feet of space to lay down their air mattresses; merely spreading out a towel over the rocks failed to provide an adequate cushion. From loudspeakers, an officious woman's voice periodically instructed "comrade vacationers" to beware of excessive exposure to the sun, and children wore the ubiquitous triangular white cloth or paper caps. A long line clogged the entrance to the only snack bar, from which one could buy large, round, stale biscuits and hot and cold drinks. During lunchtime, when the need for its services was greatest, it inexplicably closed for an hour and a half. Those still in line, no matter how long they had been standing there, were simply out of luck.

David Satter, of the *Financial Times*, and I had arrived in Sochi in August, the height of the summer season. Millions of Russians dream about spending their holidays in this Black Sea resort, which boasts generally clean air, green parks, gardens, and beaches, however rocky, and that winning combination—all too rare in Russia—of sea and sun. For those influential or lucky enough to be put up at the various sanitoriums run by government ministries, industries, or professional organizations, a Sochi vacation is luxurious by Soviet standards. It provides comfortable lodging, good meals, and beaches reserved only for those institutions. But every day, tens of thousands of ordinary vacationers, who are not taken care of by any sponsoring organization, battle for scarce living space, transportation, food, and any place at all on the public beaches; for them, everything is in short supply.

Valery, Zhenya, and Anna were back for their third Sochi vacation, and they considered themselves fortunate this time to have rented a small room in a private house. We met them on the street and they invited us for a drink in their room, saying that we should see what a real Sochi vacation looks like. All in their thirties and unmarried, they were office workers from Kiev. Anna and Valery appeared to be a couple and Zhenya a mutual friend, but the three cots in the room of the wood frame house offered no clues on that score. Daily life was communal: they cooked on a hot plate and shared the bathroom with more than a dozen vacationers who occupied the other rooms. In other houses, they said, it was common to have as many as six boarders per room.

Our hosts told us of the hurdles faced by Sochi vacationers. As soon as they arrived, they had to begin planning how to get return train tickets to Kiev to report back to work on time. Given the intricacies of Soviet railroad regulations, they could not easily arrange advance bookings. Instead, they had to choose the right moment to start standing on line. Zhenya had joined the line to the ticket office that morning, registering himself as number 156. For the next several days, he would have to show up every morning and evening to keep his place. Tickets could be bought fifteen days in advance; therefore, the trick was to get on line calculating the right waiting time to arrive at the window when tickets were briefly available for the desired day. Plane tickets, largely taken up by organized groups and held for special customers, were even more difficult to purchase. Restaurants must be practically assaulted to gain admission. David and I already knew that from our experience at the Zhemchuzhina (Pearl) Hotel, a concrete behemoth built to house 1,800 foreign tourists and well-connected or wealthy Soviet visitors. We had to raise a hue and cry before we would be seated and served because we were that bizarre specimen of foreign visitor: individuals, not part of an organized group.

But all such needs could be met more expeditiously, Anna told us, if someone had *blat*, influential connections, or money. An extra 10-ruble note, the equivalent of $14*, might procure a train ticket without the tedium of waiting days in line; it was not uncommon for a prosperous vacationer to press $5 into the palm of the doorman at the Zhemchuzhina just to get inside the lobby, since the doorman's job is not to welcome people but to turn them away, and to slip another $140 to the desk clerk to arrange for a room in the allegedly fully booked hotel. Our hosts were hardly capable of throwing around that kind of money, but

---

*To simplify, all monetary references will be given in their dollar equivalents from now on. In 1981, 1 ruble equaled $1.40.

they didn't let that stop them from enjoying themselves. They had brought about $500 each to cover expenses for their three-week stay, nearly the equivalent of three months of their regular salaries.

Was such a vacation worth the steep price? "Yes, definitely," Anna said. "One always has experiences and memories." Their only request was that David and I leave them our admission tickets to the hotel beach before we left, in the hope that they could pass them off as their own. The Zhemchuzhina beach, although crowded, was less packed than the public beach.

Corruption was the issue that had brought David and me to Sochi in the first place, but not the banal bribery that Valery, Zhenya, and Anna had described and that they said was common throughout the Soviet Union. In Moscow we had heard reports of wholesale graft involving the top political leadership, which had sparked an unusual backlash among the local citizenry. In late 1980, the Soviet press reported that Sochi's mayor Vyacheslav Voronkov received a thirteen-year prison sentence for flagrantly taking advantage of his office for personal gain. According to an article in the November 20, 1980 issue of the weekly *Literaturnaya Gazeta,* Voronkov made "apartments, jobs, services, rooms at health resorts, cars, tickets available to lackeys, careerists, and cynics with bulging purses." He charged about $2,000 for a new apartment or for a job promotion, while frequently enjoying free food, entertainment, and the company of young women at the city's restaurants and nightclubs. When the police raided his house, they discovered a box containing gold and diamond jewelry, crystal, and other valuables given as bribes; many items still had their price tags attached.

The Soviet press periodically puts out such reports in order to demonstrate that the government is serious about fighting corruption. Western correspondents routinely write their own dispatches based solely on such official accounts. But what the *Literaturnaya Gazeta* article failed to reveal was far more important than what it reported. It made no mention of the fact that Mikhail Palchekh, the original prosecutor in the case, was fired and stripped of his party membership when he began pursuing his investigation too vigorously. Nor did it mention that Voronkov would have been still at liberty if not for a courageous, small group of the city's residents, mostly retired war veterans. They had sent hundreds of letters and petitions to the press, to the Soviet Central Committee, and to Brezhnev himself detailing the corruption charges and demanding that the government take action. The article significantly failed to acknowledge that the charges implicated more than one man; the letters had accused many top party officials "who live like counts and princes" of being involved in similar practices.

David Satter and I learned all this from sources in Moscow who sympathized with the veterans and were concerned about their fate. They showed us copies of their letters that accused leaders of the entire Krasnodar region, which includes Sochi, of not only turning a blind eye to the thousands of daily illegal transactions but of personal involvement in corruption on a much more lavish scale. The authors of the letters outlined the corruption in general terms, carefully refraining from linking the local party leadership and the Kremlin. But our sources in Moscow were less circumspect. They pointed out that top Soviet leaders from Brezhnev on down regularly vacationed in the region, and local bosses entertained them in the manner to which they were accustomed. That meant, we were told, providing huge receptions, special sanitoriums whose "nurses" often were no more than high-priced call girls, and a huge network of villas, parks, and beaches for their private use. By presiding over this empire, Sergei Medunov, the first secretary of the

Krasnodar region, had attained power and prestige out of proportion to his nominal political position. He was a good personal friend of Brezhnev and had particularly close ties to his son Yuri, a deputy minister of foreign trade who drank heavily and frequented Sochi often to enjoy Medunov's hospitality.

The veterans of Sochi claimed that Medunov "systematically violates" the laws of the party and the Soviet Constitution. They were outraged by the corruption. Apparently, they fervently believed that if they could only inform the proper higher authorities, the local leaders, beginning with Medunov, would be made to answer for their crimes. When David and I arranged a meeting with two of the veterans, traces of that fervor still remained. "This group is without the weapons that belong to the party, press, and prosecutors," one of them said. "This group only has the truth."

But fear was visible on their worn faces, in their nervousness about talking to us at all. Medunov, it appeared, had offered up Voronkov as a sacrificial lamb; the mayor was guilty, but he was meant to take the blame for all the abuses; the investigation was not to continue. Medunov had no intention of allowing the veterans to push their campaign any further.

Reluctantly, the veterans we met described the price members of their group were paying for their actions. One of their colleagues had been placed in a psychiatric hospital for six months, while younger people who flirted with the idea of joining the protest were warned they would lose their jobs. Shortly before our arrival, the authorities had arrested Anatoly Churganov, the most outspoken member of the veterans' group. They also raided five apartments, confiscating all documents, letters, and petitions spelling out the corruption charges. Medunov himself reportedly warned one of the petitioners: "We will destroy your group." From prison, Churganov managed to get out a letter. "I have lived through things you would not believe," he wrote. "If I survive, I will tell you about it."

Medunov's tactics of intimidation began to succeed. One of the veterans vouched for their imprisoned colleague. "He is a patriot who is fighting against thieves who are corrupting this system," he said. The other veteran added: "They are bandits at the top who cover themselves with Leninist slogans." But before we could talk further, a neighbor came in to warn us that two plainclothesmen had conspicuously taken up positions near the apartment where we were holding our discussion. The veteran who had been doing most of the talking abruptly said, "Our letters were about internal matters that we do not want to discuss." He left little doubt that he wanted us to go as quickly as possible.

A few months earlier, there had been an encouraging sign that perhaps the veterans' efforts might produce a more positive response from the government. Some Central Committee members, like *Pravda* editor Viktor Afanasyev, had been troubled by the scope of the corruption in the Krasnodar region and the fact that this had prompted protests by people who so clearly believed in the Soviet system: it was hard to dismiss them as standard political dissidents. While his newspaper did report that it received hundreds of letters complaining about "the abuse of authority" of local officials, our sources in Moscow said that Medunov had been able to prevent other articles, which would have been more specific and damaging, from being published.

Medunov had successfully invoked his ties to Brezhnev, and the Sochi veterans we talked to were bitter about the nature of the Soviet political system. As David and I returned to Moscow, we had no way of knowing that in less than a year events would take a different turn. By then, Medunov's corrupt fiefdom would become a major issue in the internal party struggle to replace a rapidly fading Brezhnev.

Christina and the children had spent most of August in Poland, staying with her family in Czestochowa. I took a week off to join them and to visit relatives and friends in various cities. Coming from Moscow, I could easily imagine the reaction of Soviet officials to what was happening. On the nightly TV news, the Polish government criticized Solidarity's strikes, but Solidarity spokesmen issued rebuttals and accusations of their own. Solidarity offices were alive with activity in every city; the union's newspaper, bulletins, hats, pins, and posters were everywhere, for sale and display without any restriction. One popular poster showed the outline of a map of Poland partially obscured by bricks and scaffolding, with the legend: "Renovation, outsiders not allowed."

The fear of a Soviet invasion, so widespread in the West and among Solidarity sympathizers in the Soviet Union, seemed not to be shared by the Poles. They believed that Brezhnev would not dare to risk such action, for the history of Polish-Russian relations suggested that a tremendous price in blood and destruction would be exacted. The Polish Communist Party had just held a special congress that approved such novel features as voting by secret ballot for top leadership positions and open debates between contending factions. Emotional speeches were made by Solidarity supporters. But popular distrust of the party leadership remained widespread. Confrontation was in the air. A Solidarity activist told me: "My feeling from the beginning has been that we have to risk much, push things to the very edge, if we hope to achieve anything real that will not be erased at the first opportunity."

While no one doubted that the government would exploit any chance to roll back the gains that Solidarity had made, people's confidence in their new power was at its peak that summer. Our Polish friends predicted that any attempt by the armed forces and the police to abruptly turn back the clock would be met by mass resistance and would only end in failure. I wanted to share their optimism.

But danger signs were unmistakable. I had been visiting Poland for years, but I had never seen such massive lines in front of stores from morning to night, such emptiness on the shelves inside, such shortages of food, clothing, soap, cigarettes. By and large, people waited patiently, hoping that something would still be there when their turn came. However, occasional fights would break out when someone tried to cut into a line: one woman in Czestochowa became so enraged that she bit the arm of a line-jumper. People were beginning to turn their frustration against themselves. There was no easy explanation for the sudden shortages, although people began to realize that they were paying the price for the phony prosperity of the 1970s. The relative affluence of that period had been based on reckless economic policies, a mushrooming foreign debt, and the personal corruption of the top leadership that led to the wholesale squandering of the country's resources.

Although First Secretary Stanislaw Kania and Prime Minister Wojciech Jaruzelski acknowledged the mistakes of their predecessors, they increasingly blamed Solidarity for Poland's economic disarray: if there was nothing on the shelves, it was because people were striking instead of working. But many Poles were convinced that the authorities had been withholding food from distribution, allowing it to rot in warehouses, or even destroying supplies. The motive, it was said, was to exacerbate the crisis and make the population arrive at a simple conclusion: before Solidarity, life may have been difficult but most basic items could be obtained; with Solidarity, life was becoming unendurable.

I was skeptical of such suspicions, but I was as perplexed

75

as anyone by the scope of the shortages. I was also troubled by what I heard from one acquaintance who was fulfilling his military service. He talked of tightened internal discipline in his unit and the steady diet of political lectures, films, and orders that portrayed Solidarity as the enemy, an alien force that threatened Poland's security. When two soldiers fell asleep on duty, they were awakened by the angry shouts of their superior officer that "Solidarity could have already been here by now."

Nonetheless, I left Poland elated by the depth and breadth of the *odnowa*, renewal, taking place; it was impossible not to be caught up in the excitement of rediscovered freedoms and the palpable shedding of the pervasive fear that marks any police state. Christina was even more intensely moved by her stay than I was, which made her return to Moscow a week later all the more of a jolt.

She arrived with the children at almost midnight on a flight from Warsaw that had been delayed for several hours. Adam, our youngest, was falling apart and his two sisters were just as exhausted. I watched, without being able to help, as she maneuvered the luggage and the children through the long customs line. To my relief, the customs officer, a young woman, saw what kind of shape the children were in and began waving Christina's suitcases through without inspecting them. She allowed me to take them and load them into the car.

When I returned, Christina was all set to go, but at the last minute the customs official told her to open her purse. When Christina did so, the woman's face suddenly colored in anger as she plucked out a key chain: it bore no inscription, only a picture of Lech Walesa and the pope. "Bring back everything," she commanded, turning to me. A cold fury seemed to be working its way through her whole body.

For the next three hours, she took out every piece of

clothing and examined every scrap of paper in all of the bags. Her only concession was to allow me to take the children to the car, where they slept as the inspection continued. Triumphantly, she found some more Solidarity pins that Christina and the girls had collected as souvenirs, a copy of the Solidarity weekly, a prayer booklet, and a book about the 1944 Warsaw uprising. When I argued that all of those items were openly for sale in Poland and there was nothing illegal about having them, she refused to respond. She assembled everything in a pile and called over a senior inspector.

By this time, the airport was practically empty and other customs officials were looking on. Christina heard two of them talking about the Solidarity weekly, excited that they would have the chance to see a publication they had not come across before. For his part, the senior inspector began sifting through the material and, upon seeing the prayer booklet, told the woman: "You'd better give this back to her."

I asked why the other items were being confiscated. "Solidarity is not an internationally recognized organization," he replied.

"What about the book on the Warsaw uprising? You do know what happened in 1944?" In that year, Soviet troops had sat impassively on the opposite side of the Vistula River when the Warsaw underground rose up against the Germans, allowing the Nazis to crush the city and the heart of the Polish resistance, which Stalin feared would oppose his plans to impose a Communist government on Poland. The book, which was published in Poland, made no mention of that, but the Soviet authorities prefer to skip over the entire subject. "Yes, yes," he said, thrusting the book into my hands. At 3 A.M., we finally drove home. Summer was just about over.

2

*F*ALL

By the end of August and the beginning of September, the July heat wave was all but forgotten. Crisp, cool days settled in with startling speed, providing splendid afternoons of New England football weather. The frustrated jocks of the American press corps, myself included, and some of the diplomats started up what became a regular Sunday event in the park near Moscow's New Circus: a "spiers vs. liars" touch-football game. As couples out for a stroll stopped to watch before boredom got the better of their curiosity, we missed blocks, juggled passes, and occasionally put together a real play. Mothers pulled toddlers well out of range of our meandering game.

Eva and Sonia put on their uniforms, dark brown dresses with white collars, and set out for Moscow School Number 5 across the street from our housing compound. Parents were invited to the opening-day outdoor assembly, where the director read a speech about the need for world peace, frequently quoting Brezhnev's latest pronouncements. No one appeared to listen: the children giggled and pinched each other, while the parents stood proudly watching them. From the first day, classroom discipline and teaching methods were as rigid as we had been led to expect, but during breaks between classes children careened wildly up and down the halls. By and large, teachers ignored what they recognized as a necessary release of pent-up energy.

The talk in Moscow was of the nation's economic problems and the threat of war: the two were linked in the public consciousness. The message, hammered home in the state-controlled media, political lectures, and declarations of the Kremlin leadership, was that the international situation was dangerously insecure. Aside from unrest in Poland, the main source of concern was the Reagan administration. Its anti-Soviet rhetoric and commitment to higher defense spending were fully exploited to portray the United States as bent on reckless military adventurism. Muscovites needed little prompting to decipher the implications for their own lives. Anna Mikhailovna, who finally showed up to give Eva and Sonia Russian lessons, announced glumly one afternoon: "If we're getting into a new arms race, you know who will have to pay for it."

I received the same warning from Georgi Arbatov, the director of the Institute for the USA and Canada. "We are entering very lean years, both for your country and ours," he told me and two visiting *Newsweek* editors in perfect English. Arbatov is the highest official to receive American visitors regularly, and he knows exactly how to handle them. His spacious office has a Western executive look: a spotless green carpet, orange curtains, formidable desk, and large conference table all create an air of brisk efficiency, with the white molded ceiling offering just the proper touch of class. Dressed in a light gray three-piece suit, Arbatov looked more solid than portly, his sunken eyes and worn face more engaging than calculating.

He spoke of the high level of East-West tensions ("This

period is a very dangerous one and no one can guarantee it won't erupt"); of the Kremlin's frustrations with the new set of signals from Washington with the switch from Carter to Reagan ("You cannot begin from the beginning with each president"); and of the economic costs of a new arms race ("Sooner or later Washington will have to face that reality").

The connecting theme, woven into all the subjects under discussion, was the responsibility of the Reagan administration, not the Kremlin, for this sorry state of affairs. "There has been bad news from Day One of this administration." A studied pause, then a word of caution that the next part was for our ears only. "Those people seem to have come from the deep freeze of the early 1950s." Leaning forward as if to emphasize just how private a confidence he was sharing, he tapped his finger on his forehead. "They do not have it up here."

Arbatov's basic message never changed. To a steady stream of visitors from the U.S., he explained that the Kremlin had reluctantly "given up" on the Reagan administration; after his most recent actions, whether in the first year of his presidency or in his fourth, Reagan had proven himself impervious to reason and opposed to dialogue. Visiting columnists as well as resident American correspondents who kept coming back for more all produced remarkably similar stories after such encounters. No matter how many times they had been recycled, they received prominent play as a fresh analysis of Kremlin thinking. Arbatov did not have to vary his message: the same one worked again and again.

The lean years Arbatov had predicted were already a Soviet reality. The country was experiencing its third year in a row of bad grain harvests, and there were continuing shortages of meat, milk, butter, and other staples. Reports of rationing began to filter in from cities in the Ural Mountains and other remote areas, with wage earners allotted about three pounds of meat and less than a pound of butter a month. The government blamed "bad weather" for the hardships and, as that explanation began to wear thin, increasingly sought to link domestic problems to the international situation. Although officially Soviet defense spending had remained unchanged over the previous year, such pronouncements seemed to imply that guns were taking precedence over butter. They also tacitly acknowledged what everyone took for granted: that the public figures on defense spending bore no relation to actual expenditures. To personal acquaintances, Planning Minister Nikolai Baibakov admitted that two plans exist, the public plan and the real plan.

In September, several Russians told me to expect an announcement of new price increases, always a politically embarrassing move for a country that claims to have no inflation. Their evidence? The sudden appearance in the Soviet press of articles reminding readers that basic food prices had not risen in twenty years. Masters of the art of reading between the lines, Muscovites immediately began lining up at gas stations, liquor stores, and jewelry shops, the likely targets of price hikes. Right on the rumor mill schedule, Nikolai Glushkov, the chairman of the State Committee on Prices, announced that, after taking into account "the appropriate suggestions of the workers," the government was doubling the price of gasoline, raising the cost of vodka and tobacco 17 to 27 percent, and marking up the prices of just about everything else except basic foods.

Although not unexpected, the news produced plenty of grumbling. The next day, Christina overheard a woman who had been standing for two hours in line for a rare shipment of bananas and lemons. The woman complained that Glushkov had not mentioned that the government had raised the price of those fruits by 40 to 80 percent. "It's all the same to them if we know or not—they'll do what they want," she said. The government's claim that it had boosted prices of vodka and tobacco "to limit their consumption" was met with widespread disbelief. "People will drink the same amount, even if they have to eat less," said an older worker. The lines for vodka were no shorter than before even though the price was about $13 a liter. The average Soviet monthly wage was then about $230.

This episode was my first lesson in how the Soviet government refuses to confront its economic problems. The price increases solved nothing because they addressed none of the fundamental reasons for the deterioration of the agricultural sector, declining industrial growth rates, and low worker productivity. Even judged purely as a pricing decision, the new hikes came in the wrong places. But in the Soviet economy, prices bear little relation to cost. While state prices of milk, eggs, and meat had not changed since 1962, government food subsidies had ballooned to about $40 billion a year. The system of artificially low prices guarantees constant shortages: the price remains stable but the goods are unavailable much of the time. With no laws of supply and demand at work, neither collective farmers nor factory workers have any real incentives to increase production. The output of their farms or factories has almost nothing to do with their incomes, which are determined by central planners in Moscow. Soviet statistics indicate that between 1966 and 1980 the work force's total wages nearly tripled, but savings increased more than eightfold because Soviet citizens had few places to spend their money.

For political reasons, the government is reluctant to raise the prices of basic foodstuffs. After it did so in 1962, the inhabitants of Novocherkassk took to the streets in a demonstration that turned into a massacre when troops fired on the protesters.

Rents and a massive construction program to redress the chronic housing shortage are also heavily subsidized by the state. The Kremlin wants to be able to maintain that it is providing for all the basic needs of the Soviet people, even when those very policies ensure that those needs will be poorly met, if at all.

The Soviet press itself catalogued many of those economic failures. In agriculture, it reported, insufficient storage facilities, a lack of roads and transport, and inefficient or inadequate machinery ensure that about a quarter of most harvested crops are lost to spoilage; in the case of potatoes, an average 50 percent of the crop perishes. During what the Soviet press calls "the bad roads season," when unpaved roads turn into mud swamps, the majority of tractors on state farms are used for towing trucks and delivering freight. In the Russian republic, less than 1 percent of interfarm roads are asphalt covered. The railroad freight system is overloaded and grossly mismanaged; it is not unusual for two trains to pass each other carrying the same raw materials in opposite directions. Electrical power breakdowns are common, and many poultry and livestock units have no backup generators.

The one success story had been the private plots, where collective farmers can cultivate their own crops. Although such plots only occupy 1.5 percent of the cultivated land, they account for about one-third of total agricultural output aside from grain. But in the early 1960s, Khrushchev placed severe restrictions on what could be raised on private plots. In recent years, production in this sector has been largely stagnant and, in the case of milk, declining. At a time of feed shortages, the state farms were getting first call on grain supplies. The private plots were also hurt by the general aging of the farm population as younger people fled the rural life. Brezhnev loosened some of the restrictions on private plots and acknowledged their importance, but such tinkering could not reverse the negative trends. A popular joke offered this mock consolation: "There will be less to eat than last year but more than next year."

The centralization of all planning produces predictable results. With its love of statistics, the government has even quantified the red tape that clogs the system. According to the Documentation and Archives Institute, 800 billion business documents are produced each year, providing boring, largely useless jobs to millions of people. One typical result of this planning from the top is that factories are rarely sure of a dependable flow of raw materials. The ministries, not factory managers, spell out factory needs to the suppliers. The natural impulse is to hoard anything available whether or not it is needed, on the assumption that it might be needed later. The logical solution would be for managers to exchange their excess supplies to their mutual benefit, but they have no right to do so. The bureaucracy refuses to yield its power to make the decisions on allocation of resources.

The system guarantees corruption. Any administrator who wants to fulfill his plan, not to mention generate extra private income, must routinely break the rules and become involved in the "second" or illegal economy. Factory managers make private deals with suppliers, store managers pay off the factories for access to their products, and customers slip something to the saleswomen to keep items under the counter, for sale only to them. To participate in this merry-go-round, everyone has to cut corners, stealing goods and labor from the state.

That process stretches from the top to the bottom of the system. An engineer described how profits are made on road-building projects. Huge bribes are funneled to senior officials to approve a plan, providing funds for roads in a region. The specifications on such a project, he explained, might call for a sixty-centimeter base of sand and gravel below the asphalt; instead, a fifteen-centimeter base is laid, except in a couple of places where bought-off inspectors make their checks. "Everyone profits," he concluded, "the builders, the inspectors, and the officials." The plan is recorded as fulfilled, even if the road buckles during the first frost.

Officials routinely use state construction teams and materials to build their dachas, while drivers log phony trips so that they can siphon off gas and sell it privately. (The doubling of gasoline prices provided the state with little extra revenue since private cars only account for 6 percent of gas consumption, but it increased the incentive for state drivers to steal more.) Ambitious entrepreneurs have organized entire underground factories, converting part of the premises of a state enterprise into an illegal operation. Using its supplies, equipment, and labor, they churn out items like blue jeans that are in constant demand. This requires the collusion of workers, managers, and distributors, and the risks are high. Periodically, the government stages a crackdown on corruption, sending some officials and managers off to face firing squads. But even those drastic measures do little to deter.

Disregard for state equipment is widespread. If it is not stolen, it is abused or neglected, leading to chronic breakdowns. Christina saw a taxi driver angrily slam the trunk of his car down again and again, but each time it popped right back up. An old woman walking by scolded him: "Young man, you should be ashamed of yourself. You do this because it is a state car. If it were your car—"

Scowling, he cut in: "Babushka, lay off. Of course if that were my car everything in it would work beautifully."

That fall the system's shortcomings were more apparent than ever. The necessity of buying about 40 million metric tons of grain from abroad in 1981, the fourth consecutive year of rising imports, was cutting into foreign currency reserves. Soviet gold sales rose to about 300 metric tons by the end of the year, a staggering amount especially given the fact that for the first time the Soviets were selling when prices were dropping. The high cost of the SS-20 nuclear missile buildup and other defense programs, heavy Soviet subsidies for the Cuban and Vietnamese economies, and the economic crisis in Eastern Europe, with Poland at its center, were all taking their toll.

From the standpoint of economic planners, a centralized economy does have one special strength: even in difficult times, available funds and resources can be lavished on priority sectors. A strict pecking order ensures that the needs of the military and political leadership are taken care of first. Important showcase cities like Moscow and Leningrad, major industrial centers, and republic capitals are next on the list. The rest of the population lags far behind. That is where sacrifices are felt.

The country's economic situation could not be properly judged by life in Moscow, nor could Russian attitudes be properly measured anywhere but in the vast heartland, the provincial cities and towns with no particular claims to prominence or special treatment. One such place, I decided, should be my next destination.

Vologda, a province with a capital by the same name situated 250 miles north of Moscow, fit that description. If anything, it promised to be slightly better than average. It was a dairy and livestock region, dotted with old monasteries and churches that, while not on the normal foreigner's tourist circuit, attracted Russians from other parts of the country. Near my apartment in Moscow, there was a Vologda Butter Store, named after that region's well-known tasty brand; in the nineteenth century, the local product was known as "Parisian butter" and was exported to France and other parts of Europe. David Satter was once again my companion on this trip. We wanted to report on life in the provinces, but we did not want to pick a place that could be dismissed as unusually deprived, and thus unrepresentative.

We boarded the night train from Moscow and found a young couple sharing our four-berth compartment. As soon as they heard us speaking English, they picked up their belongings and disappeared. As we pulled into Vologda the next morning, a well-dressed young woman struck up a conversation with us in the corridor, explaining that she was a tourist guide and would be happy to show us around the city and the province. David thanked her and took her phone number, but we had no intention of taking her up on her offer. We were not looking for an escort.

The local authorities seemed to have other ideas. As we checked in to our hotel, a smiling, overly eager middle-aged man dressed in a coat and tie came over to introduce himself as Arkady Shorokhov, deputy editor of *Krasny Sever* (*The Red North*), the local newspaper. As a professional colleague, he said, he would be glad to help us in any way he could and offered to accompany us throughout our visit wherever we wished. We had planned to spend the first day traveling to Kirillov, a small town with a famous monastery about seventy-five miles farther north, and he volunteered to arrange for a taxi and to go with us. Since it was apparent the authorities meant to escort us one way or another, we agreed, figuring that at least with him along we would not encounter any problems getting there. We were interested in the historical sights, but our real purpose was to assess the food situation in the smaller towns of the region.

On the way up, Shorokhov talked about Vologda, giving us facts and figures about its population (260,000 in the city, 1.3 million in the province), its Orthodox churches (forty in the city before the 1917 Revolution, only two working churches now but some others preserved as monuments), and the dimensions of the province ("Belgium, the Netherlands, and Luxembourg could be fit into our territory"). I asked whether the region had felt the effect of the bad harvests. "We aren't doing badly," he replied. "Our production is not worse than last year."

He said that Vologda still shipped butter to Moscow and Leningrad and that there were occasional problems about finding it in the region's own shops. He also mentioned that there had been some hitches in the delivery of "first-category" milk, which is pasteurized and packaged to meet state sanitary requirements. "Unfortunately, there are still many unsolved problems in providing provisions to people. There are a lot of tensions in the world that make it difficult to solve them."

It was only October, but the trees along the way were already bereft of their leaves, the forests stark and forbidding. Local farmers, Shorokhov told us, were on the lookout for wolves and bears that emerged periodically to attack their cattle.

The main road connecting Vologda with the northern towns of the region, which in earlier centuries had been a major trade route, was two bumpy lanes. But at least it was paved. As soon as we turned off to see the fourteenth-century monastery in Feronpontovo, a village of one-story wooden houses painted in weather-beaten shades of blue, brown, and green, almost all of them sprouting TV antennas, I learned the meaning of the term "the bad roads season." Although it had not rained that day, the road through the village was a broad expanse of mud and puddles. The locals were apparently used to this: they trudged about wearing knee-high rubber boots. David and I wished we had planned ahead as our shoes disappeared from view the moment we stepped out of the car. Shorokhov knew better. He remained comfortably seated while we went to visit the village's solitary store. It was closed, but through the window we could see that the shelves inside were bare.

The small monastery was open. Set just above the village, its onion domes and white walls looked imposing from afar, badly aging and neglected up close. A guide explained that a hundred monks lived there until 1919, when it was closed down. They were guilty, she said, of hoarding grain and weapons for counterrevolutionaries. It was reopened in 1968 as a museum, and featured a small exhibition of artifacts that had survived. Our next stop, the Kirillov monastery, was a far more imposing stone fortress of vast expanse, although it too was run-down. In the seventeenth century, traders from Persia, England, France, Spain, and Venice used it as an entry point into northern Russia. Today, it is both a historical monument and a vocational school for the deaf.

Leaving behind Shorokhov, who looked far from pleased by our interest in current conditions, David and I walked into the town itself, a small cluster of concrete buildings surrounded by log cabins and wooden houses. Our first stop was a grocery store, whose dusty shelves featured cucumbers, pickles, moldy cabbage, and the ubiquitous cans of fish paste that, however long the lines, never seem to be bought by Soviet shoppers. Margarine was also available, but I saw no meat or butter. I asked the grocer for butter. Looking at me as if I had made the most absurd demand, a woman customer laughed. "Butter, there is none."

"Do you ever get butter here?"

Before she could respond, a young man in a black leather jacket who had followed us into the store thrust himself between us. "What do you mean no butter? Of course there is butter here."

He spun around and disappeared as quickly as he had

89

come. When I turned back to the woman to ask her another question, she drew back. "I don't know anything," she mumbled, fleeing out the door.

We tried the milk store, where milk was being ladled out into pails, but neither butter nor cheese was available or ever seemed to be. Conversations were nearly impossible because everywhere we went men in leather and nylon jackets were not far behind. The local inhabitants recognized them and fell silent. Leather jackets, which are unavailable in regular stores, are particularly popular among the young men working for the police or KGB.

"We seem to have a lot of company," I told Shorokhov as we started back to Vologda. He ignored the remark and suggested we come hear him give a speech the next day to the local chapter of the official Soviet Peace Committee. David said we'd think about it.

At our hotel that evening, the entrance to the restaurant was a battleground. People pushed, shoved, and shouted, alternately pleading and threatening as they fought to get inside what appeared to be the town's prime and probably only night spot. Inside, a percussion band played music that made up in volume what it lacked in style, and army officers danced with women in jeans. Most of the customers just drank, showing little interest in their cucumber salads and tough pieces of meat.

As hotel guests and foreigners, we were allowed in and seated. The back of my chair bumped up against a man with the look of an over-the-hill fighter who could still be dangerous. But he was as glassy-eyed as most of the crowd and his fleeting glance was friendly. At the next table, another man waved for us to join him and his companion for a drink. We motioned that they should be our guests, but a broad-shouldered waitress turned from her bouncer's duty at the door and rushed up, furiously lecturing him to stay put. Our waitress leaned over and said, "That's her husband." We assumed that the bouncer did not want her husband running the risk of associating with foreigners.

But we were not alone for long. A woman who looked to be in her thirties was seated at our table by the bouncer. Luba introduced herself as an English teacher at the local high school and she switched from Russian to English when she discovered who we were. Because nothing seemed to have been left to chance for us that day, we had our doubts about the timing of that discovery and we began to suspect that the bouncer may have already had her instructions for the evening when she had yelled at her husband. But we had no reason not to answer Luba's questions. David told her we wanted to learn about the food situation in Vologda.

Luba said that milk and butter were available in the stores, although there had been "some difficulties" in the summer because of the drought. The meat situation was worse than it had been in the early 1960s, when restrictions were placed on the cultivation of private plots. Nevertheless, she maintained that these were temporary problems and that life had improved since the 1950s. "Things may get a little worse, but we'll manage. Compared to what we've experienced, a few disruptions in deliveries are not important to us. We are more worried about other problems, the international situation. We want to preserve the peace, but Reagan is trying to build more missiles. I was very worried about his statement about a nuclear war in Europe—"

I shifted the discussion back to shortages. "You don't have similar problems in your country?" she countered.

When I replied that we had problems with rising prices but not with shortages, she looked at me doubtfully. "Well, our prices do not change. Who knows whether it is better to have higher prices or to have money and nothing to spend it on?"

The one shortage that really troubled her, she admitted, was books, particularly of the classics. She had always wanted to get Chekhov's works but had not yet succeeded.

This is a problem even in Moscow. Speeches by political leaders are churned out in massive editions, but the average Russian can only dream about getting his hands on a book by Tolstoy, Dostoyevsky, or Gogol. Small print runs ensure that such works disappear immediately, either to friends of the saleswomen or to the black market for books, where they are sold for several times their nominal price. A friend in Moscow had recently suggested that the shortage was deliberate. Ideological objections, for instance to the religious themes of the great nineteenth-century Russian writers, were only part of the explanation. The government had more prosaic concerns about the conclusions readers might draw from pre-revolutionary literature. He cited the scene in *Crime and Punishment* where Raskolnikov casually orders his servant in the late morning to run down to the pork butchers and buy him the cheapest brand of sausage. A Russian today could not help but be struck by the fact that in those times sausage was always available and there was even a broad choice. Today, on the rare occasion when sausage is for sale, the customer is grateful to buy whatever he can get, and anything available is certain to be sold out by late morning.

The next day we explored Vologda itself. The city was a jumble of old and new. Aside from the formidable monastery and churches, log cabins with white-framed windows still predominated. A few were solid, well-maintained two-story structures, with handsomely carved doors and banisters on second-floor balconies. The majority were one-story houses whose sagging roofs betrayed their age. Firewood for their owners' wood-burning stoves was stacked in yards or beside nearby outhouses; on the riverbank, near one cluster of old houses, women gathered to wash laundry. However, these picturesque but primitive houses were marked for destruction as the city methodically replaced them with standardized concrete apartment buildings. This was in response to a definite demand, but increasingly Vologda was losing its character and coming to resemble any number of Soviet cities.

From a survey of the city's stores and from brief conversations, the dimensions of the food problem were readily apparent. Red meat had largely disappeared from the state stores beginning in the early 1960s, and only chickens could be bought there now. The only red meat we saw was in the farmers' market, where it sold at double the state price, putting it out of bounds for average workers. When I asked one woman for directions to the city's own Vologda Butter Store, she replied: "We don't see our Vologda butter here anymore." She did not exaggerate; butter was nowhere to be found. Word that "first-category" milk was about to be delivered created huge lines, and supplies quickly sold out. "Second-category" milk—the kind that is usually served up from open pails—is neither pasteurized nor packaged and is often thought to be dirty and diluted with water. While the meat problem was nothing new, shortages of butter and cheese products had only occurred in the last couple of years, and the milk problem had only recently grown serious.

We had lunch in a blini restaurant, a steamy ground-floor establishment where women in stained white aprons pitched tin dishes with the servings across the counter to customers standing in line. The menu listed blinis with margarine, cabbage, sour cream, and *tvorog*, a farmer's cheese, but that last item was not available. A sign in the restaurant read: "Bread for lunch; just take your norm. Bread is a great value; preserve it."

At local party meetings, citizens were told that these

"temporary difficulties" were occurring because Vologda province had to send more of its products to other parts of the country and abroad, to unspecified countries, at a time when everyone was suffering the effects of the bad weather and poor harvests. Judging by what we heard, many people seemed satisfied by that explanation and accepted the rationale that somehow increased tensions between the superpowers were to blame.

When we introduced ourselves to two older women on the street, they launched into a political lecture. "We don't have enough food here because America is attacking us," one said. But what, I asked, had that to do with the shortage of Vologda's own butter? "It goes elsewhere." Elsewhere? "To the army," she said.

Our discussion went no further because a young man who had been lingering nearby burst in at that point demanding to know what we were talking about, telling the women they should not be speaking with foreigners like us. I told him to leave us alone, but he had done his job. Sheepishly, the women excused themselves and left. When I tried to take a picture of a milk line, another young man jumped in front of my camera. As we kept walking, other men kept shadowing us.

The irony of the situation was that, like the two older women, people we were able to talk to largely accepted and echoed the government's official rhetoric. A taxi driver complained that the food situation was deteriorating but said that this was because "we are helping many countries," although he had no idea which countries. A cashier in a bookstore shrugged: "Problems, problems, there are difficulties everywhere. After all, we are the first socialist state and Moscow was not built in a day."

Most people knew that ten miles outside of Vologda there was a special store for the elite that stocked fresh meat, butter, milk, fruit, vegetables, and other delicacies that were not available elsewhere, but no one seemed to question the right of the *nachalniki* (bosses) to shop there. They also knew about the contrast between Vologda and Moscow, which is so much better stocked with food that Vologda factories organize periodic shopping trips there for their workers. I asked one man whether he resented this disparity. He looked at me quizzically and said, "Of course it's better in Moscow. It's the capital."

In the afternoon, we skipped Shorokhov's discourse on world peace and took a taxi to Cheropovets, an industrial city of 270,000, a little more than an hour away. We made similar rounds and found the same basic food situation, with one exception. Milk was being sold by prescription: one liter a day for babies up to a year old, a half a liter a day for infants between the ages of one and two. Parents with older children had to find milk when it was delivered at the stores for general sale, but while we were there none was available.

By the time we prepared to head back, the rust-colored sky had turned pitch black. A few miles outside of Cheropovets, in darkness among open fields, our taxi broke down. The driver tried in vain for half an hour to fix it. The temperature was dropping, and our driver offered to help us flag down another car. As for himself, he would have to spend the night in his taxi on the side of the road until a repair truck came. "If I abandoned it here, nothing would be left by morning," he said.

Headlights flashed by, mostly of large trucks. Another taxi finally stopped and agreed to take us. We gratefully hopped into the back seat, where a woman was already seated; the front seat was occupied by a male passenger. The driver asked us a couple of questions about what had happened, and a silence descended on the cab. From our accents, they knew we were not Russians but the driver and the woman took some time before they cautiously began to feel us out. The man, who was well dressed and whom the driver addressed respectfully as if he were someone of rank, never turned his head. When we explained who we were, he kept looking ahead, never acknowledging our existence. I imagined him wondering where we had ditched our parachutes before emerging from the dark, empty landscape to infiltrate that remote corner of his country.

On our third and final day in Vologda, Shorokhov reentered our lives. In one case, it was indirectly: we had to use the deputy editor as a reference. I had been taking pictures of the log cabins I had found so colorful, when a policeman demanded to know who we were and what we were doing. I explained that we were American correspondents on a working visit, with the full knowledge of the authorities. But he remained skeptical. Why would I want to take photographs of such ugly sights instead of the city's monuments or new construction? Surely this was unauthorized, he concluded, and asked for my film. David showed him Shorokhov's card; the deputy editor could confirm that we were on an official visit. The policeman hesitated, took the card, and left.

But not for long. After we crossed to the other side of the river, he was back trailing us. He approached me again, this time more insistent that I give him my film because he had seen me continuing to take pictures. We repeated the same arguments and gave him our calling cards so that he could show them to Shorokhov or anyone else he wanted to check with. Just then, a young man who had been standing around a building site with a hammer in his hand called the policeman over and they exchanged a few words. He probably was no ordinary construction worker. After their chat, the policeman left us alone, apparently having been told that we were in other people's hands.

Shorokhov was with us when we went to interview Mayor Vladimir Parmenov at City Hall. The mayor was prepared with pictures of new apartment buildings and a variety of facts and figures. Sixty percent of the city's families lived in their own apartments, while the remainder were equally divided between communal apartments and private housing, the wooden and log houses. These were being destroyed at the rate of 200 a year, while 4,000 new apartments were being built annually. The housing problem and alcoholism were the primary reasons for divorces. "Alcoholism is a problem," he concluded, "but I wouldn't say it has any effect on productivity."

What were our impressions of Vologda, he asked. David volunteered that we were surprised by the extent of the food shortages in a dairy and livestock region. Parmenov nodded, acknowledging that meat and dairy products were not in evidence in the stores. "We had inadequacies of some supplies, but this does not mean we do not have those products. It means we do not have a surplus. The population, however, is guaranteed an adequate amount."

We pursued his surplus theory for a few minutes with little success. His point, it appeared, was that the foods were supplied to the stores but were immediately sold. That was why the shelves appeared to be empty. "If you go to any family on a birthday or a wedding," he added with a smile, "everything is there."

As for the reasons for this lack of "surplus," he reeled off the familiar litany. "We are still suffering the consequences of the Great Patriotic War. Also, there are such international tensions that resources are needed to allow an improvement in the situation. But despite that, every year the situation gets better."

David mentioned that we had heard about a special store for the elite. Parmenov stiffened. "There is no such store."

I asked if the shortages had produced any popular discontent. "Some discontent may exist if someone does not have an apartment, but this does not lead to any campaigns. People understand miracles don't happen."

In Poland, I continued, such discontent gave birth to Solidarity. Was anything similar possible in Vologda?

"A Russian is a Russian. We all understand very well what happened. There is no family here that did not suffer during the war—no nation suffered as much during the war as we did."

I was not trying to minimize the suffering of the Russian people, I said, but Poland had lost an even greater proportion of its population during the war.

"No, no. No nation has suffered what we suffered. People understand that we have to do everything for ourselves, that no one will help us. Socialism in the Soviet Union was built by Russians, by our own people."

"Not like in Poland?" I asked, alluding to the fact that it was the Soviet Army, not the Poles, who installed a Communist regime in Warsaw at the end of the war.

"Yes," he replied.

Walking back to our hotel with Shorokhov, we passed a long line of people waiting to buy detergent. A shipment had just come in and customers were buying up to ten boxes each.

Shorokhov conceded that they were stocking up because detergent, too, was in short supply. "But," he said as we parted, "these problems will be solved during the current five-year plan."

"A Russian is a Russian," Mayor Parmenov had said. It was a statement loaded with implications: that a Russian believes in his government, will obey it, endure any hardship that is imposed on him by the Soviet system; that he is naturally passive and draws upon vast pools of patience in the face of adversity. Despite all the attempts to interfere with our reporting and especially to intimidate people who were willing to talk to us, I left Vologda with no reason to doubt that the attitudes expressed to us by local citizens, supporting the mayor's conclusions, were authentic. I felt that in my travels I had already journeyed from one end of the Soviet attitudinal spectrum to the other. Lithuania had provided a picture of near-universal opposition, both active and passive, to the Soviet government and everything it represented, while Vologda had provided an image of complete support.

But was I to conclude from this that Russians, as opposed to other nationalities within the Soviet Union, had an infinite capacity for obedience to the state, even if their living conditions were worsening?

There was much more evidence other than my personal observations in Vologda that life was becoming harder for the Soviet population in general. A recent U.S. Census Bureau report* had produced startling findings about the deteriorating physical well-being of Soviet citizens: the Soviet Union had become the first industrialized country in the world to experience a rise in its infant mortality rate and a decline in life expectancy, reversing previous trends. Christopher Davis and Murray Feshbach, the authors of the study, had methodically analyzed all available Soviet demographic data in an attempt to explain Moscow's failure to publish figures on life expectancy since 1972 and infant mortality since 1974. They concluded that the infant mortality rate had risen by 36 percent between 1971 and 1976, and life expectancy for Soviet men had declined from 66 to 63 years while the figure for women, 74 years, had leveled off.

The authors pointed to a broad range of factors that

---

*Christopher Davis and Murray Feshbach, *Rising Infant Mortality in the U.S.S.R. in the 1970s*. U.S. Department of Commerce, Bureau of the Census (June 1980), 1 and 31.

helped explain the infant mortality statistics. Pregnant women, like the rest of the population, are drinking more heavily than ever before. Birth-control devices are generally unavailable, producing a staggeringly high abortion rate: they cited evidence that the average Soviet woman has at least six abortions in her lifetime. Nearly all Soviet women work, performing a disproportionate share of the strenuous jobs, and they usually keep working until their seventh month of pregnancy, heightening health risks. Other factors include overcrowding in housing and child-care centers, the Soviet inability to produce properly nutritional formulas, poor sanitation, and the declining quality of medical care.

Ever since I arrived, I tried to test the accuracy of those findings. If true, they pointed to the existence of a health-care crisis of considerable proportions in the Soviet Union. The official view was spelled out in the first press conference I attended. Alexander Smirnov, the deputy director of the state planning organization Gosplan, argued that infant mortality was not on the rise and that any figures that indicated otherwise were the result of improved statistical data from the Central Asian republics, where health care had traditionally been limited. But Davis and Feshbach had demonstrated in their report that infant mortality was increasing all over the Soviet Union. Smirnov, moreover, failed to explain why, if Soviet statistical gathering capabilities were improving, the government had withheld figures on infant mortality and life expectancy, when in the past it had published them.

Soviet officials were willing to concede the dimensions of the alcoholism problem. "Alcoholism is one of our most serious problems for the birthrate, the death rate, and the economy in general," Smirnov said. Reports in the Soviet press indicated that, despite strict rules against drinking before driving, about one-third of all traffic accidents are caused by drunk drivers and one out of every four pedestrians involved in road accidents is drunk, and by some estimates overall economic productivity could be raised by 10 percent if the nation sobered up. But the sale of alcohol is a major source of state revenues, and I saw no convincing evidence that the government wanted to curtail consumption. *Molodoi Kommunist,* the monthly magazine of Komsomol, the Young Communist League, reported that in new towns in remote regions of the country per capita annual consumption of alcohol reaches fifty liters. Excluding children, such a figure means "that each worker drinks a bottle a day."*

The impact on people's health of such intake of hard liquor is easy to imagine, but the problem in the Soviet Union is exacerbated by the quality as well as the quantity of the alcohol consumed. I quickly learned that the best gift for anyone was a bottle of Stolichnaya or Moskovskaya vodka, the brands that are exported to the West and sold in the hard-currency *beriozka* shops for foreigners. In normal liquor shops, Russians rarely see those brands, although they were sometimes featured in display windows. (As one popular ditty summed it up, "What is in the window is not in the store.") Customers had to content themselves with coarser vodkas and cheap fruit wines. Among doctors I met, there was a widespread conviction that the declining quality of these products—wines were often made with spoiled fruit, for example—was one reason for the poor health of many patients. In addition, they pointed out, people were employing an increasing amount of dangerous substances in *samogon,* home brews. Anything from alcohol products for industrial uses to eau de cologne was going into the mix.

Other bits and pieces of evidence were falling into place that appeared to confirm the gravity of the health crisis. I

Molodoi Kommunist, February 1980, 65.

learned from reliable sources that letters written to the Communist Party before its 26th Congress in February 1981 had focused on poor health care in hospitals and clinics; before the previous party congress in 1976, most people complained about the housing shortage. Doctors privately told me that the U.S. Census Bureau's findings were generally accurate and that these health problems were directly linked to the nation's deteriorating medical care.

I visited a retired woman surgeon who was a patient at Moscow City Hospital Number 59, a hulking five-story building from the Stalin era. It was considered one of the best orthopedic facilities available and Nina, the woman I had come to see, told me that special arrangements often had to be made to get someone admitted. What kind of special arrangements? She said it helped to know the right people.

Nina made it clear that she was not about to criticize her former colleagues or to discuss such issues as corruption in the medical profession. But she was concerned about the problems she had seen growing during her recently ended career. The problems were evident even in Hospital 59 with its excellent staff of doctors, she said. I had only to look down empty corridors to understand what it was that the hospital lacked: any sign of nurses or orderlies.

Nor was this unusual, she said. Orderlies received $98 to $126 a month, and even nurses were paid only $140, less than most factory workers. Since few people wanted to work as orderlies for such minuscule wages, nurses had to perform most of their duties, changing linen and patients, for which they received small additional pay. The reward was hardly worth the heavy work load, and many nurses preferred to work in clinics where they only had to deal with out-patients. While Hospital 59 was still reasonably well maintained, sanitary conditions in other institutions were becoming a health hazard in themselves because of the lack of support staff. Nurses who must perform menial cleaning jobs also find less time for monitoring patients. "Even if an operation is done well, there is no one to take care of the follow-up," Nina said.

Other doctors I talked to were less reticent about discussing the implications of the poor funding of the health services, which they pointed out affected their own salaries as well. A doctor straight out of medical school earns $154 a month and, even when more experienced, does not make much more than the average wage of $230. This had spawned a "second economy" in medicine. To obtain basic services, sometimes even to be admitted to a good hospital, families of patients pay bribes to orderlies, nurses, and doctors: $1.40 may guarantee a change of linen, while $700 may be needed for a major operation. In provincial towns where there is little to buy, doctors may prefer gifts of chickens or chocolates to cash.

Practices vary throughout the country. Bribery is less common and more modest in the far north, where doctors' wages are higher because of hardship duty allowances, than in southern republics like Georgia, where many doctors make several times their official salaries in bribes. Corruption is pervasive. A Leningrad nurse maintained that any family that could not or would not pay bribes at the hospital where she worked was risking the health and very life of the patient. After a routine appendectomy, she recalled, an eighteen-year-old boy developed an infection that was noticed but initially ignored because his parents had not paid up. By the time proper attention was given it was too late to save him.

A doctor I knew well and respected for his professionalism maintained that, despite such stories, whose accuracy he did not dispute, "if there were no second economy in medicine, health services would be much worse." Illegal fees and gifts are what prompt doctors, nurses, and orderlies to work conscientiously; any blame for this state of affairs, he argued, should be assigned not to individuals but to the system, which fails to provide a minimal livelihood for anyone who works according to the rules.

Almost by accident, I learned of a rich source of data that provided evidence confirming many aspects of the Western findings about the health crisis: statistics collected by Moscow research institutes on Soviet women. These were for internal distribution and had never been published, since they contradicted the government's claim that sexual equality had been achieved long ago in Soviet society. Even doctoral dissertations on such sensitive subjects as the role of women workers in labor-intensive industries are filed away as "closed materials." But women who collect such information have their own views on the subject. Natasha, for example, an established social scientist in her mid-thirties, publicly had to adhere to the official explanation that exploitation of women is purely a capitalist disease. Privately, however, she offered scathing commentaries on the changing role of women in Soviet society. "Before, a woman had no rights and she was dependent on her husband, who was obliged to support her," she said. "Now she is still responsible for all the work at home, but the husband is no longer obliged to support her. That is what equality has led to." Her bitter opinions were shared by others.

It was not surprising to find that, as in other countries, there were people interested in leaking information on what the government had learned from its research institutes. Their studies firmly established a link between strenuous manual labor of mothers and their children's health problems. Alcoholism was rising fastest among women with heavy physical jobs. Only about 15 percent of the children born to women in higher skilled jobs were found to have significant health problems, while nearly 75 percent of children born to unskilled and semi-skilled workers suffered from health problems. The incidence of abortions among working women was 2.5 times higher than it was for unemployed women. According to Soviet statistics only 8 percent of Soviet able-bodied women were unemployed.* As a rule, they stay home out of choice: they can afford to do so. Most Soviet women do not have the option not to work because their families can barely survive on one salary. For a working woman, an unplanned pregnancy portends a significant drop in her family's income, at least during the period of her maternity leave.

Employment patterns for women were found to be as unbalanced as Western researchers assumed. About 70 percent of the jobs rated in the lower half of professional skills levels are filled by women, while men outnumber women by 2 to 1 in the jobs that are rated in the upper half of the professions. That is particularly so in such industries as construction and forestry. In new high-rise housing projects, women do almost all the finishing and decorating work. Since the elevators are often not functional when that work is performed, women carry heavy buckets of paint and plaster up the stairs to the top floors. With millions of men tied up in the army, the police, and the KGB, women are needed to handle a majority of the arduous civilian jobs.

Despite constitutional guarantees of equal pay for equal work, men earn more than women in 75 percent of Soviet households, while women earn more than men in only 5 percent of households (70 percent of Soviet doctors are women precisely because medicine is a low-paying profession, although that fact is often cited as evidence of sexual equality in Soviet society). After a full workday and often a long commute, women are expected to put in a "second shift"

*Sovetskaya Rossiya, February 4, 1983.

at home. The average Soviet male remains firm in his conviction that household work is a woman's responsibility: women spend 20 more hours a week on household tasks than men, and 15.5 hours less for sleep and relaxation. Women also take more responsibility for raising children. For example, when children are sick and cannot go to day-care centers, women tend to stay home, thus decreasing their chances for promotion. The day-care centers themselves have proved to be breeding grounds for diseases because of over-crowding and inadequate staffing.

The quality of Soviet life had begun to decline. Soviet citizens, accustomed to a slow but steady improvement in their living standards and the services provided by the state, were increasingly aware that in many crucial areas of life they were worse off than a few years earlier. The 6 percent annual economic growth of the 1950s and early 1960s had slowed to about 2 percent, and the allocation of resources ensured that the civilian sector absorbed all losses. The CIA and others in the West have periodically revised their estimates of Soviet defense spending and estimates of the Soviet budget are always subject to dispute, but the broad outline of spending patterns was clear. Soviet military defense spending—which is usually put at 13 to 14 percent of GNP, about double the U.S. figure—continued to grow while the percentage of GNP allocated to health and other human services declined. Figuratively, if not literally, the woman who told me in Vologda that the local butter was now going to the army was right.

Outsiders looking at those trends are tempted to come to one of two conclusions: either that the Soviet system is heading toward a crisis, perhaps even a collapse, since domestic discontent must inevitably come to a boil, or that the Russian *narod,* the people, will suffer these and other setbacks indefinitely because of their inherently passive historical character. Sometimes, these two seemingly irreconcilable views are fused. Harvard professor Richard Pipes, who served on the National Security Council at the start of the Reagan administration, believed that Soviet economic failures and problems within its empire in Poland and elsewhere were building to a major crisis. Yet he was also the author of *Russia Under the Old Regime,** in which he strongly argued that Soviet communism was a natural outgrowth of Russian traditions. "Unlike most historians who seek the roots of twentieth-century totalitarianism in Western ideas, I look for them in Russian institutions," he wrote. Working from that premise, Pipes provided an interpretation of Russian history that offered virtually no hope that the Russian people would ever oppose their government, no matter how incompetent or despotic it proved to be.

Pipes's thesis that Russians have never been able to impose restraints on their political rulers, allowing them to enjoy absolute and arbitrary powers, is the focal point of a major debate. It is one that concerns not just historians but everyone trying to understand the forces at work in the Soviet Union today, for at its heart is the question of who the Russian people are and what accounts for their past and present behavior. The arguments of that debate were a constant murmur in the back of my mind as I tried to make sense of the sights and sounds of Soviet society.

Sitting in the comfort of my Moscow apartment after my Vologda trip, I could easily be seduced by Pipes's line of reasoning. I was reading *Journey for Our Time*† by Mar-

---

*Richard Pipes, *Russia Under the Old Regime* (New York: Charles Scribner's Sons, 1974), xxi and 294.
†Marquis de Custine, *Journey for Our Time* (New York: Pellegrini and Cudahy, 1951), 128–29, 146–47, and 181.

quis de Custine, a Frenchman who traveled to Russia in 1839 and wrote a wonderful account of his journey to the land of "an absolute government and a nation of slaves." His reflections on Russians and Russia provide ready ammunition for those inclined to share Pipes's views on "the continuity of the police mentality in Russia irrespective of the regime."

Any sampling of de Custine's irresistibly quotable book offers observations that just as easily could have been written about Soviet society today: "In Russia, the tyranny of despotism is a permanent revolution. . . . In Russia, fear replaces, that is to say, paralyzes thought. . . . Actually, this country lends itself marvelously to all kinds of fraud. Russia is always governed by deceit—here admitted tyranny would be a step forward. . . . If freedom of press were accorded to Russia for twenty-four hours, what you would see would make you recoil with horror. Silence is indispensable to oppression."

Such a reading of Russian history enrages nationalists like Solzhenitsyn. In his famous impassioned attack on Western scholarship on the subject in the Spring 1980 issue of *Foreign Affairs,* Solzhenitsyn accused Pipes and others of choosing only the darkest chapters in Russian history to support their theories. Solzhenitsyn wrote:

In this presentation of pre-revolutionary Russia, Western historians succumb to a persistent but fallacious tradition, thereby to some extent echoing the arguments of Soviet propaganda. Before the outbreak of war in 1914, Russia could boast of a flourishing manufacturing industry, rapid growth, and a flexible, decentralized economy; its inhabitants were not constrained in their choice of economic activities, significant progress had been made in the field of workers' legislation, and the material well-being of the peasants was at a level which has never been reached under the Soviet regime. Newspapers were free from preliminary political censorship (even during the war), there was complete cultural freedom, the intelligentsia was not restricted in its activity, religious and philosophical views of every shade were tolerated, and institutions of higher learning enjoyed inviolable autonomy. Russia, with her many nationalities, knew no deportations of entire peoples and no armed separatist movements. This picture is not merely dissimilar to that of the Communist era, but is in every respect its direct antithesis.

The relative merits of these two diametrically opposed interpretations of Russian history can be argued at length, but I found myself uncomfortable with either view, especially after my first few months in Moscow. Solzhenitsyn's rosy portrayal of Russia before the Revolution glosses over the considerable evidence of early police state tactics and the accompanying climate of fear and subjugation that struck visitors like de Custine. But Pipes makes the evolution from czarist Russia to the Soviet Union appear inevitable, as a mere extension of earlier policies. That there was fertile soil for the Bolshevik Revolution seems unquestionable, whatever Solzhenitsyn maintains, but it is no less true that what emerged in this country represents a quantum leap from its pre-revolutionary antecedents.

Repression under the czars was inept compared with the Stalinist terror or even the more refined methods of today's KGB. Imprisonment and Siberian exile for opponents of the regime were not a Soviet invention; even so, the Gulag Archipelago, the vast network of labor camps that has claimed millions of lives, constitutes a dimension of suppression of a wholly different order. A visit to the Lenin Museum of

Moscow brought those vital differences home for me. Despite the attempt to demonstrate the brutality of the pre-revolutionary government and secret police, it produces the opposite effect. I was struck by the ease with which the dissidents of those days printed newspapers and pamphlets abroad and smuggled them into the country, as illustrated by a map of the smuggling routes, and by the austere but humane conditions of their Siberian exile when they were caught. The scope of Lenin's activities, carefully explained by the photographs and documents of the time that were on display, attested as much to the laxness and inefficiency of the authorities as it did to his organizational skills.

Such comparisons must be kept in mind when judgments are passed on the Russians of today. Solzhenitsyn's most valid argument is that too often in the West Russians are written off as "a herd of sheep," thus ignoring the numerous manifestations of resistance to the Communist authorities. Those included, as Solzhenitsyn pointed out, the "counter-revolutionaries" who battled the Red Army from 1918 to 1922; the Russians who, along with Ukrainians, Byelorussians, and the Baltic peoples, initially welcomed the Nazi invaders as liberators in 1941, some of whom joined the German Army in their desperation to rid their country of Stalin; the inhabitants of Novocherkassk who protested the food price increases of 1962; and countless acts of opposition by small groups and individuals that continue to this day, despite the authorities' repeated crackdowns on the dissident movement.

My initiation into Soviet life had taught me not to rush to judgment on a people who had survived as much as the Russians had. The death and destruction brought by Hitler's armies were only the smaller part of it; most of the suffering had been inflicted on them by their own rulers. Solzhenitsyn, who has chronicled the suffering of his people more thoroughly than anyone else, contends in the *Foreign Affairs* article that the Soviet system has claimed the lives of 60 million victims, three times the official number of Soviet soldiers and civilians who died during the Second World War. The gruesome statistics of mass murder are never precise and some Western scholars believe Solzhenitsyn's estimate may be too high, but there is little doubt that Stalin outdid Hitler within the Soviet Union itself. As British historian Robert Conquest wrote: "Stalin, simply because he had a longer period to operate in and a larger pool of potential victims, killed a good many more than Hitler did."*

This has left a lasting legacy of intimidation. To this day, many Russians are nervous about admitting that members of their own families were victims of Stalin's terror. It was only after I got to know Yuri well, an economist in his fifties, that he was able to tell me of his father, a Red Army officer who disappeared in 1937 when Yuri was a young boy. Not until Khrushchev came to power seventeen years later did the family receive confirmation of their suspicions in the form of a death certificate, which Yuri removed from the cupboard and carefully unrolled to show me. The year of death was filled in as 1937, but the spaces after "Cause of death" and "Place of death" were blank . . . evidence that he had been executed in Stalin's purges of that year.

A Moscow writer, who considered himself a Russian nationalist of the Solzhenitsyn school, argued that Stalin's systematic destruction of everyone who could be suspected of independent thought obliged Westerners like myself to measure Russians by different standards. "You shouldn't be surprised when almost no one speaks up when a Sakharov is sent into internal exile in Gorky," he said. "Instead, you

*Robert Conquest, *Kolyma: The Arctic Death Camps* (Oxford: Oxford University Press, 1979), 116.

should be amazed when one in a thousand is able to recognize that this is a gross injustice."

Among Moscow intellectuals I knew, this was a minority view. Others were far more willing to condemn the average Russian for his docility. At a large banquet to celebrate the opening of an exhibit by a prominent artist, a painter sitting across from me maintained that the key difference between Poland and the Soviet Union was that the gap between Polish intellectuals and workers had been bridged. His voice was testy. "There are no real ties between intellectuals and workers here. They threw out Solzhenitsyn, and so what? They exiled Sakharov, and so what? There was that incredible outpouring when [balladeer] Vysotsky died, but if he had lived and been thrown into prison, no one would have done anything here."

That harsh assessment would have been difficult to refute, but a visit to an informal art exhibition shortly afterward raised new questions in my mind. The exhibition was in the apartment of a woman who considered herself a patron of the arts; she allowed recognized and "unofficial" artists to show their works there. The authorities must have known about these exhibits, but for some reason they had made no move to prevent them. As usual, theories abounded to explain the anomaly. To some, the woman was a true benefactor; to others, she was a possible KGB informer with the mission of flushing out independent artists. But proponents of both theories took full advantage of her hospitality.

I was more interested in how the woman described the artistic island she had created in her house. "We do not live by politics," she said as we drifted among oil paintings of brightly colored devils and terrified faces that had no chance of being officially exhibited. "We make our own little worlds and we live in them. That way we survive." Could that also be part of the reason for the gap between intellectuals and workers in Soviet society? Did workers feel that intellectuals were just as indifferent to their plight as the painter at the banquet maintained workers were to what happened to intellectual dissenters? Despite their separate worlds, weren't both groups wrestling with some of the same demons?

As my circle of friends and contacts grew wider, it became increasingly apparent that the monolithic face that Moscow presents to the outside world was not at all an accurate reflection of reality inside the Soviet Union. Many voices, with different stories to tell, were trying to make themselves heard. They refused to be stilled.

What intrigued me most were ordinary citizens who did not consider themselves dissidents but insisted on airing their individual grievances. Their most common recourse was to write letters to Soviet newspapers; major papers like *Pravda, Izvestia,* and *Trud* received thousands of letters every week. They printed a handful that happened to fit in with the political campaign of the moment, such as attacks on bureaucratic red tape and factory theft, and editors claimed that all unpublished letters were answered. But sources familiar with the procedures said that many of those responses are more perfunctory than helpful. Another aspect of this process, they said, was that newspapers keep unpublished letters for up to ten years and periodically the KGB checks those files for troublemakers.

To demonstrate what was contained in such files, those sources provided me with a sampling of letters received, but never printed, by two major Soviet publications. I was intrigued both by what they had to say and by the fact that people had taken the risk of writing them at all. With help from a friend in deciphering the various kinds of handwritings, I began working my way through about a dozen long letters.

A worker involved in the construction of a hydroelectric · power plant in a remote site in Eastern Siberia wrote to complain about the difficulty of obtaining adequate food, housing, and clothes. He cited a case of massive food poisoning at the workers' cafeteria, and another instance when the cafeteria was closed for two days in order for the manager of the cafeteria to hold a wedding party. "Despite shipments sent by the government, the local store has never once stocked canned meat or buckwheat, whereas a certain boss managed to get red caviar, smoked sturgeon and other delicacies for a family wedding," he wrote. Meat and the consignment of sheepskin coats were sold only to friends of those bosses or "on the left," in illegal private deals. Of the magazine subscriptions received, not one was allotted to the workers. "Distribution of apartments depends on the whims of the bosses. [One boss] gave an apartment in a building built for the workers to his daughter. [Another] gave an apartment to his mistress." When workers were ordered to help on neighboring state farms, he concluded, payment for that work never reached them.

Several letters spoke of life and violence in labor camps for juvenile delinquents and dry-out centers for alcoholics. A man who had worked for twenty-seven years as a projectionist in a Byelorussian camp for juvenile delinquents claimed he was fired from his job because he had protested the "arbitrary rule and tyranny" of the camp's new director. He accused the new director of misappropriating funds, pocketing wages that prisoners should have received for logging and potato-harvesting work, selling off carpets intended for the camp, and systematically brutalizing people. "He personally beat prisoners. Once, on a warehouse construction site, he struck an inmate, sending him into a ditch. He punched a second delinquent in the ear, who then hit his head on the corner of a metal chest as he fell and lay unconscious on the floor for some five minutes. All this took place in full view of other inmates."

A twenty-seven-year-old letter-writer from a "therapeutic settlement" for alcoholics in northern Russia complained about the treatment there: heavy doses of drugs that are designed, when mixed with alcohol, to produce an allergic reaction. "There are a number of deaths here only because the doctors do not pay sufficient attention to the patients. The task of the doctor is to poison your body—after which, the chances of your living a long life are not very great. Many people have already died here because they were filled with these drugs."

Two members of the "Truly Orthodox Christians," a breakaway sect from the Russian Orthodox Church that is not accepted as legal by the authorities, wrote in separate letters from a town in central Russia about the persecution of their group. "As believers in God, we get saddled with everything: with supposedly opposing [Soviet] power, opposing the law, humanity, with slaughtering children, drinking blood at Communion, with making human sacrifices. The people have been armed with hatred against us. We are beaten endlessly. There is not a place on our bodies that has not been beaten. Fines have been levied up to [$70] for getting together on holidays. You go to the store and come across types who holler, 'We'll get you sectarians.'"

Children, they claimed, were victims of brutal treatment by their peers: one fifth-grader had been "deformed" by the beatings he received over a three-year period, and afterward screamed at night. "What have our children done to deserve being beaten by the others in school? The teachers have eyes to see and ears to hear and still pay no attention." The believers said they were threatened when they tried to complain. "The chairman of the town council said to me in public: 'I've got enough bullets to handle the lot of you.'"

Attached to the file copies of these two letters was the following reply from the newspaper: "Article 52 of the Constitution of the U.S.S.R. grants citizens the right to profess any faith. That same article, however, also speaks of the citizens' right to spread atheist propaganda. Why should it upset you, then, when various individuals object to your attempts to preach religion in public among people not.inclined to listen? In our opinion, they took perfectly legitimate action."

Another letter began: "We know that what we have to say will not be published, nor will this letter be of any help in solving our problem. But even so . . ." It was from two Russian veterans of World War II. "War veterans in this country are respected only in the newspapers. More than thirty years have passed since the end of the war and we still have no real benefits. . . . Imagine how happy we were when a decree was issued promising war veterans telephones and medical aid. But how unreal it turned out to be. . . . What about sanitoriums? In all the twenty years and more we've been working at our factory, neither of us has had the chance to visit one, while the boss' wife and the boss himself go regularly, and they're both under 40. Or take telephones. Here lots of people have asked to have them installed. So have we, and not as a luxury item—there are times you have to call for emergency medical service late at night. But they keep telling us the same thing: 'Can't do anything about it just now,' 'Give it another two or three years,' 'There's a long waiting list.' . . . What's the use of issuing decrees if you can't possibly live up to them? And what a poor country this must be if it can't even install a phone for a wounded veteran at his own expense?"

Finally, a *kolhoznik*, a collective farm worker, returned to the corruption theme. "All my life I've worked in the country. What do you see everywhere you look? Everyone from the measliest boss to the highest ranking officials without a twinge of conscience shoving his hand in the public purse every chance he gets." His examples of corruption on the farm: "I need a car but I haven't 'earned' one, so it's fork out [$700] or [$840]. . . . Say I need roofing slate. 'Coming right up,' [the chairman of the state farm tells me], 'providing you bring me ten heads of sheep.' . . . It is hard to bring up kids these days when there is all this corruption going on and they drink it all in. I thought it was only like that here [in the country], but I went to visit my son in the city and it's even worse there."

Only a small fraction of such individual grievances, whether pursued in letters to newspapers or in petitions to party or state organizations, give birth to political or social protest in the Soviet Union. But that is still the most common route to dissent. Very few dissidents are of the Andrei Sakharov mold, whose special prominence as a renowned nuclear physicist combined with his general concerns about Soviet internal and foreign policies placed him in open conflict with the authorities. As a rule, the first step on the path of dissent is often a disagreement with the authorities over a personal grievance, which then may lead, over time, to protests about broader issues.

For writers, the first clash usually comes when the government refuses to publish their works. Georgi Vladimov was able in the early stages of his career in the late 1950s and early 1960s to write reviews and articles for Soviet publications. His first novella appeared in *Novy Mir,* the same journal that published Solzhenitsyn's *One Day in the Life of Ivan Denisovich.* In 1965, Vladimov submitted the manuscript of his most acclaimed work, *Faithful Ruslan,* a brilliant novel about a prison camp guard dog who is bewildered by the closing of his camp during Khrushchev's de-Stalinization program. It was turned down, but his works began appearing in samizdat publications and abroad. In 1977, Vladimov resigned from the Writers Union and joined the Moscow branch of Amnesty International.

During my stay in Moscow, Vladimov's apartment was

one of the few remaining enclaves of the human-rights movement of the 1970s, which had been nearly obliterated by
the imprisonment, commitment to psychiatric hospitals, and
exiling of its members. Writers and others already in conflict
with the authorities, along with those on the fringes of the
dissident movement who were sympathetic to its goals but
nervous about jeopardizing whatever positions they had established for themselves, showed up there for companion-
ship, advice, and occasionally for contacts with Western
correspondents.

A more troubled enclave of dissidents whose personal
grievances had put them on a collision course with the authorities was the communal apartment of Vasily and Galina
Barats. Vasily, who was only in his mid-thirties but whose
broad face and heavyset features made him look considerably older, had been an army officer until his conversion to
the Pentecostalist faith. Along with his wife, Galina, he had
become an ardent believer. After his conversion, he found
himself harassed by the authorities, who on one occasion
had him committed to a mental hospital. The only job he
could find was as a watchman at a garage. But the more the
authorities tried to punish him, the more committed both
Vasily and Galina became to helping others suffering similar
ordeals for their religious beliefs.

They formed the Committee for Emigration with members of various religious denominations who were convinced
that they would only be able to practice their faith freely
outside of the Soviet Union. Traveling around the country,
Vasily and Galina gathered information on the treatment of
believers, passing whatever they learned along to any correspondent who would listen. When I visited their Moscow
apartment, I usually found several visitors from the provinces, simple people in plain, worn clothing who exuded
both faith and fear. Like the Truly Orthodox Christians,

whose letters I had read, they belonged to churches not officially registered and controlled by the state, which made them illegitimate in the eyes of the authorities. They talked of beatings, arrests, and confiscations of Bibles and other religious literature.

The Baratses were hardly popular with their neighbors, three other families who shared their four-room apartment. Their activities brought constant surveillance, and the apartment's single phone was frequently disconnected to make it more difficult for them to keep in touch with their scattered colleagues and correspondents. People would arrive at all times of day and night after long train rides from the provinces. The sense of danger was palpable; the scent of trouble to come was in the air.

From the government's standpoint, the most dangerous kind of dissident was the worker turned activist, someone whose sense of outrage about his particular working conditions had prompted him to try to change them. Their fate helped to explain why, even if Russian workers shared many of the grievances that prompted their Polish counterparts to organize Solidarity, such a movement would have no chance of developing in the Soviet Union under current conditions. I never met such workers because they were all under some form of detention during my stay in Moscow, but family members and friends recounted their stories and kept me informed of whatever news there was about their treatment.

Aleksei Nikitin, a mine engineer and Communist Party member, began protesting lax safety regulations in the Donetsk mines in the early 1970s. Ever since, he had spent most of the time at the Dnepropetrovsk Special Psychiatric Hospital, where he was treated with powerful drugs like sulfazin, a preparation of purified sulfur that causes severe pain and high fever. In January 1980, after he was released, Nikitin continued his protest. By discussing mine conditions with Western correspondents he sought to pressure the authorities. At the same time, Anatoly Koryagin, a psychiatrist who was a consulting physician to a small "working commission" of human-rights activists monitoring Soviet psychiatric practices, examined Nikitin and found him sane. That did not provide Nikitin with any protection: he was sent back to the Dnepropetrovsk Hospital. Shortly after my arrival in Moscow, Koryagin was sentenced to seven years in labor camps and five years of internal exile for "anti-Soviet" slander, forcing his wife and three children to fend for themselves. Other workers, like Vladimir Klebanov, a coal-mine foreman who went from complaining to his superiors that his men were dying in accidents because they were exhausted from too much overtime work to announcing the formation of an independent union in 1978, also ended up in psychiatric hospitals.

Throughout the 1970s, the only people who petitioned the authorities and with some consistency had their requests granted were Jews, ethnic Germans, and Armenians seeking to emigrate. More than 250,000 Jews were allowed to emigrate on the grounds of "repatriation to their historic homeland," although about 100,000 of them settled in the United States instead of Israel. About 2 million ethnic Germans, mostly the descendants of Germans who heeded the invitations of the czars for them to settle along the Volga River in earlier centuries, live in the Soviet Union. Most are now scattered across the country as a result of wartime deportations to Central Asia and Siberia when they were considered Nazi sympathizers. After the signing of a nonaggression pact between West Germany and the Soviet Union in 1970, more than 60,000 were allowed to resettle in West Germany during the following decade. In the same period, about 20,000 Armenians were allowed to leave.

Such government actions appeared to signal a greater

sensitivity to Western public opinion in the era of détente and a desire to open up pressure valves for select groups of citizens; it also provided a convenient means of ridding itself of "undesirable elements." But allowing large numbers of people to leave went against every natural instinct of the regime. It created new problems for the security apparatus: despite censorship, those who emigrated often managed to maintain communication with their relatives and friends who stayed behind. Phone calls, facilitated by the introduction of international direct dialing in certain sections of Moscow at the time of the 1980 Olympics, were particularly difficult to control. The outside world—and images and ideas that did not correspond to official Soviet propaganda—kept filtering back into the country.

From the Kremlin's perspective, all this was distinctly troubling. Except in special cases—for the privileged and the outcasts—borders were meant to keep Soviet citizens in and foreign ideas out. The exodus of minorities permitted in the 1970s was an aberration, the exception that proved the rule. Those who left had to renounce their Soviet citizenship, making their departures an anti-Soviet act. There was never any question of allowing the free movement back and forth across borders: the treachery of those who asked to leave had to be demonstrated to all. Otherwise, others might start wondering why they could not travel.

That fall, Vadim Kreydenkov, our Russian teacher in California, had developed serious health problems. His mother, a retired physician in her early seventies who lived in Alma-Ata, the capital of the Central Asian republic of Kazakhstan, desperately wanted to visit to help him and his family through the crisis. The authorities refused her requests, saying that the only way she could leave was on a one-way ticket. Her whole professional life had been spent in Alma-Ata, her friends were there, and, unlike her son, she had never wanted to leave, but she was forced to choose between emigrating and not being able to go to the aid of her only son. She did what any mother would have done. Christina and I assisted her as she forlornly stumbled through the final departure arrangements in Moscow. She could not understand why she was treated as if she were betraying her country. Her modest belongings were turned inside out by customs agents and her most prized personal possessions—the stethoscope, reflex hammer, and syringe she had used throughout her long years of medical practice—were confiscated.

For ordinary Russians it is a considerable feat even to obtain permission to travel on tightly policed tours to pacified Eastern European countries. The vetting process is long and laborious—and can be full of unpleasant surprises. A taxi driver who was taking Christina and me to the airport one afternoon launched into an angry denunciation of "the garbage" who emigrate. But when Christina suggested that some people would not leave if they had the freedom to travel abroad and return, he softened a bit and recounted his own recent attempt to take a trip abroad for the first time. He had managed to sign up for a short excursion to Czechoslovakia, and he had been immensely excited by the prospect. But when he went to get a required medical clearance, he was turned down on the ground that he allegedly had a weak heart. He shook his head in bewilderment and frustration. "I sometimes work twelve hours a day behind this steering wheel and nobody worries about my heart, but it's not good enough to go to Czechoslovakia for a few days' vacation."

During my stay in Moscow, Kremlin policy-makers were returning to more familiar behavior in dealing with the emigration issue as well. The situation was changing for all the groups involved in the outflow, particularly for the Jews.

Jewish emigration had peaked in 1979 at 51,000; in 1981, the figure was just under 10,000 and the monthly rate was dropping precipitously. Those who had been trying to join the departing waves but failed were further demoralized by that trend. People we knew had been waiting for up to ten years to emigrate, collecting one refusal after another. They lived in limbo, having lost their professional standing in society once they had applied to leave. In order to survive, doctors became night watchmen, physicists tutored high school students in elementary science, writers ghosted other people's articles and research papers. The strains and tensions in their uncertain lives were enormous.

The son of a well-known Soviet composer, Vladimir Feltsman, had been a brilliant rising star in the Soviet music world. He had won major international piano competitions in Prague and Paris while still a teenager. But in 1979, he and his wife Anna applied to emigrate and everything was transformed overnight. His recordings instantly disappeared and he was banned from the major concert stages in Moscow and Leningrad where he had once been acclaimed. Their emigration applications were turned down, and as far as the authorities were concerned Vladimir's musical career had ended well before his thirtieth birthday. The only concerts he gave were for his friends in their cramped one-room apartment on Moscow's inner ring road.

At the time when Christina and I became good friends of the Feltsmans that fall, their plight was somewhat relieved. As a result of protests organized by outraged musicians in the West, Vladimir was booked for appearances in a few remote provincial towns. But these were token, scornful gestures. Vladimir was still effectively denied an audience and the necessary stimulus of preparation for a real performance. He worried incessantly about his ability to maintain his skills at the top level, and he knew that every

123

month spent in his current state was subtracted from the new career he had hoped to launch in another country. A strikingly handsome young couple, they also had hoped to start a family once they had embarked on a new life. They had already put this off longer than planned. Even the most personal of decisions could not be separated from the authorities' refusal to permit their emigration.

Discouraged by what was happening to refuseniks like the Feltsmans, many Jews reluctantly decided not to apply to emigrate. Some still hoped for an improvement in U.S.–Soviet relations, on the theory that détente was what prompted Moscow to allow the emigration in the first place. Others shelved their hopes altogether. Ethnic Germans were experiencing similar setbacks: those who still persisted in applying to emigrate were vilified and threatened, in some cases arrested on trumped-up charges. The country's doors were drawing shut once again, and only a crack of an opening was left.

On a cold, blustery Sunday morning in late November, David Satter and I set out to visit a mutual friend in Berendeevo, a small town about 100 miles northeast of Moscow. It was the kind of trip that was highly unusual for Western correspondents, both because Berendeevo was a tiny backwater light-years from the capital in terms of the primitive lifestyle of its 3,000 inhabitants, if not in distance, and because foreigners rarely would get to know someone from such a town, much less be invited to visit him. But Adolph Muhlberg, our host, was no ordinary Soviet citizen: he was a person who had made a serious mistake as a teenager and had kept on paying for it ever since. In an effort to undo the damage, he had decided to tell his story to anyone who would listen.

Born in independent Latvia in 1930 of German parents,

Adolph moved westward with his mother after Soviet troops occupied the Baltic states in 1939, staying first in German-occupied Poland and near the end of the war moving to Germany itself. After his mother died in 1945, he struck out alone to make his way in postwar Europe.

Adolph had dreamed of becoming a merchant seaman and he traveled to Hamburg and other ports but found no one wanted to hire him. He worked briefly as a clerk, a coal miner, and a farmhand, flitting illegally across the various occupation zones of Germany and even across borders into neighboring countries. He had several scrapes with the law, escaping from a juvenile delinquent camp in Germany and spending a couple of months in a Belgian prison for illegal entry. Finally, he was classified as a displaced person by a Latvian committee in Germany that should have allowed him the possibility of emigrating to the United States or Canada, but since he was not yet eighteen no one would give him a visa.

Adolph then met a Russian who suggested that he could go to the Soviet Union and work on a ship there. Enthralled, Adolph went to the Soviet military mission in Baden-Baden, where he declared himself a Latvian. He was shown glossy magazines of the U.S.S.R. and told that, yes, he could choose his profession if he returned to the land of his birth, which was now a Soviet republic, and there would be no problem about becoming a seaman.

In 1948, Adolph arrived in the Latvian capital of Riga. His family records were found in the archives and he was brusquely told that, since his family had renounced its Latvian citizenship in 1939, he would be treated as a foreigner—and foreigners had no right to live in the Baltic states. Without access to the Baltic ports, Adolph watched his dream of a life at sea evaporate and he quickly realized the magnitude of the mistake he had made. After working as a ditch digger in a Russian town near the Latvian border, he went to Moscow in 1949 to complain that he could not survive on the meager salary he was receiving and to ask to be allowed to return to Germany. The passport office told him that he had no right to be in Moscow and that he had better leave immediately. Instead, he went to the Australian embassy, hoping to find out how to emigrate there. He was arrested before he ever entered the grounds, and he was sent to Latvia to spend a year and a half in prison. Later he would resume his drifting within the Soviet Union, picking up sundry jobs. In 1955, he was forced to accept Soviet citizenship: the alternative was a twenty-year prison sentence.

But Adolph, who was now living in Berendeevo with his wife and four children, never accepted his fate: he kept trying to find an escape hatch. That was why David and I were driving that morning in my conspicuous blue Volvo station wagon to see him. He had visited us many times in our adjoining offices and he wanted us to reciprocate. The fact that two Western correspondents were concerning themselves with his situation, he hoped, might do some good; he was long past the stage where he worried about the possibility of things getting worse.

Our plans to visit Adolph were of course known to the authorities. As required, we had filed our itinerary with the Foreign Ministry ahead of time, detailed down to the license plate of my car and the road we would travel. Passing the police checkpoints that abound on every road leading out of Moscow, we were never stopped since we were clearly expected; each policeman along the way dutifully recorded our presence so every moment of our journey would be accounted for. At the larger town of Perslavl-Zalessky, we turned off onto a dirt road leading the last thirteen miles to Berendeevo. A few miles farther, we had to stop. Two large piles of sand and a bulldozer blocked the road in both directions. The sand had clearly been dumped there just moments before we arrived: traffic had been flowing freely in both directions until we reached this impediment. More cars drove up and waited with us.

David and I were not particularly concerned. There was a man in the cab of the bulldozer and we assumed he would scoop the sand to one side and let us pass. Instead, he climbed down, got into a waiting car, and drove off back in the direction of Berendeevo. Other drivers began to complain. This was the only road to and from Berendeevo; no detours were possible. For us, another route was out of the question anyway because we were wedded to the travel plans we had filed with the Foreign Ministry. If we had departed from these plans, we would have been sent back to Moscow by the first policeman. Were David and I being blocked on purpose? I dismissed the notion as preposterous. But we were stuck.

Then, we had some luck. The driver of a large truck forced his high-suspension vehicle over the sand. That flattened the sand piles a bit and a taxi driver fought and swerved his way across, clearing a path for the rest of us.

We reached Berendeevo and parked near the corner of Novazaprudnaya Street where Adolph lived, not daring to drive down the narrow, muddy lane for fear of getting stuck. As we locked the car, three young men, similar in their casual dress and demeanor to the "interested citizens" who had kept us company in Vologda, approached us. "Whose house are you going to?" one of them asked. We ignored them, leaving them standing around my car. We then walked to number 13, Adolph's address. It was a dilapidated log cabin, listing to the left at such an angle that it appeared to be sinking into the ground. The neighbors' houses were more stable structures, made of evenly cut boards instead of logs, with picket fences demarcating property lines.

Adolph opened the door and, as we made our way through a dimly lit hall to the main room, he whispered without elaboration that he had other visitors. There, two men were sitting: one with a beard and sporting a tie and the other, looking much less comfortable, in his overcoat. Adolph's four children were watching, not quite sure what all these visitors meant, and his wife was trying to stay as far away in the cramped quarters as possible.

"These are my friends, correspondents," Adolph said, gesturing toward us as we entered. "You should have something in common."

The bearded man nodded and introduced himself as Shiryayev. He said he was a reporter for *Severny Rabochy* (*Northern Worker*), the district newspaper. He added with a wave of his hand toward the man in the overcoat: "You have here a representative of Soviet authority: the mayor of Berendeevo, Afinon Alexandrovich Pavlov. We are here because this person," he said of Adolph, who was still standing, "has just received his emigration visa."

"It was completed Friday, so we came by," the mayor chimed in eagerly, attempting to make it sound as natural as possible that he would be visiting one of the town's citizens on a Sunday for such a purpose.

Adolph had been waiting more than thirty years for this moment, and it just happened to occur as he received the first foreign visitors in his Soviet lifetime. But Adolph was far from elated; he seemed nervous, perhaps doubting that what he was hearing was true.

Sitting in the dank room amidst the Muhlbergs' paltry belongings, Shiryayev proposed we take advantage of our "chance meeting" to chat. "It's interesting for me professionally. Why have you come here?" He smiled and his eyes surveyed our surroundings. "So you can see how a Soviet citizen lives?"

"Because he's our friend," David replied.

"Your friend? What do you see in him? There are so many interesting people I could introduce you to, who could tell you things that would make you stand with mouth agape. Why him?"

David said Adolph was an interesting person, someone with a Western outlook but extensive Soviet experience. He asked if Shiryayev had ever visited the West.

"Yes, Helsinki in 1973." A sure sign, if any were needed, that Shiryayev had more than simple journalistic responsibilities. A simple reporter for a small provincial newspaper would have little chance of ever traveling abroad, especially outside of the Soviet bloc; such a reward would go to someone who had performed valuable duties for the security services. Later, when we asked Shiryayev more precisely whom he represented, he pulled out his documents, with the mayor obediently following suit, and insisted that we look at them, saying: "Otherwise, you might get the idea that we are from the KGB."

"We have good things and bad things in our country. There, I admit it," Shiryayev said as if he were making a dramatic concession. "The same is true of the West. So why listen to someone who just tells you bad things?"

The mayor suddenly asked Adolph: "What don't you like about our country?"

Adolph objected to the lack of democracy. When Shiryayev began pressing him to explain, he described his high hopes for democratization and his later disillusionment at the time of the 20th Party Congress in 1956 when Khrushchev exposed Stalin's crimes.

"What do you mean by democratization?" Shiryayev asked.

"The right to emigrate—why keep people here by force? In West Germany, people can go anywhere, they can get fresh rolls in the morning, and the people in the West can read newspapers that criticize their own leaders. You'll find cartoons making fun of Reagan. Here, if you say anything they lock you up."

"Now, that's not true," the mayor interjected.

Shiryayev, the more polished of the duo, took a different tack. "Your notion of democracy is silly. You think of fresh rolls. I speak my mind here and for fifty years no one has ever touched me."

"I've been imprisoned twice."

"There must have been a reason."

I later asked, when Shiryayev persisted in questioning why we should visit someone like Adolph: "Why are you so afraid of our meeting him?"

"No, we're not afraid of anything."

I asked the mayor the population of the town.

"Why are you asking this?" he demanded.

At that, Shiryayev laughed, seeing a chance to demonstrate his sophistication. "Go ahead, it's not a military secret," he said. The mayor sheepishly answered my question.

We had brought the obligatory bottle of vodka along and, although David hardly ever drinks, he suddenly insisted on pouring everyone a round. The mayor looked pleased for the first time since our arrival. When everyone had a full glass in hand, David offered his toast: "To Adolph's new life in the West."

The mayor paused, his already aroused impulse to throw back the vodka momentarily fighting his discomfort at the toast. He looked at Shiryayev, who hesitated briefly but then drank up. The mayor did the same.

We were interrupted by a knock on the door. A policeman entered. "Whose blue Volvo is parked down at the corner of the street?" he asked. He just happened to notice it had a flat tire.

He asked for our documents. I showed him my passport and press card but David, who is wonderfully oblivious to such things, had nothing with him except a wallet containing money and an American Express card. He pulled out the latter, saying it was the only identification he had. Our Berendeevo policeman curiously fingered the green plastic. Shiryayev stepped in, saying that in the West such cards are used for identification. "As a colleague, I can vouch for him." I couldn't help but think about the commercial possibilities of this scene—"Don't leave home without it!"—but who would believe it?

Adolph escorted all of his visitors out of the house. The policeman suggested we leave soon: it was snowing and the roads were getting dangerous. "How did you find the road coming here?" he asked.

"Not bad," I said.

"I had heard there's some repair work going on." The policeman continued, now in a confidential tone. "You could have done better in picking a friend. In Moscow there are so many fine people, why did you pick him?"

As we approached the car, Shiryayev and the mayor said their good-byes. David and I changed the tire, which had been cut by a thin blade. I mentioned the three young men whom we had left standing around the car.

"No, no, I'm sure people wouldn't do anything like that here," said the policeman.

"Our car will be safe now?"

"Of course."

I was quite certain he meant it: after all, the authorities had already made their displeasure about our visit known, but they would not want us stranded in Berendeevo by arranging for another flat tire. So Adolph, David, and I set out for a walk through the town. Adolph was quick to tell us his poor quarters were not typical, that the larger wooden houses were more common. But many held several families, and none had indoor plumbing. As snow swept down, blanketing the fields, the town seemed particularly isolated and desolate. The railroad station looked abandoned, as did a string of wagons parked on its sidings. The belfry of the only church had been decapitated; Adolph said the building was now used for movie showings in the evenings. At the town's center, recognizable by the fact that the wooden houses there were more tightly clustered together, the obligatory World War II monument of a Soviet soldier was the only landmark.

We parted, driving uneventfully back to Moscow as the snow and early darkness added to our sense that we were leaving another planet and leaving behind an uncertain Adolph, who did not know whether he had been the victim of an elaborate ruse or was finally on his way with his family out of the Soviet Union.

Two weeks later, he phoned. "I'll be leaving this socialist heaven in a few days to live in that capitalist hell." He could barely contain himself: his whole family had been granted permission to emigrate "to Israel." The authorities had refused to categorize him as an ethnic German, preferring to label him as Jewish instead. This is a relatively frequent occurrence. By the bizarre criteria of Soviet emigration policies, many non-Jews are considered as Jews. The state does this in order to conceal their real reasons for leaving. Someone like Adolph can be easily dispatched in this fashion without any troubling discussions of what motivated him to seek to emigrate, his disillusionment with the Soviet system. The emigrants play along with this fiction until they cross the border and head for their true destinations. At the end of December, Adolph and his family were in

West Germany. It had been three decades since he had left.

Before his departure, Adolph passed along a bit of information about that day we visited him in Berendeevo: he had confirmed from people in the town that the dump truck with sand had been sent out for the specific purpose of blocking our arrival.

3

WINTER

Winter sneaks into Moscow well before it is acknowledged by the calendar. It makes runs at the city as early as October, sending chilly blasts of wind across the wide boulevards in the late afternoon when darkness has already settled in, catching you by surprise on a morning when dawn seems to have forgotten to arrive. Then, it lies low for a week or two of balmy fall weather before it insinuates itself into your bones, still mild and unassuming even with the first snows of early November, but with the promise of stronger doses in every dip of the thermometer, in the rapid contraction of the hours of pale sunlight. Except for the snow, all is gray, brown, and black. By December, it has settled down for the long siege.

Muscovites, as if trying to pacify winter's wrath, blend in with those surroundings. Their heavy overcoats, of coarse wools and harsh polyesters, come in the same background colors of the streets and buildings. At the first hint of winter in October, all heads are covered with genuine or ersatz fur hats. They remain religiously covered for five or six months, even when temperate days are interspersed with the frosty ones. Foreigners like myself who refused to do so were regarded scornfully or with pity; if we took the children out with their heads uncovered, Christina and I would receive reproving glances, sometimes a stern lecture from an older woman about our responsibility as parents. When the temperature plummeted, I would again be out of step, pulling down the ear flaps of my sheepskin cap and tying them tightly under my chin. Men with similar caps always kept the ear flaps tied over their heads; using the ear flaps seemed to violate the local macho code, no matter how red your ears had turned.

It is the long hours of darkness on the seemingly endless succession of days when the sun makes only the faintest appearance that offer insights into the brooding nature of the Russian *dusha* or soul. But then an overnight snowfall enfolds everything in a white blanket of sparkling purity, providing a clue to its romanticism and giving substance as well to the feelings both that nothing will ever change and that everything can be transformed, God willing. (Sonia came home from school one day beaming about the admonition her class received from their rigidly ideological teacher: "You can't throw away bread because God will punish you, even though there is no God.")

Individuals may feel powerless to influence the elements, but there is a sense of reassurance in the power of the elements themselves that transcends anything temporal. Gliding on cross-country skis through the forests of Peredelkino, the writers' colony where Boris Pasternak wrote *Doctor Zhivago,* or ice skating on the magnificent flooded, frozen pathways of Gorky Park, I felt as though I had touched the source of Russian dreams. I felt a communion with the dreamers. Nature, an implacable foe and ally, had helped to shape, even to nurture, the dreams and hopes of an entire people that no one, no political organization or campaign, had ever managed completely to stamp out.

But those were fleeting moments. The raw reminders of life as interpreted by the powers that be kept the upper hand. Late on a frozen, translucent night, our black-and-white collie ignored my imprecations and continued to romp on the snow-covered playground near our building. She was only a few months old and my half-hearted training techniques had done little to restrain her rambunctious spirit. The policeman on duty at the guard booth in the parking lot watched my futile efforts to grab her and snap the leash back on. "It's always that way," he volunteered. "When you give people freedom, they don't know when to stop—they just run and run. What can you expect from animals?"

Christina went to the market with Basia, a Polish woman who lived in Moscow and spoke perfect Russian. They were buying *tvorog,* a farmer's cheese, when another woman approached them and demanded to be served. Basia told her that they would be finishing in a moment and she should wait her turn. As Christina recalled, that led to the following exchange.

Turning to Basia, the woman said, "You should not be here at all. It's impossible to breathe with your perfume."

BASIA: "So you don't like my perfume?"

THE WOMAN: "No, and the cheese is going to smell with your perfume."

BASIA: "Is it written in the Constitution that you cannot wear perfume at the market?"

THE WOMAN: "Yes, if people don't like it, it should be forbidden."

BASIA: "And who are you? Maybe you work for the KGB?"

THE WOMAN: "That's exactly where I work."

BASIA: "Oh, how you frighten me."

THE WOMAN: "Just two more words and we'll go for a walk."

BASIA: "Now, you really frighten me."

THE WOMAN: "I'm telling you just one more word . . ."

Her voice trailed off as it began to dawn on her that she was not dealing with a Russian. Most Russians would hardly have dared to taunt her because they would have had no way of knowing whether she really had the authority to threaten them with punishment; it would be prudent to remain silent. She took a closer look at Basia's clothes, particularly her obviously foreign boots, mumbled something about having an allergy to perfumes, and left without waiting for her turn.

The most likely explanation for her behavior was that the woman did work for the KGB in some minor clerical post, and that she was used to exploiting her position when it suited her. Flaunting one's power, however minor, whenever possible, is the golden rule of Soviet society. In this case, she had miscalculated.

The members of the aging Brezhnev team followed the same principle, trying their best to exercise their own power. The failures of the Brezhnev era were increasingly evident: the Polish unrest, the inability of the Soviet Army to achieve a decisive victory in Afghanistan, and the successive economic setbacks. Even in showcase Moscow, butter had disappeared from the stores for about two weeks just as winter was making itself felt. But the more depressing the news, the more frantic were the efforts to portray Brezhnev as a heroic leader, firmly in command. With the approach of Brezhnev's "glorious" seventy-fifth birthday on December 19, the glorification campaign assumed all the trappings of a personality cult.

Presses spewed out new biographies, anthologies of his

reports and speeches, and the fourth slim installment of his autobiography. These volumes, written in trite prose, containing doctored recollections of Brezhnev's past, had nonetheless won him the Lenin Prize for literature. The Soviet leader had already collected more medals than any of his predecessors, including military decorations that normally are awarded to those who have led troops into battle. As a political officer during World War II, Brezhnev had no combat experience. On his birthday, party ideologist Mikhail Suslov, who himself was seventy-nine, pinned an eighth Order of Lenin and a fourth Hero of the Soviet Union on his overcrowded chest.

The Politburo had begun reacting much earlier to the growing intimations of Brezhnev's mortality—his increasingly slurred speech, his halting movements—by drawing in the wagons around him. The men in the Kremlin seemed to believe that if they acted as though nothing would ever change, nothing would. The possibility of change—any change—could not be admitted. The 26th Party Congress in February 1981 had provided the spectacle of a gerontocracy that refused to yield a single top leadership position to a younger man. Nothing had changed since.

When Brezhnev traveled to West Germany in November 1981, on what turned out to be the last foreign trip of his life, a mere allusion to his health could send sparks flying. At a joint press conference, Soviet spokesman Leonid Zamyatin took offense at a comment by Kurt Becker, his West German counterpart, that his government's leaders were "impressed" by Brezhnev's ability to participate in a long program without displaying any signs of fatigue. Announcing that he wanted "to illustrate that Mr. Becker's comments were not correct," Zamyatin told the surprised reporters: "I can assure you that his physical health is good, and that he is fully capable of working. That was proven by the seven hours of talks he held yesterday with the leaders of West Germany."

If anything, such episodes and the endless tributes to Brezhnev only deepened the lingering sense of mortality in the air. They also spawned new, sometimes cruel jokes. At the meeting with Brezhnev, so one story had it, which began circulating among Muscovites immediately after the trip to Bonn, Chancellor Helmut Schmidt asked the Soviet leader to explain how he had managed to depose Khrushchev. Brezhnev answered: "Who's Khrushchev?" As Brezhnev walked away, an aide congratulated him on his clever reply to Schmidt. "Who's Schmidt?" Brezhnev asked.

Another joke was about a mute who was taking a test for party membership. When asked who Marx was, he gestured to show a large beard and made writing motions. When asked about Lenin, he outlined a goatee and raised his right hand in the pose of a revolutionary orator. For Stalin, he made shooting gestures. For Khrushchev, he pretended to pound the table with his shoe. For Brezhnev, he mimicked someone picking out ribbons and medals and pinning them on his own chest.

"You'll be there for the succession," one editor in New York told me as I was preparing to go to Moscow. He paused. "But I've told our last three correspondents that and they've come and gone and Brezhnev is still in power." As winter settled over Moscow and Brezhnev shuffled through his lavish birthday celebration, I began to think that perhaps in this, his fourth prediction, the editor might be proven right.

The cocoon of privilege that envelops the Soviet elite, which was not invented by Brezhnev but thickened markedly during his tenure, is largely hidden from the Soviet people and outsiders. The only visible sign of it may be the Zils, the sleek black limousines with Politburo passengers that race down the city's reserved center lanes. (Brezhnev and several other bulky comrades were compelled to ride in the front seats of their Zils because negotiating the low back seats proved too difficult.) About thirty Zils are manufactured each year by a special factory. They are assigned only for the use of the top leaders. The cars, which each cost about $140,000 to produce, cannot be purchased at any price by a Soviet citizen.

That winter I saw other privileges of the elite that are ordinarily invisible. It was common knowledge that party and government officials shopped in special stores, thereby avoiding the lines and shortages that plague ordinary citizens. But as far as I know, Satter and I were the first Western correspondents to see the inside of such a store. A person with access to the store offered to take the considerable risk of getting us in by using his family's extra passes. He instructed us not to say anything at all because he was afraid our accents would give us away.

The store we visited is located in "Government House," the building immortalized by Yuri Trifonov in his novel *House on the Embankment* and in the play of the same name. Located just across the river from the Kremlin, it is a massive gray edifice whose outer walls are covered with plaques bearing the names of old Bolsheviks who once lived in its spacious apartments. They make no mention of the darker memories of those walls: the police raids during the Stalinist era, when many of those same Bolsheviks were dragged out of their apartments to prisons and firing squads.

On the street side of the main facade of the building, there is an ordinary *gastronom* or food store, with the usual paltry collection of dry goods, only the lowest grade of meat, and standard items like vinegar and the inevitable, inedible canned fish pastes. But our walk through the gate of the building next to the store led to a different world.

A semicircular structure stood to the right of the large courtyard of the building. The only clue to its function was the chauffeur-driven black Volgas, the cars used by officials of medium rank, that had pulled up, or the occasional delivery truck parked off to the side. The plain wooden door was guarded from the inside by a woman checker, who admitted no one without a coupon marked "store for special dietetic food."

I had heard many stories about such institutions, but I was still not prepared for what I saw. Affluent matrons in furs or sheepskin coats, younger women in imported, fashionable boots, and a few male customers placed their orders at various sections of a long, semicircular marble counter. The service was courteous and efficient. No money was used, only tiny coupons that are made available to such privileged customers at a fraction of their real value. Into the women's *sumki* (bags) and men's briefcases disappeared large numbers of packages discreetly wrapped in plain brown paper.

On the shelves behind the counter or when a customer inspected his purchase, the contents were visible: choice cuts of smoked tenderloin, ham and Hungarian salami, fresh fish, cakes and chocolates, butter, Greek orange juice, lush pears and tomatoes, Indian coffee, even an open crate of suckling pigs. At a side counter, customers picked up prepared orders in large, wrapped boxes. To maintain the fiction that this was all for "dietetic" purposes, a poster on the wall provided advice for those suffering from kidney ailments.

Among Muscovites, the fare of such stores is known as the *Kremlevsky payok,* the Kremlin ration. But the store in Government House is not at the summit of the pyramid of Soviet special stores. It is for officials at the deputy minister level. Central Committee members do their shopping at a more exclusive shop on Granovsky Street, close to the Kremlin. Such stores contain a variety and a quality of food most Soviet citizens will never see in their lifetimes.

If I as a Westerner living in Moscow felt somewhat dazed by my visit, it was hard to imagine what emotions an ordinary Russian would experience if he were suddenly allowed to step into that fairyland. I had two immediate questions for the person who took us to that store. First, I wanted to know what those unbelievably courteous saleswomen and other employees felt when they daily witnessed the benefits bestowed on government officials.

That was no problem, he assured me. They simply stole a few grams of butter here, a few slices of ham there; such petty pilferage was expected and tolerated so long as it stayed within reasonable bounds. The average saleswoman would leave work with only a tiny fraction of what any of the special customers would take as a matter of course, but that would be enough for her to feel lucky to have the job—and to feel infinitely superior to her neighbors who could not dream about such luxuries. That is what the system is all about, he concluded; it gave everyone a reason to feel that he too has privileges, however minuscule, that elevated him above the next person. This is Soviet Marxism's own version of the trickle-down theory.

My second question concerned the customers themselves: How did they feel about the privilege of shopping there? He shrugged. "These people see nothing unfair about the system. On the contrary, they complain that they are not as well supplied as they used to be. Before, red and black caviar were always available; now they aren't."

Our meeting did not last long and I could not ask more questions. But David and I were able to get another view of the world of privilege from two Russians who were ready to talk at length. They were Nadezhda and Nikolai Pankov, an intensely religious couple in their mid-thirties who had lost their jobs as projectionists for Goskino, the Soviet state film organization, in a "staff reduction" earlier that year. In reality, they were fired because they had applied to emigrate, a common occurrence. But the Pankovs took the unprecedented step of fighting for their reinstatement in the courts on the ground that Soviet labor laws stipulate that both wage earners in a family cannot be fired in a staff reduction. Their efforts, which stretched out several months well into 1982, predictably ended in failure. But the court sessions provided a forum for them to talk about what they had observed during their six years at Goskino, where they handled special screenings for selected audiences.

Embittered by the government's refusal either to permit them to emigrate or to rehire them, the Pankovs decided to break the unwritten rule of silence that all those who serve the elite observe. They had a lot to tell. They had screened hundreds of films and had access to the logs of who saw what and when. David and I had told a couple of other correspondents about this opportunity to cover this unusual story, but they showed no interest. Nikolai told me that the one other American correspondent he had talked to earlier had mentioned the possibility of writing a piece after he left the Soviet Union, but he had ruled out writing anything from Moscow for fear of government retaliation.

The information revealed by the Pankovs about the elite's taste in movies could hardly be described as flattering. At the 26th Party Congress in February 1981, delegates would unwind after a long day of turgid speeches about five-year plans and Leninist ideology by spending the evening watching an American movie like *Dirty Harry,* or *Natural Size,* a French-Italian film about a dentist whose mistress is a life-sized rubber doll. After planning military operations in Afghanistan, members of the Red Army general staff preferred escapist fare like *The Cassandra Crossing.* After viewing

Soviet films all day to determine which would get the Lenin Prize, jurors enjoyed a change of pace by seeing the likes of *The Godfather, Last Tango in Paris,* and *The Towering Inferno.* "No one passes up the chance to see a good Western film," said Nikolai. "The same people who write about the moral degeneration of the West then ask to see sex films."

According to the Pankovs, Goskino uses a variety of means to satisfy such demands. Films that are sent to Goskino as distributors' samples are widely shown and, in many cases, illegally duplicated. Films purchased by Eastern European countries with more liberal cultural policies, such as Yugoslavia and Hungary, are sometimes passed on to Moscow after they have been shown there. A certain number of outright pornographic and "anti-Soviet" movies are obtained through undisclosed means, and they are kept in a special safe. In the period before the Pankovs' dismissal, that Goskino safe contained prints of *The Deer Hunter* and a documentary about the pope's visit to Poland in 1979.

Access to those prized films is arranged strictly according to rank. Politburo and Central Committee members have first call on any new film obtained by Goskino, and KGB projectionists screen the movies in the privacy of their apartments or dachas. Officials from ministries, institutes, publications, and other state and party organizations wait their turn to see them in Goskino's screening rooms. This order is extremely important: it not only determines who will see the film first but also the quality of what will be seen. Most distributors' samples have to be returned eventually, and duplicated copies are of poor quality. When the samples are sent back, the explanation provided is that they are of no interest to Soviet audiences; frequently, however, the returned copy is badly worn and frayed from repeated showings. The ranking of officials also determines what films they will see, since not everyone admitted into Goskino is allowed to see the full range of offerings. "The higher up and the more potentially useful a person is, the more likely it is that he will be shown something titillating," Nadezhda explained.

Christina was once taken along by a Russian friend for a screening at Goskino of a Soviet film that had failed to make it past the censors. This, too, was a special treat for elite audiences: to see Soviet productions banned from regular movie theaters. What struck Christina about the evening was both the luxury of the setting—the small screening room was outfitted with deep comfortable armchairs and ringed with heavy red velvet curtains—and its atmosphere of an intimate, private party. There were about fifty people, and everyone exchanged casual greetings. The people who attended such screenings were members of the same club and saw each other constantly.

Contradictions between public posture and private behavior appeared to pose no problems for members of the club. While a Soviet delegation at the 1980 Cannes Film Festival ostentatiously walked out of the showing of *The Deer Hunter* because of its depiction of the Vietnam War, the same film went on to enjoy great popularity in private screenings in Moscow. The editors of the ponderous Communist Party journal *Kommunist* have been particularly fond of mystical productions like *The Exorcist* and *The Omen*. James Bond movies and pornography from *Emmanuelle* to hard-core Scandinavian and Japanese productions are major attractions.

Much of what Goskino shows is neither particularly racy nor political—just foreign. That is enough to convince Soviet censors that the films cannot be shown in regular movie theaters. Nadezhda, whose own longing to leave the Soviet Union may have been subconsciously strengthened by seeing Western films, understood the reasons of the censors. "For an ordinary person, to see how people live, shop, and dress in the West would be too much," she said. Infection from Western productions is considered dangerous at any age. Under lock and key in a special Goskino archive is a complete set of Walt Disney films, available only to the children of the elite.

Lyona is a serious poet with a light, deft touch; his stanzas exhibit a stylistic range rare for someone in his twenties. He had managed to get some of his poems published, but he knew that his undercurrents of pessimism and alienation were suspect. There had been more rejections than acceptances, although no one questioned the quality of his work. Whatever frustrations he felt he kept in check somewhere behind his dark green eyes and bushy beard. He felt at home in Moscow and could not imagine living, especially writing, abroad as some of his former friends were doing. "I need the Russian air," he would tell me. "I need to feel myself a part of what I am writing about." The rejected poems went into the drawer, not to publishers in the West who had signaled their interest.

For Lyona and other Moscow intellectuals we knew, the events in Poland inspired an emotional mix of exhilaration, hope, fear, and something more complex. Lyona claimed that he felt a distinct ideological tightening in Moscow because of the Polish situation, dooming his recent efforts to be published. But he left no doubt that his sentiments were completely with the Poles. Another writer, who had made a respectable career for himself within the Soviet publishing world but still chafed at its restrictions, argued that what the Poles had achieved in terms of artistic freedoms affected Russian self-esteem. "Many of us feel an angry envy because Poland is such a small country and it is doing what a big country like ours should have done much earlier. We wish the Poles luck and success, but at the same time we feel a sense of inferiority—and that is where our anger comes from." He grew more animated as he talked. "If a person thinks less of himself because someone else is doing what he wishes he could be doing, he feels angry with himself. Because he is afraid, he doesn't know what to do or where to start."

The fear came from their reading of the signs that the Soviet leaders' fury at the drift of events in Poland could at any moment be transformed into action to crush Solidarity. Those signs had been multiplying throughout the previous summer and fall, particularly after Solidarity held its congress in September. That meeting had produced strident resolutions calling for free elections, workers' self-management, and the establishment of independent trade unions throughout the Soviet bloc. The Kremlin had repeatedly warned the Polish government to put a stop to "actions hostile to the Soviet Union." The attacks on Solidarity "extremists" and "counterrevolutionaries" in the Soviet press took on an increasingly shrill tone and Poland and the Poles were progressively isolated from their neighbors.

The kinds of measures I had witnessed in Lithuania to cut off previously routine contacts with Poland were being instituted elsewhere. New travel restrictions denied Poles easy access to Czechoslovakia and East Germany for shopping trips. This was justified on the ground that the Poles were buying huge quantities of goods they could no longer find in their own stores. It also was an effective form of economic sanction, registering Prague's and East Berlin's disapproval of developments in Poland, and it served as a further safeguard against the spreading of the Polish political "disease."

Despite intensified jamming, most Russians we knew kept abreast of Polish events by tuning into Western radio broadcasts. Some would wait until the early morning hours when jamming was less effective to catch the BBC, the Voice of America, Radio Liberty, and other stations. I first became aware of these listening practices when friends would comment about my articles in *Newsweek* immediately after their publication—and long before I had received my own mailed copy of the issue a week later. They had heard my stories read on the Russian language services of those stations.

For Russians, a good short-wave radio is a prized possession. The best Soviet models are sold only abroad or in the hard-currency stores for foreigners. But old consoles are painstakingly maintained and if a more limited newer model can be made to tune into foreign broadcasts at any time of day or night it is considered serviceable. One of the great missed opportunities of Western governments has been the lack of sufficient investment in the strengthening of their transmissions. The Voice of America, for instance, still uses transmitters from the 1930s. "Two rockets less and two strong transmitters more," was the advice of one friend who twirled the dials of his radio incessantly in search of Western broadcasts. The potential audience was there, but many people did not have the patience of Moscow intellectuals to spend hours trying to pick up weak transmissions.

On Sunday morning, December 13, Russians did not need to hear Western stations to learn about the imposition of martial law in Poland: it was carried on regular Soviet broadcasts. I had been awakened at four by a call from *Newsweek*'s New York office after the first wire-service bulletin and, numb and discouraged, I had stumbled through the day, learning little beyond the official announcements. Christina was stunned and disbelieving as most Poles still were. The Soviet press and television moved quickly from merely reporting Jaruzelski's speech justifying martial law to expressing Soviet satisfaction with the action. "Hundreds if not thousands of letters have been sent to Soviet television asking when Polish Communists would do away with the violent conduct of anti-Soviet elements," television commentator Aleksandr Kaverznev said on the evening news. "A step has now been taken in that direction."

Many Russian friends took the unusual step of risking phone calls. They did not identify themselves by name, but in muffled, pained voices expressed their sorrow, which was as much for their sense of loss as for what they knew would be our own. Everyone felt an increased sense of vulnerability. A Latvian dissident paid a short visit, his eyes betraying an inner anxiety that could not be suppressed. "If they can destroy an organization like Solidarity with 10 million people, they can do anything with people like me without worrying about any consequences," he said, knowing that I would have nothing to say to contradict him.

Lyona sent a message that he wanted to see me. He looked pale and tired, but his voice was steady. He had been analyzing the situation endlessly and had come to certain conclusions. "Jaruzelski has to give the order to shoot—without that, martial law is nothing. If he holds back from that step, then gradually power will slip away from him and the process of August 1980 will start all over again." I could not quarrel with his premise about the nature of Jaruzelski's power, but I did not want to believe his prediction about turning guns against the people: the risks of a backlash, I tried to convince myself as much as Lyona, would be too great.

Lyona characterized his government's attitude as one of caution and fear at that point because the Soviet leaders were not quite sure where the Polish events would lead. "The main thing now is to avoid Soviet intervention," he said. Unlike several other Russian friends who had been equally sympathetic to Solidarity, he did not expect any act of reconciliation by Jaruzelski once the resistance to martial law had been ended. Instead, he anticipated continued political repression and no substantial economic progress. He pointed out that a right-wing military dictatorship can at least get the economy of a nation moving by ending labor unrest and giving businessmen a free hand; a Communist military dictatorship could impose the same political control and prevent strikes, but it could not offer the necessary economic incentives.

Jaruzelski's strategy, Lyona concluded, would be to make sure that at least vodka was available, even as other shortages persisted. "Better that they drink and forget politics. I'm sure that they're getting plenty of advice from here on that—our officials are experts at demoralization. Look at the somber faces of people on the street, the passivity. That's what Jaruzelski is trying to achieve."

Was this what Soviet power had been reduced to, retaining power by keeping people addicted to the bottle? It was the extension across Soviet borders of the concept first suggested to me by Misha, the social scientist. I did not argue with Lyona, but I felt reluctant to accept his conclusions completely.

The next day Western stations broadcast the first reports of Polish security forces firing on miners in Silesia; seven had been killed. I also learned that a ban on liquor sales instituted with the imposition of martial law had been lifted.

In lines at Moscow stores, there were occasional remarks that echoed the official line praising "the restoration of order" in Poland. The months of media reports portraying Poland as on the brink of anarchy had some of their desired effect. But in the weeks that followed martial law, I found my assumptions about the divisions between Soviet workers and intellectuals on the Polish issue tested and sometimes refuted.

A university professor in his fifties recounted his exchange with a younger colleague about a report she had heard that claimed that the families of those interned in Poland were receiving state aid.

"It's horrible, we are feeding them and the government is spending money on their families."

"Where should they get their food?" the older professor asked.

"That's their problem. If their husbands are guilty, they are also responsible."

When the older professor pointed out that those interned had not been convicted of any crimes, she replied: "That's not so. If they are interned, they are guilty. In '37, many were not charged in our country but they were clearly guilty."

By this time, the professor recalled, he could barely control himself. He had lost two family members in Stalin's purges of that period. "Doesn't it bother you that the Poles do not want this system?" he demanded.

"And who's asking them? They are a Soviet country."

"You mean a socialist country?"

She shrugged. "What's the difference?"

One evening at Gorky Park, I was standing off to the side of an ice-skating rink watching my daughters when another father asked me about my new Canadian skates, a source of constant curiosity. He presented the unmistakable picture of someone from the provinces, with his cheap gray coat and worker's cap. His round face beamed with pride as he pointed out his daughter in a red coat skating near Eva and Sonia. He asked me where I was from and commended me for managing in Russian. "We Russians don't speak other languages—we have no opportunity to practice them."

I mentioned that Russian had been somewhat easier for me to learn than for the average American because of my

Polish background. He nodded grimly. "It's a real tragedy what happened in that country. They've really tightened the screws. They do this and it's only worse for us." He described the chronic shortages of meat and other foodstuffs in his region. "Go to places like Rostov and Gorky—there is nothing, absolutely nothing. In Rostov a cooperative enterprise is selling sausage, but for $16.80 a kilogram."

He clearly linked his own grievances with those of the Poles, and had understood the basic motivation for the protests; he had seen in Solidarity a flicker of hope, now extinguished. All this in spite of the best efforts of the Soviet media to turn average Russians like him against the Poles and to keep them ignorant of even the most basic information. The fact that Solidarity had 10 million members was never mentioned, for example, and some Russians had no idea that it was anything more than an "extremist" movement. But encounters like the one I had in Gorky Park convinced me that pockets of sympathy for the Poles existed among some workers, just as the exchange between the university professors in Moscow indicated that intellectuals were far from united on this issue.

An economist in Moscow told me that he had found more sympathy for the Poles among ordinary people than there had been for the Czechs in 1968. "The basic reason," he said, "is that the situation has become worse here. The corruption and demoralization the Poles are fighting against are something everyone recognizes as widespread in the Soviet Union." I had no illusions that Solidarity was a popular cause among Russians as a whole, but I was increasingly wary of making sweeping generalizations about their attitudes.

Some of my colleagues approached this matter differently. During a taxi ride with a newspaper correspondent, the driver treated us to an anti-Polish diatribe. "That's my piece," the correspondent happily proclaimed as we reached our destination. He meant it: he wrote his article that afternoon characterizing the attitudes of the average Soviet citizen toward Poland based on that single conversation. After recounting our talk with the taxi driver, who was simply identified as a Russian, he wrote: "The conversation, initiated spontaneously at a chance meeting, was typical of what Ivan Ivanovich, the average Soviet man-in-the-street, knows about and thinks of Poland." Shortly after the imposition of martial law, a reporter for another major newspaper told me that he had taken his own informal survey of local attitudes toward Poland. He said that everyone he talked to had echoed the official line, and that he had not found a single dissenting voice. Since I knew that he spoke little Russian, I asked him how he had done his reporting for the story. The answer: he had gone out on the street with his UPDK translator.

The government itself remained nervous about the possible repercussions of the Polish situation long after December. Instead of letting up, the effort to discredit Solidarity intensified. In February, I attended an evening of lectures for the workers of the Moscow Ballbearing Factory. A Foreign Ministry official presented a report on Poland that, aside from pushing the standard line that Solidarity was a CIA creation, indicated that such political lecturers had been instructed to go further than the press in spreading fabricated stories to buttress their arguments. In this case, the speaker stated flatly that the pope in private talks with Josef Glemp, the Polish primate, had declared that martial law was necessary to prevent a civil war.

Soviet television aired a special program on Solidarity that featured shots of American diplomats, with footage of the alleged capture of a woman diplomat transporting bundles of Solidarity literature in the trunk of her car. While they were sabotaging the Polish economy and bringing it to the brink of ruin in accordance with CIA instructions, the Solidarity leaders were described as living lavishly on the money they received from the West and unsuspecting union members. Restaurant receipts for drinking bouts and huge meals flickered across the screen. For the first time, Lech Walesa and other Solidarity leaders were shown. They were characterized as the fiddlers while Poland burned.

A few days after the program was shown, Christina and I were invited to a small dinner party hosted by Warren Zimmerman, the American chargé d'affaires, and his wife in their elegant apartment in the embassy. Zimmerman had served in Moscow before and he was adept at picking out the more interesting Soviet officials from the pool of those authorized to make the rounds of the diplomatic social circuit. That evening, Christina found herself seated next to a prominent, highly polished editor. Always impeccably dressed in sharply tailored suits, he nevertheless had a thoughtful, somewhat diffident manner that was more appealing than the forced joviality or somber lecturing pose assumed by other officials in the presence of foreigners. Christina let the editor know exactly what she had thought of the program on Solidarity. "You of all people should not be angry—you know what the truth is. That was not meant for foreigners like yourself," he said in a tone that suggested any intelligent person would not deign to pay the slightest attention to such a production. "It was meant for our people who heard too much about Solidarity and maybe had some ideas about organizing their own Solidarity here." By Soviet standards, his response was remarkable for its honest cynicism.

At an earlier encounter just after martial law was declared, the same editor had offered another observation that shed some light on the Kremlin's thinking about Poland. He discounted Western fears that the Soviets might invade should

Jaruzelski have problems controlling his resentful people. "We must let the Poles settle this themselves even if it comes to fighting," he said. "I know nothing would unite the army faster against the government than us coming to its aid." If the Polish regime were on the verge of being overthrown, he and everyone else I talked to in Moscow assumed that the tanks would roll, but he argued that anything short of that would not prompt such a reaction. In fact, throughout the entire Solidarity period, the Kremlin was much more reluctant to resort to the use of its own military might than most Western analysts had assumed.

As martial law was grudgingly swallowed by the Polish population, it was tempting to conclude that the Soviet leaders had painstakingly calibrated their responses every step along the way to the inevitable crackdown and that they were always confident that in the end they would regain control of the situation. What I had seen and heard since my arrival in Moscow convinced me that the truth was quite different. The Kremlin was caught as much by surprise as the rest of the world by the transformation of the initially scattered protests into the first genuine workers' movement in a Communist society, and the speed with which the Polish Communist Party and its organizations crumbled under the pressure of long-suppressed popular demands. I remembered the signs of a nearly palpable sense of panic about Poland when I first arrived: it was almost as if the Soviet rulers themselves recognized that the prophecies about this spelling the beginning of the end of their empire might prove to be devastatingly accurate.

Moscow found itself lurching about, trying to employ any tactic to reassert control. This included a mixture of political and military threats. Warsaw Pact troops were sent on maneuvers and heavily reinforced along Poland's borders, but the Kremlin's reluctance to invade stemmed from several considerations. There was no Suez crisis or Vietnam War to distract the West's attention as had been the case when the Soviets invaded Hungary in 1956 and Czechoslovakia in 1968. In addition, an invasion would have doomed Soviet efforts to encourage peace movements in the West, a major foreign policy objective at the time. Moreover, the Afghanistan war was already draining men, resources, and morale. But the most compelling reason was the near-certainty that the Poles, unlike the Czechs, would fight back against a Soviet invasion force, whatever the odds. The long history of Polish-Russian warfare was not forgotten by either side. For the aging Brezhnev team, the idea of unleashing such mayhem in the heart of Eastern Europe, with all its unpredictable consequences, must have given them pause.

After martial law, some of our Russian friends argued that these constraints on the Kremlin offered Jaruzelski the opportunity to demonstrate still a measure of independence and salvage a portion of what Polish workers had achieved with Solidarity. Having decisively proved that the government still held the power in Polish society, they reasoned, he could have worked out a compromise with Solidarity, preserving the concept that workers had the right to organize themselves, but placing strict political limitations on their activities. In theory, I was convinced that was possible. If Jaruzelski had moved quickly in that direction after martial law, the Kremlin might have felt compelled to accept such a solution. Moscow's vital interests would have been safeguarded, even though Poland would have carved out a more independent niche for itself than Moscow would have liked.

But after reviewing the events leading up to martial law, I saw little reason to believe that Jaruzelski harbored such intentions. Increasingly, I found myself sharing the bitter skepticism of people like Lyona or of the Poles I had met the previous summer who had claimed that the authorities were deliberately exacerbating Poland's economic problems in order to discredit Solidarity and wear down national morale. Western officials had frequently argued that the Soviet Union had a large stake in keeping the Polish economy afloat in this period, but the truth was that Poland's deepening economic crisis was advantageous to the Soviets once the basic decision had been made that simple political pressures could not bring about a turnaround. The threat Poland posed to living standards throughout Eastern Europe, the fear that its economic disintegration would undermine the economies of its neighbors and chief trading partners, also served as Moscow's most effective weapon in fanning popular resentment against the Poles.

The fact that after martial law more goods suddenly appeared on the shelves of Polish stores for a brief period suggested that the warehouses had not been as empty as the government had claimed. Much later, Polish sources confirmed that back in September and October, when preparations for martial law had already begun, stocks of canned meat and other products were pulled out of Warsaw stores in the middle of the night. But for public consumption, the Soviet Union and its allies had to be portrayed as doing everything possible to rescue the Polish economy. Shipments of supplies from the Soviet Union, Czechoslovakia, and others were given prominent attention in the media, while the massive flow of private aid from the West went largely unreported. Such selective reporting served the additional purpose of further convincing the Russians, the Czechs, and the East Germans that whatever economic problems they were having were on account of the Poles.

Just how much the Kremlin and Jaruzelski did behind the scenes to accelerate the process of economic disintegration in that period will probably never be known. Similarly, it is difficult to pinpoint the exact degree of responsibility the Soviet Union bears for Poland's long-term economic problems. But ever since Moscow refused to allow Poland's participation in the Marshall Plan after World War II, the Soviet Union has been more of an obstacle to sound economic development than a help. While the Poles did get Soviet oil at below market prices for many years, an honest full balance sheet of Polish-Soviet trade, should it ever emerge, would hardly place Moscow in a positive light.

Throughout the 1970s when the Polish government was borrowing massively from the West, the country's economy kept churning out goods with expensively acquired Western parts and technology for the Soviet market. The Gdansk Lenin shipyard, for example, spent vast amounts of hard currency to install the latest Western equipment for ships under construction, which went straight to the Soviet Union. The Soviets would pay the Poles with "transfer rubles," a currency that could only be used for bilateral trade and had no market value anywhere else. Aside from contributing to Poland's hard-currency squeeze, it was a highly questionable arrangement even in purely bilateral terms. During the Solidarity period, a Polish study of the "transfer ruble" arrangement concluded that successive Warsaw governments had allowed the Soviets to use payment formulas that systematically overvalued Soviet exports to Poland and provided inadequate compensation for Polish goods sent to the Soviet Union.

The changes sweeping Poland threatened to produce not only unacceptable political reforms but also the public scrutiny of the economy as a whole, something that the Kremlin would hardly welcome. Pressures also were growing for decentralizing industries and allowing private business activity on a broader scale, which would have meant taking a major step away from Soviet principles. Those measures may have been what the economy needed to get back on its feet, but that was a secondary consideration for the Soviet leaders and Jaruzelski. They were determined to regain political control at all costs, and by that fall they were fully committed to a strategy of rejecting any compromise with Solidarity in favor of a confrontation they intended to precipitate once all preparations were carefully made.

Could Solidarity have triumphed under such circumstances? Probably not, at least in the short term. The union's own internal divisions provided the government with numerous opportunities to exploit. The union was easy to infiltrate and easier still to provoke when provocation was in the regime's interests. However, the indecisiveness that characterized Moscow's response to Solidarity in the early stages suggests that nothing was preordained about the outcome. The question is what, if anything, could have produced a different result.

A common analysis in the wake of martial law was that the Solidarity activists had pushed too hard, too fast, and thus had sealed their fate. There was some truth to that, particularly at the point when Solidarity had its congress and issued its sweeping appeals for free elections, workers' self-management, and the establishment of independent trade unions throughout the Soviet bloc. But at an earlier stage, more not less militancy may have been needed. Reluctant to intervene militarily, the Soviets encouraged the Polish party to launch the crackdown itself. Even that was a risky gamble, and if Solidarity had demonstrated more convincingly that this would result in unified resistance, the government might well have hesitated. However, in a crucial standoff in March 1981, after Polish police beat rural Solidarity members in Bydgoszcz, Walesa went along with the recommendation of the Catholic Church and called off a nationwide strike designed to show that the Poles would no longer passively accept such brutality. On the eve of martial law, Jaruzelski won in an outright test of force when he ordered riot police to take a Warsaw fire fighters' academy where students had been staging a sit-in. The ease of that victory indicated that martial law would not spark unmanageable opposition.

For all its weaknesses, Solidarity still produced the most sweeping changes ever witnessed in the Soviet bloc and mobilized the bulk of the Polish population behind its efforts for sixteen months. That is far more astonishing than the crackdown that Moscow finally orchestrated after a long period of confusion and uncertainty. The Polish "renewal" planted the seeds of dissent in a whole new generation of Poles, and it provided a brief glimmer of hope to some of the Soviet Union's own citizens. Before my visit to Poland the previous summer, I had asked a Russian friend whether there was anything I could bring back for him. "A little freedom," he replied. If somehow the reform movement had succeeded in surviving longer and also coming to grips with Poland's economic crisis, it would have provided an even more attractive model for a broader range of Eastern Europeans and Russians. That is precisely why Moscow was determined to abort the process.

Lyona spelled out the only conclusion that could be drawn. We were sitting in his cramped kitchen, drinking tea. I had waved away the vodka and he had not insisted; turning to the bottle at that point would have been more of a surrender to gloom than a ritual of our friendship. Instead, he soberly stated the obvious: all of us—by that, he meant himself, Christina, I, and others in Moscow who had been swept up in the optimism of the Poles—had underestimated the power and tenacity of the Soviet system's instinct of self-preservation. Solidarity had proven that the system was vulnerable, but the Poles had learned Lyona's lesson the hard way.

The holiday season contained little joy. We had planned to spend Christmas with Christina's family in Poland, but the travel restrictions introduced with martial law made that impossible. Forced to stay in Moscow, we drummed up as much Christmas enthusiasm as we could for the children's sake, although our hearts were not in it. Our thoughts were elsewhere; Christina had no word from her family because communications were still cut.

We spent New Year's Eve with pianist Vladimir Feltsman and his wife, Anna, in Krasna Prakha, a lovely settlement of dachas and rest homes for the members of the artistic elite. Vladimir's father, Oskar Feltsman, a composer of popular songs who made no secret of his disapproval of his son's desire to emigrate, had a beautifully crafted two-story dacha there. Vladimir was making use of it that evening to entertain a few friends. Although the settlement was only a short drive from Moscow on an excellent road, it had a luxuriously rustic feel. The rambling houses were set back behind sturdy fences and gates, with large yards and enclosed patios just barely visible. The narrow roads were paved and kept free of snow. If he had not applied to emigrate, Vladimir probably could have counted on eventually getting a dacha of his own. It was not hard to see why the government always had plenty of musicians, writers, and artists willing to conform to its dictates.

At first, the evening did not look promising. The shadow of the Polish events along with Vladimir's and Anna's frustration that another year had passed with them no closer to their goal of beginning a new life in the West contributed to the glum mood. The New Year's Eve program on television did not help either: it featured second-rate music and dancing by performers from all the republics and greetings from border guards shown on nighttime patrol, checking the terrain with powerful searchlights. But before midnight, someone suggested we go outside to pop the champagne and our spirits revived in the crisp, cold air and frosted snow. We toasted each other and embraced, celebrating the bond that had come to link us so closely in such a short time.

In February, I took the family, minus only our youngest, to Tallinn. We felt ready for a weekend outside of Moscow, and the Estonian capital with its medieval old town on the Gulf of Finland promised a more traditional European setting. Like its sister Baltic republic of Lithuania, Estonia has a long nationalist tradition and enjoyed a brief interlude of independence between the two world wars. Its religious heritage is Protestant, not Catholic, a result of its cultural links to the German states and Scandinavia rather than to Poland. Although I had intended to spend the weekend sightseeing and relaxing with the family, I was curious about the popular mood. In discussing the issue of discontented minorities, Western analysts pointed to the smallest of the three Baltic republics as a prime example.

Upon our arrival at Tallinn's airport, we looked around for someone from Intourist because we had ordered a car to take us to the hotel. Not seeing anyone we took our places in a long line of people waiting for taxis. But in a few minutes a young man came straight up to us and asked if we were the Nagorskis, introducing himself as the Intourist representative and steering us toward a waiting car. "How did you know who to ask in that long line of people?" Christina asked. He grinned. "You were the only ones without hats on. When I saw the children with their heads uncovered, I knew you had to be foreigners." Some customs, it appeared, were the same in Tallinn as in Moscow.

Others were distinctly different. We wandered the cobblestone streets admiring the castles, churches, and heavy stone Teutonic buildings of the old town, which, unlike Vilnius, had been meticulously restored because Tallinn had been the site of the yachting events of the 1980 Olympics, prompting a major sprucing-up campaign. We ran into numerous foreign tour groups with guides speaking French and German. Outside an Orthodox church, a man in a Finnish parka approached us. "Do you have dollars?" he asked. We saw other tourists detaching themselves from their groups and making quick exchanges on the street, with the black marketeers taking minimal precautions to disguise what they were doing. Foreign currencies were fetching about four times the official rates. I knew that a flourishing black market also existed in Moscow, but I had never seen it operating openly as it was in Tallinn.

The biggest business was provided by the Finns. When we returned to the Viru Hotel, an incongruous modern skyscraper, a large number of Finns were checking in, having just disembarked from the ferry from Helsinki. We had visited Helsinki from Moscow before and liked both the city and its people, but this group of Finns was not an uplifting sight. Their main purpose, it turned out, was to drink themselves into oblivion. By selling their Finnmarks, jeans, or anything else on the black market, they could get all the liquor they wanted, pay for their stay, and still come out ahead of what it would have cost them in Finland for such a weekend bender. Some were already tanked as they came off the ferry. In the morning, they would start with beer for breakfast and continue all day long. After an interminable wait for an elevator—modern showcase Soviet hotels like the Viru never manage to keep elevators working properly— we would step in and find ourselves with four Finns drinking champagne or vodka straight from the bottle.

The local authorities were eager for their hard currency, however it was spent. They did nothing to discourage behavior that, even by Soviet standards, pushed the limits of drunken decorum. But while turning a blind eye to men and women stumbling through the corridors, the hotel enforced peculiar rules. We could not find a restaurant in town that would admit us with the children in the evening, presumably because liquor was being served, and back in the hotel we were refused admittance to the main restaurant for the same reason. We were finally given a separate room for dinner. When I ordered a beer, the waiter primly informed me that he could not serve alcohol in the presence of children.

Another strange ruling, in this hotel designed primarily for foreigners, pertained to the television sets in the rooms. Since Finnish signals can easily be picked up in Tallinn, the TVs were all locked on one local channel; this created the paradoxical situation of foreign guests not being able to turn the dial to Finnish stations that most Estonians could catch. When the children switched on the TV, we were treated to a concert from Moscow's Patrice Lumumba University given by Dean Reed. An American who never found an audience at home, Reed has made a highly successful career for himself in the Soviet bloc by claiming to have been blacklisted in his native country because he had championed the cause of oppressed American workers. He lives the life of a pop star in East Berlin with his East German wife, an actress who had recently played the role of Jenny Marx in a Soviet film about Karl Marx, and travels frequently to the Soviet Union, where he has his most ardent fans. Clad in jeans and strumming his guitar, he sang that evening of heroic Soviet workers opening up Siberia and finished his performance with "We Shall Overcome." The audience of Third World students studying Marxism-Leninism loved him.

Tuning into the world beyond their borders far more easily than most Soviet citizens, Estonians had a different outlook and were less likely to applaud such a performance. Their postwar history was punctuated by protests against Russification, the name they applied to the policies of the government designed to promote the Russian language and to increase the percentage of non-Estonians living in their republic. Student protests were staged in 1980, and in November 1981 pamphlets had circulated calling for work stoppages on the Polish model. Estonian dissidents periodically circulated letters condemning the government's policies, warning that Estonians were in danger of losing their cultural identity.

The Estonians I talked to took such predictions quite seriously. They pointed out that the percentage of ethnic Estonians in the republic's population had steadily declined and now stood at 64 percent of a total of only 1.5 million inhabitants. The wartime and postwar deportations of Estonians had taken a heavy toll as similar measures had in the other Baltic republics. Most of the population increase in recent years had come from immigrants from other parts of the Soviet Union, while the Estonian birthrate had remained low. Estonia was still not as Russified as neighboring Latvia, where ethnic Latvians make up 53 percent of the population, but it was heading in the same direction. Lithuania, with its relatively large population that was 80 percent ethnic Lithuanian, was the only Baltic state holding its own.

I spent several hours with one couple; Gabriela was a librarian and Viktor was a factory worker. "The average person understands everything about our situation," Gabriela said. "There is so much information from abroad and contact." Lutherans, Methodists, and Baptists, the three main Protestant denominations in Estonia, were sheltered somewhat by their ties to churches elsewhere. "They never deal with us the way they deal with religious groups in Russia," she continued. Both of them were Methodists and both feared that the relative strength of the religious denominations would be challenged as the cohesiveness of Estonian society eroded further.

Their alienation from the system was every bit as deep

as that of people I had encountered in Lithuania, but their response was fatalistic, less defiant. Viktor said that the planned strikes had fizzled after a few people distributing pamphlets were arrested. "In my factory people say that if we do the same things as the Poles, it will only produce the same reaction. People live relatively well in Estonia compared with the rest of the country and they are not ready to risk arrest or lose their jobs for some political action."

There was anger, however. Viktor recalled how a couple of years earlier, when meat was suddenly in short supply, a political instructor came to his factory and consoled the workers by saying that they could buy chicken instead and it had the added benefit of being a bargain at $1.50 a kilogram. "The workers nearly killed him because chickens are available at that price only at the special stores for people like him."

Both of them compared the economic situation with Poland. "When the Soviets took over in 1945, people still kept working the way they had in bourgeois times. But then they learned there was no need to work, no incentive, and now they don't work. They put in their eight hours and that's it," Gabriela said. Viktor nodded. "No matter how much money is invested, there are no results."

The conversation drifted to their eight-year-old son, who was playing nearby. They switched the subject when he came closer, with Gabriela offering an explanation when he had moved again. "He is only in the second grade but he already has political lessons: they tell him about Reagan and the American threat. We have to be careful how we talk around him because they ask children provocative questions at school and want to know what we talk about at home. We are teaching him from the very beginning to lie. That's horrible, but what can we do?"

I asked if Estonians saw any hope, any attainable goals

that would improve their plight. Viktor frowned. "The aim is to buy something in the store, and it would be nice if it were something imported."

Gabriela harkened back to her faith in God. "If we were not believers, it would really be a nightmare. At least we believe that we'll have rewards later. But what non-believers hope for, I don't know. I don't know what their aim in life is."

Walking back to the hotel, I thought that perhaps if I had visited Lithuania after the Polish crackdown rather than before I might have met the same bitterness and resignation I was finding in Estonia instead of bitterness and defiance. Perhaps it was a matter of Protestant realism as opposed to Catholic romanticism. Perhaps I had not had a chance to meet the truly defiant ones; my sampling of local opinion was minuscule because of the brevity and circumstances of my visit. But I could not suppress the thought that, while the Kremlin was understandably nervous about the depth of Estonian national discontent, its existence was hardly threatened by such a disheartened, tiny minority.

In the long battle between dissenters and the government, Andrei Sakharov occupied a singular position. A top physicist who helped develop Soviet nuclear weapons, he had abandoned his career and privileges to promote humanist views that transformed him into his country's most famous dissident. In January 1980, after Sakharov had denounced the Soviet invasion of Afghanistan, he was sent into internal exile in Gorky, a city 250 miles east of Moscow that is closed to foreigners. There never was a trial or legal justification for that action; the authorities had simply decided that he had to be isolated so his protests would no longer have the audience provided by Western correspondents and others in Moscow. Although his wife Yelena Bonner continued to bring out messages for him, the government's action did succeed in making his contacts with the outside world much more difficult. He felt lonely and cut off, frustrated by the surveillance and harassment, including the theft of his personal documents.

I had never met Sakharov but I attended press conferences given by his wife at their apartment on Moscow's inner ring road. Bonner would be flanked by the one or two other members of the Moscow group for monitoring Soviet compliance with the Helsinki Accords still at liberty. A thin, young woman with arresting Eurasian features, dark eyes and high cheekbones would quietly watch but not participate. She was Yelizaveta Alexeyeva, twenty-six at the time and the wife-by-proxy of Sakharov's stepson who had emigrated to the United States. Early that winter, she became the focal point of an extraordinary contest of wills between Sakharov and the government. In late November, Bonner announced that she and Sakharov would fast until the government reversed its decision barring Alexeyeva's emigration.

For Sakharov, the personal risk was considerable. He was sixty and suffered from a heart condition, making even a short hunger strike a dangerous affair. He could reason that the government would fear the international outcry if he died, but he also knew that in a confrontation between one individual and the Soviet state there rarely was any contest. Moreover, the authorities—who had not hesitated to deny permission to emigrate to Russians legally married to foreigners before—did not recognize Alexeyeva's proxy marriage as legitimate and therefore maintained there were no grounds to justify emigration. More than fifty friends and fellow dissidents signed a letter backing Sakharov's demand and asking that in addition he be allowed to return from Gorky, but other dissidents were surprised by his decision to stake his life on this issue. Some suggested, not without a touch of bitterness, that he should have chosen a larger cause.

In the kitchen of Sakharov's Moscow apartment after Bonner had gone to join her husband in Gorky, Alexeyeva offered her own explanation for Sakharov's action. She was earnest and nervous, frightened by the sacrifice made on her behalf but insistent that this was more than a purely personal affair. "Before deciding on a hunger strike, he thought about all other alternatives but saw none. He cannot fold his hands and do nothing. This is a continuation of his battle for human rights—in a very concrete case. He has always dealt with concrete cases."

The origins of the case were complex. She and Alexey Semyonov, Bonner's son, had decided to get married before Semyonov had officially divorced his first wife. Then, Semyonov was summarily dismissed from Moscow's Pedagogical Institute in what Sakharov was convinced was part of the authorities' campaign against him. The next likely step for Semyonov, having lost his student status, would have been to be drafted; if he refused to serve on grounds of conscience, he would have been sentenced to a labor camp. When the government suddenly offered Semyonov the opportunity to emigrate in 1978, Sakharov urged his stepson to leave. Alexeyeva was in full agreement. "In that situation, there was no choice," she said. After his divorce was official, Semyonov married Alexeyeva in a proxy ceremony in Montana. It was Sakharov's conviction that he was the cause of the young people's separation that prompted him to take his desperate action.

Thirteen days after their hunger strike began, Sakharov and Bonner were hospitalized. Four days later, the authorities capitulated and informed them that Alexeyeva would be allowed to emigrate. With the whole world watching, they had been forced to accede to the demands of one stubborn man.

Even those dissidents who had questioned Sakharov's stand were relieved, but no one believed this victory heralded a softening of the government's attitude toward dissent. Sakharov's international prominence offered him protection others could not hope for. While the physicist was recovering from his ordeal, several dozen people gathered in Moscow's Pushkin Square to silently observe Human Rights Day; about thirty were immediately rounded up by the police. Anatoly Koryagin, the psychiatrist who had been condemned to a labor camp for declaring a dissident worker sane, managed to get a letter out appealing to his professional colleagues in the West not to forget those "condemned to spend years in the nightmarish [for a healthy person] world of psychiatric wards, exhausting themselves in a debilitating struggle to preserve their psyches." Koryagin himself, relatives told me, had been placed in a special punishment cell for his continual defiance. Two writers met me at a subway stop to pass on word of the arrest of Yevgeny Kozlovsky, who had published a short novel in the West, and KGB raids on the apartments of three other authors, resulting in the confiscation of papers, notebooks, and typewriters. All of that happened in December, the month of Sakharov's victory. The balance sheet left little doubt which way the wind was blowing.

In February, Serge Schmemann of *The New York Times* called to say that KGB agents were conducting a search at Georgi Vladimov's apartment. Along with Tony Barbieri of the *Baltimore Sun,* we went over as the nine-hour search was ending. "They seemed to know where everything was," the author told us as he assessed his losses. His Amnesty International files had been confiscated along with research materials for a new book, old letters from Solzhenitsyn and Sakharov, the calling cards of correspondents like ourselves, and manuscripts of aspiring writers who came to Vladimov for his evaluation of their work. The agents also had attempted to pin responsibility on Vladimov for the smuggling abroad of Kozlovsky's short novel, although they had no evidence. While Vladimov was interrogated in his apartment, his wife, Natasha, had been taken for questioning at Lubyanka, KGB headquarters. As we left the Vladimovs' apartment a black Volga with four young agents was still parked outside.

Open dissent, which had blossomed in the late 1960s and 1970s, was wilting under the sustained campaign of intimidation. The belief was fast disappearing that public challenges to the government on legal and moral grounds, asserting rights theoretically guaranteed by the Soviet Constitution, could produce positive results. I heard of small study groups forming that produced typewritten journals, but these were assuming a conspiratorial nature by necessity. Unlike earlier dissidents, they did not want their essays to circulate widely and to reach Western correspondents. For their own protection, they wanted to be islands unto themselves. They weren't; gradually, with the help of informers, the KGB began zeroing in on their activities.

But a steady stream of people continued to believe that Western correspondents were the key to their salvation. Probably because word had spread of Adolph Muhlberg's emigration after Satter and I visited him, I heard from many ethnic Germans during the winter. One group of Volga Germans, who had been trying to emigrate for years, sought me out after failing to make contact with any West German correspondents. It appeared that they were getting the brush-off from correspondents who preferred not to be bothered with their problems, although their plight was a natural story for West German publications.

They were desperate. As we walked along Kutuzovsky

Prospekt, a conspicuous group of mostly middle-aged men and women clustered around me, announcing in uncertain terms that they planned to stage a protest in Red Square. They asked me to cover it and bring my colleagues along as well. It was an accepted practice among Moscow correspondents to pass on information of this nature to colleagues so that dissidents organizing a press conference or protest would not have to increase their risk of exposure by contacting each reporter individually, but this struck me as a different situation. Their eyes searched my face for my reaction, and it was obvious that their determination to go ahead with their protest depended to a large extent on my response. I told them that such an action was suicidal. Even if I and other correspondents came, there would be no guarantee we would see anything before they were arrested and disappeared; if we did, it would be at most a brief, quickly forgotten news item. They reconsidered.

For Soviet citizens, the risks of contacting or associating with correspondents were growing. One evening in January, Christina and I were driving back with three Russian friends from a small neighborhood theater where we had seen *Dragon*, a play about a medieval despot who bore an unmistakable resemblance to Stalin, in a production that was remarkable for its impassioned allusions to contemporary Soviet society. As soon as we turned onto the main road leading out of the wilderness of drab apartment buildings where the play had been staged, a police car drew up parallel with us and the disembodied voice from its loudspeaker ordered me to pull over. The policeman asked for my documents but made no pretense that I had committed any offense; instead, he stuck his head through my window and looked at the other passengers in the car. "I want to see who your friends are." That was all he said, but it was enough to have a chilling effect on at least two of my passengers who wished they had taken the bus home.

One woman recalled afterward that in a second she had taken a mental inventory of everything in her purse to make sure she did not have anything that could possibly be considered incriminating. She didn't, but she still felt a momentary panic that she would be searched and something would be found. That kind of vague feeling of guilt is commonplace, putting completely innocent Soviet citizens on the defensive whenever they have to deal with the authorities. Another friend once recounted the story of a respected scientist who was allowed to go abroad for the first time when he was about sixty to accept a prize in London. The morning after his arrival, he got up, opened the window of his hotel room to look at the city, and had a startling thought: "I'm not guilty, not guilty of anything." For the first time in his life, he had shed that pervasive sense of guilt that was always with him in Moscow.

I realized that the warning in the car was also intended to put me on the defensive, not just my passengers. It suggested that the authorities were displeased with the company I was keeping and my reporting habits. There had been previous signals to that effect in the Soviet press. After my trip to Lithuania, a short article appeared in the Lithuanian daily *Tiesa* charging that my reporting consisted of a collection of gossip from old women at the market. My trip to Vologda was followed by a lengthy piece in *Krasny Sever* by Arkady Shorokhov, the deputy editor who had attached himself to David Satter and me whenever possible. Entitled "Don't Get Yourselves into a Mess, Gentlemen!" it portrayed *Newsweek* as working with the Reagan administration to inflate a bogus "Soviet military threat." Shorokhov wrote:

> It has become very difficult to convince the American readers that it's necessary for the U.S. to substantially reduce expenditures on social programs and drastically

increase its nuclear potential. *Newsweek* needs "sensational" arguments and "irrefutable" evidence that the Soviet Union, if you will, is desperately arming itself, and is preparing for aggression and nuclear war. But where does one get the facts? One can get into a mess by telling lies. An alternative method appears—*Newsweek* decides to speculate on certain food problems in our country. Here, if you will, is the incontrovertible evidence that the Soviet Union is arming itself . . .

The methods of the foreigners were so despicable and provocative that they immediately aroused indignation and bewilderment on the part of the Vologda residents. The journalists operated on the principle of "the dirtier, the better." And, understandably, their attempts were met with justifiable resistance by the Soviet people.

The article then cited testimony of various citizens, like the young man who interrupted our talk with the two elderly women on the street, about our "insolent" behavior, our asking "provocative" questions, and my taking pictures of "unattractive buildings," "an old, neglected shack," and "a pile of rubbish." Shorokhov reported with indignation my asking the mayor "straight in his face" what he thought of Solidarity. In a subsequent issue, several letters were printed echoing the same themes, focusing primarily on the pictures I took of log cabins—none of which appeared in *Newsweek*. The conclusion was that the cabins should be "cleared from the face of the earth" to prevent Americans using them for anti-Soviet propaganda.

Shiryayev, the journalist who had been waiting for us along with the mayor when we visited Adolph Muhlberg in Berendeevo, had written an article for *Severny Rabochy,* his newspaper. Never mentioning Adolph's German background, it portrayed him as a drifter and a bum, a slothful, disreputable character. It never explained why he had received permission "to leave for Israel." The only conclusion the reader could draw was that he was Jewish. "Disrespect for public and civic duty, the running down of the ways of our country, a desire to give little and get a lot, moral uncleanliness and finally overt parasitism—these and other 'qualities' in Muhlberg apparently turned out to be to the liking of the foreign correspondents," Shiryayev wrote. "That is why Nagorski, having taken along his British colleague for authority, had driven a hundred miles to sniff, to put it bluntly, the smell of a rubbish heap."

He ended by citing Shorokhov's article about our visit to Vologda. "In short, in their trips in our country Andrew Nagorski and his colleague clearly behave tendentiously, use unworthy and impermissible methods, misuse the hospitality extended to them. For shame, gentlemen!"

I constantly marveled at Misha's matter-of-fact cynicism. Dismissing the official pronouncements and the genuflections toward ideology he had to make at conferences he attended in his position as a prominent social scientist, he gradually won me over. I shed much of my early skepticism about his theories on alcoholism, for example, and accepted his perspective as logically consistent in the Soviet context. He still had his moments when he became uncharacteristically defensive. Brushing back his hair and leaning his long frame forward, he insisted on one occasion that Muscovites were just as well dressed as Parisians, Londoners, or New Yorkers, and he looked genuinely unhappy when he pressed me for confirmation and found none. But his baggage of illusions was exceptionally small and his assessments of Soviet society were uncannily accurate.

At the beginning of the winter, we had talked about the

latest in a series of anti-corruption drives that had been launched with great fanfare. The press featured numerous articles on the subject, and a letter from the Central Committee that had been read at closed party meetings had announced that stern measures were being taken to punish the guilty. It reported that a city official in the Georgian capital of Tbilisi had been executed for taking bribes for allocating apartments. But, Misha pointed out, the targets of the drive were, as usual, relatively minor officials and middle-level managers, while senior officials were left untouched. This prompted people to dismiss the campaign as no more than a routine show designed to prove that the government was serious about fighting corruption without attacking the source of the problem. "A fish rots from the head," Russians were fond of saying when pressed to identify that source.

The campaign in progress, Misha told me, had backfired. By zeroing in on the likes of store managers who make deals "on the left" with suppliers, the authorities hindered rather than helped the economy. "During an anti-corruption campaign like this, you can get five years in prison for taking a $70 bribe and a lot of people are hurt. But the authorities discovered that without bribes and the second economy the system doesn't work at all." Supplies were disappearing, customers used to paying a "commission" for a decent suit now found that the store manager had no suits available since he was afraid to take bribes and pay off the distributor, workmen failed to do their repair work for standard wages, and plans everywhere were not being fulfilled. Within a couple of weeks, Misha said, complaints were so widespread that the government had quietly begun backing away from the entire campaign. Later in the winter, however, the anti-corruption drive would be revived for quite different reasons, and Misha and I found ourselves repeatedly returning to the subject.

What began to change in the interim was the leadership itself. At the end of January, just a month after he had pinned the seventy-fifth-birthday medals on Brezhnev, Mikhail Suslov died. The party ideologist's gaunt body was still lying in state at the House of Trade Unions, the same place where Brezhnev's body would be on display ten months later, when I visited historian Roy Medvedev at his apartment on the outskirts of Moscow. Medvedev had been expelled from the Communist Party in 1969 for his attacks on Stalinism and his books were only published in the West, but he insisted on his belief in socialism and was cautious about participating in dissident protests. As a result, he had maintained a unique position in Moscow, writing for publications abroad and openly meeting with Western correspondents to discuss political developments without retaliation from the authorities. He was normally cool and detached in presenting his analysis of the topic of the day, but this time his voice betrayed excitement. After years of answering the obligatory questions about the Soviet Union after Brezhnev, he sensed that with Suslov's death the action was finally beginning.

Suslov had been the keeper of a rigid faith. Totally dedicated to Stalin, he was provincial party chief of Rostov-on-Don in the 1930s and carried out purges there with a vengeance: they were said to be so sweeping that at some party meetings it was difficult to come up with enough members to fill abruptly vacated seats. During World War II, he supervised the deportations of minority groups from the Caucasus that Stalin had accused of collaboration with the Nazis, and later he imposed Soviet rule on Lithuania, exiling entire villages to Siberia. Under Khrushchev, he demanded the continued ostracism of Yugoslavia for its independent policies and advocated the suppression of the 1956 Hungarian revolt with Soviet tanks. When Khrushchev's power base began to erode, it was Suslov who led the attack against him in October 1964, and orchestrated his replacement by Brezhnev. Gradually emerging as the number two man in the Brezhnev hierarchy, Suslov continued to be a proponent of hard-line policies aimed at crushing dissent within both the Soviet Union and Eastern Europe.

Medvedev thought that Suslov's death was less important for Soviet policy than for its impact on the succession. Suslov had never commanded enough support to give him a shot at the top job, something he was savvy enough to realize. Instead he had devoted himself to maintaining stability under Brezhnev, working arduously and effectively to quash any open politicking for the succession. Now, his stabilizing influence was gone and rivalries were likely to emerge.

Most Western speculation until then had focused on two men: Andrei Kirilenko, who had often chaired Politburo meetings when Brezhnev was absent, and Konstantin Chernenko, who had been Brezhnev's aide-de-camp and upon whom the Soviet leader had increasingly relied as his own strength waned. Younger Politburo members like agriculture specialist Mikhail Gorbachev and Leningrad party leader Grigori Romanov were viewed as possible future, not current, candidates.

Medvedev dismissed Kirilenko as a strong contender because of his age, seventy-five at the time, and his reputed health problems. As for Chernenko, Medvedev doubted that an apparatchik so utterly dependent on Brezhnev, with no power base of his own, could mount an effective campaign when Brezhnev's grip on power began to loosen. Instead, Medvedev predicted that Andropov would make a bid for Suslov's position as chief ideologist, which would catapult him into front-runner status. "It would be a good step to get him out of the KGB," Medvedev said. By formally shedding his fifteen-year association with the Soviet Union's most feared instrument of power, Andropov could remind people that he was a politician, not a policeman, by trade.

That scenario was at first deemed highly improbable by Western Kremlinologists. They argued that no KGB chief had made it to the top before, and the "laundering" period as chief ideologist would be too transparent a power play, which potential rivals would move to block. Standard Kremlinology also assumed that there must be friction between the military and the KGB, and without the support of the nation's top brass no one could be made general secretary in the Soviet Union. Finally, Brezhnev was believed to be strong enough to prevent someone he didn't want from openly positioning himself for the succession.

These assumptions looked perfectly reasonable, but in the end they overestimated Brezhnev and underestimated Andropov. No one anticipated the impact of the corruption issue on the succession struggle. In the weeks and months that followed, that struggle spewed out an unusual number of clues that offered a rare glimpse of what was happening behind the scenes in the Kremlin.

There were a couple of early hints that events were taking an unexpected turn. In an issue dedicated to Brezhnev's seventy-fifth birthday in December, the Leningrad literary magazine *Aurora* published a short story entitled "Jubilee Speech" on page seventy-five. It was about a very old writer who "is living and does not plan to die," although everyone thinks of him as practically dead. The author describes his elation when he hears an erroneous report that the writer has died, adding: "The joy was premature, but I think we won't have to wait for long." The "old writer" being lampooned was clearly Brezhnev. Shortly after Suslov's funeral, Brezhnev, while attending the funeral of Colonel General Konstantin Grushevoi, a close friend who was also seventy-five, broke down and wept. That in itself was not unusual but the moment was shown on the nightly television news—which was highly unusual. It violated the unwritten Soviet principle of never permitting Soviet leaders to appear vulnerable. It served as a dramatic reminder of Brezhnev's own mortality.

Bob Gillette of the *Los Angeles Times* broke the story that would prove to be a crucial part of the succession puzzle. Acting on a tip from a dissident source who was shunned by many other correspondents, he visited the headquarters of the famed Soviet circus. On the third floor, he found the office of Anatoly Kolevatov, the general director. The door was carefully sealed with orange wax and an official stamp, Kolevatov's nameplate had been removed, and a notice hung on the wall announcing that a special Ministry of Culture commission had been established to examine the operation of the circus organization. People in the circus spoke of a mushrooming scandal involving Kolevatov and an associate, Boris Buryatia, who was in turn linked to Galina Churbanova, Brezhnev's daughter.

Here was a story that begged investigation. I scrambled to learn what I could and found, to my delight, knowledgeable circus sources and people who knew Boris Buryatia and his habits. Between the time I filed my first story on the scandal and the second one the following week, I reconstructed the verifiable facts and heard the unverifiable rumors that purported to fill in the blanks of this plot. In true Russian fashion, the tale grew increasingly complex and contained a long list of characters who had to be carefully catalogued to keep them straight. But the important point was the connection to the country's first family.

Everything revolved around the circus, for which Brezhnev had always had a special fondness. During his days as a rising party official in the Ukrainian city of Dnepropetrovsk, he often took his children to performances. Galina took to the circus even more passionately than her father: her first two husbands were circus people, and even after she married a policeman, who quickly rose to the rank of deputy minister of interior, she continued to maintain close ties with the circus crowd. Boris Buryatia, her lover at the time, was also a habitué of the circus milieu and a partner of Kolevatov in the schemes that were his undoing. Known as Boris the Gypsy, he was a minor singer at the Bolshoi Ballet and one of Moscow's flashiest young men. He wore a diamond-encrusted crucifix prominently displayed under his unbuttoned sport shirts and drove a green Mercedes.

Probably by coincidence, Galina was present when the first in a bizarre chain of events occurred leading to Boris's arrest. The occasion was the funeral on December 27, 1981, of Nikolai Asanov, a former Moscow circus director. Aside from Galina, the mourners included Irina Bugrimova, a retired lion trainer who owned an extremely valuable collection of diamonds, some of which had belonged to old Russian noble families. When Bugrimova returned to her apartment after the funeral, she found her door ajar and her most valuable diamonds stolen. The police later discovered the gems in Boris's apartment. Finding himself in that seemingly hopeless position, Boris reportedly claimed that any action against him would drag in Galina as well.

At this point, the case became murkier and impossible to verify. But according to the version of events then widely circulating in Moscow, General Semyon Tsvigun, the first deputy chief of the KGB, ordered Boris's arrest, prompting an angry confrontation with Suslov shortly before he died. Suslov was supposed to have told Tsvigun that he had vastly overstepped his authority by issuing the arrest order for someone that close to Brezhnev's family, indicating that by doing so he had ruined his career. Boris was not picked up immediately and Tsvigun abruptly showed up in the obituary column, a rumored suicide. The obituary notice was signed by Andropov and almost all of the KGB leadership, an almost unheard-of occurrence. Brezhnev pointedly did not sign it. After Suslov's death from natural causes, the KGB took the offensive once again, arresting Boris on the very day of Suslov's funeral when Galina would be unable to reach her father to intervene.

Kolevatov was picked up next and found to have $200,000 in hard currency and $1.1 million in diamonds squirreled away in his apartment. Hot diamonds, it appeared, were a specialty he shared with Boris. The source of most of those riches was bribes he extorted from performers who wanted to travel abroad, a routine Soviet practice. Since the national circus operates more than 80 troupes, ice shows, and traveling zoos and employs 20,000 people, including 6,000 entertainers, Kolevatov's revenue potential was virtually unlimited. Aside from its other attractions, a trip abroad offers Soviet citizens ample opportunities for instant enrichment: almost anything they manage to purchase during a trip can be resold in the Soviet Union at several times its original cost. As a result, Soviet travelers will barter whatever they have, skip meals if they can get their food allowance in cash, or do virtually anything else to provide them with the hard currency they need to make their trip a commercial success. To get on a trip in the first place, they consider it normal to invest in a suitable payoff to the appropriate officials.

As other correspondents and I pieced together what had happened, it was evident that we were engaged less in investigative reporting than in following tracks that had been intentionally left uncovered. The speed with which the scandal broke and reports about it spread left little doubt that somebody high up wanted things that way. Even Russian-language Voice of America broadcasts, which normally were jammed by the Soviets, came through clearly when reporting the details of the scandals based on our stories. The Soviet press never reported any of this, but the scandal was the talk of Moscow.

That "somebody," I was convinced, had to be Andropov. The KGB was behind the arrests that "unmasked" the scandals, and only such a powerful organization could arrange for the satirical piece in *Aurora* and the "inadvertent" film footage on TV of Brezhnev in tears; it also had responsibility for the jamming of foreign radio broadcasts. By these actions, Andropov was proving that Brezhnev was no longer fully in command, since he demonstrably could not squelch a scandal touching on his daughter. The KGB chief was also reminding potential opponents that he had dossiers on everyone. The circus director's activities must have been known to the KGB for a long time, but he wasn't arrested until it served Andropov's interests to do so.

The bland official explanation was that the circus arrests were part of a new anti-corruption campaign, but that fooled no one. Misha, whom I visited just as the scandal had become widely known, observed that the pervasiveness of corruption in the Soviet system made everyone theoretically vulnerable. When an anti-corruption drive begins to strike at important people, their affiliations serve as key political indicators. "It makes no difference what they catch you for, it's just an excuse," he said. Andropov had a powerful weapon to wield in his drive for power.

How was Brezhnev to fight back, banish the speculation that he was losing his grip on power, and maneuver his own candidate, Chernenko, into Suslov's post instead of Andropov? It was a tall order, especially for someone as physically frail as Brezhnev.

I had developed a guarded, infrequent contact with someone who could provide reliable information on Brezhnev's health. I had learned from him that the Soviet leader had suffered heart spasms in late February, just when the circus scandal had broken. It was not a heart attack, but hospitals and medical teams of the Ministry of Health's "Fourth Department"—which oversees the network of special medical facilities for the Soviet elite—had been placed on full alert. Yevgeny Chazov, a cardiologist who served as Brezhnev's personal physician and as a deputy minister of health in charge of the Fourth Department, was taking no chances with his patient. (Chazov, incidentally, has other responsibilities: he travels frequently to the West to speak at conferences sponsored by International Physicians for the Prevention of Nuclear War, which he co-founded with Harvard's Bernard Lown. When he speaks in the West, he likes to be introduced simply as a Soviet doctor concerned about the arms race, with little or no mention of his government position.)

Brezhnev recovered quickly and decided to demonstrate that the Politburo, despite the swirling rumors, was still united. In early March, he arrived at the Moscow Art Theater accompanied by Chernenko, Andropov, Defense Minister Dmitri Ustinov, and Foreign Minister Andrei Gromyko. The play was *Thus We Shall Triumph,* a drama about Lenin's twilight years, but the evening was less than a success. As one of the actresses later told me, Brezhnev had a problem with his hearing aid. Like many people with hearing problems, he overcompensated by raising his voice. "That's Lenin. That's Stalin," he said in his gravelly voice that could be heard throughout the theater. Chernenko motioned to him to lower his voice, but Brezhnev ignored him. The result was to make Brezhnev look more feeble than ever, and no one was impressed by the ostensible display of unity.

Given these dramatic developments, my editors and I decided that a cover story was needed to examine the succession struggle and Brezhnev's legacy. Originally scheduled for the second week in March, it was postponed several times as often happens with newsmagazine projects. I kept updating the story every week, but I had the frustrating feeling that interest was waning back in New York. We had given more play to the infighting than many other publications and we had been alone in reporting Brezhnev's heart spasms but, with a lull in the action, my arguments for going ahead with the cover were not making much headway.

Brezhnev himself changed that. Instead of taking a vacation in March as he had been increasingly prone to do to rest from the rigors of the Russian winter, the Soviet leader undertook a vigorous political schedule to counter the growing impression fostered by Andropov that his political and physical health was dramatically weakening. In late March, he took a tiring, four-day trip to Tashkent. When Soviet television and newspapers failed to carry the customary photographs of Brezhnev's return to Moscow, rumors spread that the Soviet leader had been carried off the plane on a stretcher and immediately hospitalized. Nothing was officially acknowledged, but a planned visit by President Ali Nasir Muhammad of South Yemen was abruptly canceled and Chazov, Brezhnev's physician, scrapped a trip to England. My editors revived the cover story.

But I was faced with a problem. The one major reporting task I had left, to learn what I could about the seriousness of whatever had happened to Brezhnev at the end of the Tashkent trip, was proving extraordinarily difficult. I had heard the rumors that he might have suffered a stroke, but I could not confirm them. When I needed him most, my key source on Brezhnev's health was impossible to reach.

As the cover-story deadline approached, my foreign editor called to say that our Washington bureau had obtained the contents of a highly classified U.S. intelligence report.

Brezhnev had suffered a "very serious" stroke, according to the report, and even if he survived he would be unable to stay in power beyond a Central Committee meeting in May. As a result, *Newsweek* was considering changing the cover headline from "The Succession Struggle" to "Brezhnev's Final Days." Although I could neither confirm nor deny the intelligence report's information, I argued against the change on the ground that it would put us in the position of appearing to predict Brezhnev's imminent demise. No matter what the state of his health, that was risky and unnecessary. It would also make it look like the only reason for our cover was his latest illness, which was not the case. I had one more day to learn what I could before the deadline passed. Meanwhile, the cover line would be discussed.

Late that night, I took a walk with a U.S. diplomat who was one of the embassy's best analysts and also someone I felt would give me an honest response on such a sensitive matter. I told him about the Washington intelligence report and asked if it had originated in the embassy. He insisted that it had not and that the embassy had no information to confirm its contents. Then what would explain the report? He thought there were two possibilities: Washington may have picked up something directly through independent means like radio intercepts from the plane coming back from Tashkent, or the author of the report might have taken the cables from the embassy reporting the speculation in Moscow about Brezhnev, stripped them of their qualifiers, and presented the rumors as facts.

That was hardly reassuring, and it made me more anxious than ever to reach my source who could provide me with an accurate assessment. But the next day I had no more luck than before. That evening, however, he appeared at our usual meeting place and I could barely conceal my relief: it was the last possible moment for me. What he could tell me was not conclusive either; Brezhnev's doctors were still uncertain about their diagnosis. But they were focusing on two possibilities: either he had suffered a mild stroke or a transient prestroke condition called "spasms of the cerebral vessels." The medical team was leaning toward the second, less serious possibility. If they were right, my source said, Brezhnev could reappear in a few weeks.

I rushed back to the office and filed just in time to get that information into the story. The Washington intelligence report was still given the most prominent play but my conflicting news was also provided, and no definitive judgment about Brezhnev's health was made. However, before I had reported back, the cover line was set as "Brezhnev's Final Days."

The *Newsweek* cover prompted the first official explanation of Brezhnev's disappearance. A Foreign Ministry spokesman angrily denied that Brezhnev was fading and declared that he was "on his regular winter rest." A few days later, my source provided me with the latest report of Brezhnev's doctors. They had revised their diagnosis, concluding that his collapse had been prompted by a new attack of heart spasms, stronger than the ones he had suffered in February. That was less ominous than their earlier suppositions, but the episode had further weakened Brezhnev's constitution and had heightened the chances that the next incident could be his last. While the doctors believed that he would be able to make a public appearance after a reasonable recuperation period, the long-term prognosis was guarded. "This was an alarm bell," my source concluded. "He may be able to survive for a good while yet, or at any moment the final bell may ring."

Instead of taking his "regular winter rest," Brezhnev was bedridden and under constant medical care at his dacha on the outskirts of Moscow, which had begun to resemble a mini-hospital. During the nearly four weeks that Brezhnev was out of sight, rumors swept Moscow that the Soviet leader had died. They could be heard in the subway, at beauty parlors, in shopping lines. They also could be heard, presented as reliably confirmed information, from known KGB informers in conversations with Western diplomats. Another account making the rounds described Brezhnev as still alive but just barely, a "vegetable" kept breathing by sophisticated life-sustaining equipment. Andropov, it seemed, was convinced that even such patently false rumors helped him by reinforcing the impression that the Soviet leader was no longer in command. Chernenko, who had been making numerous well-covered public appearances while Brezhnev was active, had vanished from television news broadcasts and the front pages of Soviet newspapers.

Brezhnev finally reappeared on Lenin's birthday in late April. Andropov delivered the birthday speech. When Andropov finished, there was a revealing moment that was not caught by the television cameras but which I could clearly see through my binoculars from the press balcony. Andropov returned to his seat, his usually stern countenance suddenly breaking into a broad grin as he was congratulated by a cheerful Dmitri Ustinov, the powerful defense minister. Ustinov's backing, and that of the generals, was probably already lined up. Chernenko had to console himself by chatting with a frail-looking Brezhnev.

4

SPRING

It was on the day in March when I took Eva and Sonia out to the woods of Peredelkino and our skis kept sinking into slushy wet snow that I recognized, both with relief and a tinge of regret, that winter was finally ending. The beginning of spring was less a flowering, since greenery did not reappear until later, than a soggy limbo between the cold of the recent past and the promise of warmth yet to come. Dirty clumps of city snow subsided, trickling their moisture onto streets and sidewalks. Mud was tramped onto the floors of steamy windowed cafes, beer halls, and the aisles of the gloomy food stores. The park near the New Circus was too wet to resume our "spiers vs. liars" football game, and I was left to jog occasionally along the concrete Moscow River embankment to revive my sluggish circulation.

The days felt strange and uncertain, with politics as much in limbo as the weather and Moscow witness to a bizarre social protest. Brezhnev was back, but no one knew for how long. The Western press discussed the possibility of a Reagan-Brezhnev summit, but my source who had proven accurate in his previous reports on Brezhnev's health told me that the Soviet leader never would be capable of traveling abroad again. Stories circulated about a baffling "Fascist rally" in Pushkin Square commemorating Hitler's birthday on April 20. When I first heard this, I was convinced that I had misunderstood something or that my informant had let his imagination get the better of him. But neither was the case.

Many Russians I knew had heard some version of what had happened: a group of teenagers had apparently gathered by prearrangement in Pushkin Square and attempted to hold a Hitler birthday rally. By some accounts, the group numbered about 100 and many wore black shirts or black ties. Other groups of youths heard about the gathering and came out to fight the Fascists. There were reports of scuffles and somewhat belated police intervention, resulting in a few arrests. But the rally had fizzled out before it actually began. What was astounding was that in a country that had suffered so much during the war, there should be any young people who considered themselves "Fascists." I was told, however, that this was a phenomenon that had existed for some time.

At most, it appeared, the Fascists were a fringe movement of a few thousand youths scattered in several cities. An older economist claimed that it was a genuinely political movement "which shows that young people are unhappy with disorder, the lack of food and goods, the corruption of officials, and the poverty of spiritual life." He also said it contained overtly racist overtones, urging the maintenance of white supremacy over Asian minorities and the exiling of all Jews. But a Jewish high school student compared the Fascists with the tiny Soviet hippie movement that had emerged in the 1970s, calling both apolitical protests against the system by teenagers primarily from well-off families. The hippies had taken on the trappings of their counterparts in the West—long hair, deliberately sloppy dress—and also were more interested in dropping out of society than in reforming it. A young acquaintance who had himself gone through a brief hippie phase, while conceding that the Fascists expressed more of a yearning for order, described them as "attracted to purely the exterior forms of Fascism and not much interested in ideology."

I did not know what to make of any of this, and older Muscovites were shocked and equally perplexed. The authorities, high school students claimed, knew of the existence of these groups but had taken few steps to break them up. By contrast, they had taken harsh measures against the hippies in the 1970s, who were seen as a threat to the social order: there had been arrests, beatings, and placement in mental hospitals. The explanation for the different official reactions remained elusive, although the former hippie I knew argued that the security forces felt more sympathy toward a group that expressed authoritarian leanings of any stripe than toward groups that to them represented the forces of anarchy.

I was on more familiar if depressing ground in following the latest assault on the battered dissident community. The authorities were conducting what amounted to a mopping-up operation of what remained of the Helsinki group, the small band of activists who had sought to pressure the Kremlin into respecting the agreements they had signed in the Finnish capital in 1975. Those accords had included broad human-rights provisions such as freedom of conscience, equal treatment under the law, free trials, free choice of place of residence, and freedom to travel in and out of one's country. They also called for the reunification of families living in different countries, a greater exchange of information, and improved working conditions for journalists. Each of the thirty-five nations had pledged themselves to observe all these provisions. But Soviet activists, like Ivan Kovalyov, who tried to monitor their country's failure to do so found themselves targeted by the authorities. In April, Kovalyov was sentenced to five years in prison plus five years in exile. He was twenty-seven and the third member of his family to be dispatched to a labor camp; his father and his wife had preceded him.

That same month, the KGB conducted a sweep of the apartments of people suspected of involvement in Russian nationalist activities, the printing of underground publications stressing Russia's religious heritage. Religious literature, Bibles, and icons were confiscated and thirteen people were arrested. In May, Leonid Borodin, a writer with views on Russian nationalism similar to Solzhenitsyn's, was also arrested.

Borodin had already spent six years in labor camps and prisons as a result of his involvement with a militant nationalist group in the 1960s that had advocated the creation of a theocratic state. Upon his release, he had continued to write fiction and philosophical articles that circulated in samizdat and appeared in émigré journals, but his outlook had softened considerably. As his fellow writer and friend Georgi Vladimov put it when I visited him after the arrest, "Borodin became a completely different person. Like Dostoyevsky, he renounced his early revolutionary phase." The irony of the situation was that he was picked up again at a time when his personal dissent was muted; the tragedy, according to Vladimov, was that his previous imprisonment had left him with major digestive problems that would make it difficult for him to survive another sentence, although he was only forty-four.

The diffuse movement sometimes referred to as the "Russian party" troubled the authorities at least as much as the more vocal, better-known human-rights activists. It was not a party at all and there was no single viewpoint or set of beliefs, only a general commitment to preserving the Russian cultural and religious heritage, elevating that which is Russian above that which is Soviet. But that was enough to put anyone suspected of participating in its activities in jeopardy, despite persistent claims that even some members of the political elite sympathized with its goals.

Those goals, like the movement itself, are far from clearly defined. Critics, both among the remaining dissidents within the Soviet Union and in the heavily Jewish Soviet émigré communities, charge that this longing for a return to the nation's Russian roots constitutes an appeal for chauvinistic policies based on expansionism, subjugation of other nationalities, and anti-Semitism. Proponents like Solzhenitsyn argue that these are the characteristics of the Soviet system and that, by returning to its true self, Russia would become a more tolerant and peaceful nation, allowing other nationalities to choose their own destinies.

Whatever the relative merits of those two conflicting interpretations, Vladimov believed that this was the one group, precisely because of its amorphous nature and broad appeal, that could not be easily destroyed. "The point is that the human-rights movement as represented by Sakharov can be written off. It was a narrow group without support among the people and it has been destroyed by emigration and arrests. The Russian party has greater roots in the population, more sympathizers, and for the authorities it is more frightening. It consists of philosophers concerned about Russian history and it will not be weakened by emigration. Those people want to live here."

Natasha Vladimov agreed, citing her experience a day earlier when she went with Larisa Borodin to ask a policeman to pass a package of food to her imprisoned husband.

"Well, we are all Russians," the policeman had said as he agreed to the request. Natasha read into that remark a glimmer of sympathy, a recognition of a bond between him and Borodin. What struck me was how little was needed, just the slightest sign of humanity, to give people grounds for hope.

Galina Barats had witnessed a more impressive gesture. She called me in late April to report that her husband, Vasily, the former army officer turned Pentecostal activist, had been put in a mental hospital. When I arrived at their apartment, she described how he had been taken by five KGB agents to the local police station. While Galina watched, the officer in charge called for an ambulance, which arrived with a woman psychiatrist. The psychiatrist briefly examined Vasily and declared: "We do not take healthy people." With that, she turned around and left with the ambulance. The psychiatrist's refusal to compromise herself did not save Vasily, who was dispatched to another psychiatric hospital where doctors had fewer scruples, but that only underscored the magnitude of that rare act of courage.

At the insane asylum that took him in, Vasily was given an injection that had left him temporarily almost speechless, his mouth dry, and his body lethargic. He told Galina that a doctor had explained that he was being held because the authorities wanted him kept away from a religious conference scheduled for May sponsored by the Russian Orthodox Church. Entitled "The World Conference for Saving the Sacred Gift of Life from Nuclear War," it was to be attended by representatives of a broad spectrum of churches and countries, including evangelist Billy Graham. The KGB did not want Barats trying to reach delegates with his message about religious persecution of Protestant sects in the Soviet Union. Upon hearing this, Galina had threatened the doctors that she would personally demonstrate outside the congress

194

if her husband was not released. "What kind of congress is this that is to prevent nuclear war but starts by putting a sane man into a psychiatric hospital?" she demanded.

Galina's persistence in calling attention to what was happening to her husband and her threat to embarrass the conference produced results: Vasily was released shortly before the foreign delegates began to arrive. When I met the reunited couple, Vasily was more determined than ever to publicize the fate of believers. He asked me to pass on word to other correspondents that he would meet with them on the eve of the peace conference. In the press stand at the May Day parade in Red Square, just beside the Lenin Mausoleum where Brezhnev and the rest of the Politburo stood reviewing the performance, I wrote out directions for the few correspondents who were interested.

When we arrived at the Baratses' apartment two days later, Vasily described the stepped-up persecution of members of his group who wanted to emigrate to worship freely. "Today our situation is critical. Even while the authorities are preparing this peace conference, they are trampling on the rights of all believers," he said. "We want to call attention to our problems." He reported searches and confiscations of Bibles and other religious literature in the Voronezh region, and the commitment of an Orthodox member of the group from Smolensk to an insane asylum. He also showed a picture of the badly bruised body of Leontiya Timoshuk, a young man from the Ukrainian city of Ternopol who, along with his wife and baby, had applied to emigrate. Vasily maintained that the unexplained death of this member of his group smacked of foul play, although no one knew what had happened. His body had been dumped in an empty gas cistern.

I asked Vasily about his own experiences in the psychiatric hospital: what was the explanation given for his release? He mopped his broad brow. "They said they would deal with me later—after Graham leaves."

Peace conferences sponsored by the Russian Orthodox Church are normally routine, completely predictable affairs. Orthodox leaders have long been characterized by their subservience to the government, and no one expects them to do anything but endorse Soviet foreign policy as "peaceloving" and denounce American "imperialism." That is the price they feel they must pay to preserve the church as a legal entity. For the KGB, however, that is not assurance enough of its loyalty: dissident sources within the church maintain it also has maneuvered clerics in its direct employ into top leadership positions.

Thus, previous peace conferences, which had consisted of Soviet church leaders plus a good-sized contingent of amenable Third World representatives and a smaller group of like-minded Westerners, went virtually unnoticed by reporters like myself in Moscow. But this time there was a major difference: the conference had attracted a big name from the West—Billy Graham. An Orthodox Church spokesman, a veteran of twenty years of such affairs, noted with satisfaction at a press conference packed with Western correspondents: "I've never seen such interest."

Reagan administration officials had attempted to dissuade Graham from attending, arguing that he would only be lending credibility to a Soviet propaganda show. But Graham had recently taken up the theme of nuclear war in his sermons and found receptive audiences even on college campuses where he had once been dismissed as a right-wing extremist. Brushing aside the administration's warnings, he declared before his departure for Moscow: "If the Gospel is not more powerful than anything I'll hear over there, then I ought to quit preaching."

Graham set the tone for his visit with his Sunday sermon at Moscow's only Baptist church, his first public appearance. Preaching through a translator, he denounced sin and nuclear war but made no reference to religious persecution within the Soviet Union. Instead, he quoted St. Paul on the need for obedience to the state: "God can make you love people you normally would not love. He gives you the power to be a better worker, a more loyal citizen because in [the] thirteenth [chapter] of Romans we're told to obey the authorities."

The church held about 1,000 people, a congregation that was heavily dominated by KGB agents, reporters, and peace conference delegates who had been given special tickets to attend. A couple of hundred of the faithful, who had come from all over the country, were left singing their hymns on the street because they were denied admission. On a normal Sunday, adjacent rooms are opened up to accommodate more people, but this time they remained firmly closed.

Despite all these precautions, genuine voices of the Soviet Protestant community did make themselves heard. Many Soviet Protestants, believed to number about 2 million, have to practice their faith covertly and often take tremendous risks. With a famous American preacher on hand, some evidently felt that they had to do so again. After Graham finished his sermon, a young man held up a sign saying: "Deliver those who are drawn away to death." Just opposite the balcony where I was sitting along with other reporters, a young woman draped a banner for several minutes over the railings: "We have more than 150 prisoners for the work of the Gospel."

I looked to see if Graham had seen the banner, since many eyes were turning to witness this act of defiance. One of the preacher's aides did look up and quickly whispered something to Graham, who fixedly kept his eyes down. Another woman tried to hold up a sign as Graham was leaving, but a plainclothesman ripped it out of her hands. Later, Graham said that he had not seen any of the signs because he was thinking about his next appearance at an Orthodox cathedral. "I was too busy thinking about what I was going to say."

At the end of the Baptist service, as several of us watched, a plainclothesman led away the woman who had draped the banner over the balcony. Outside, Bob Gillette of the *Los Angeles Times* caught up with Graham as he was getting into his limousine and told him about the crowd of the faithful that was denied admission and was anxiously waiting to catch at least a glimpse of him. "Oh, I didn't know that," he said. But he drove off in the opposite direction without making any effort to reach them.

At the peace conference, Graham was provided with maximum exposure. The American preacher, who in his earlier days had called communism "Satan's version of religion," was given a prominent seat on the dais, where the cameras could easily focus on his suntanned face. Soviet television featured excerpts from his speech and even a separate interview with him. In both cases, Graham avoided assigning blame for the arms race and the threat of nuclear war on the United States alone—but that presented no problems for his Soviet hosts. All they had to do was put his general comments praising the conference and decrying the threat of nuclear destruction in the context of what others were saying.

There was plenty of appropriate material to choose from. Patriarch Pimen of the Russian Orthodox Church had opened the conference by assailing the West for "blackening the honest and peaceloving policy of our fatherland" and by offering a standard condemnation of U.S. plans to install medium-range missiles in Western Europe, never mentioning the Soviet deployment of SS-20s aimed at Western Europe. In a message of greetings to the conference participants, Prime Minister Nikolai Tikhonov declared: "The proponents of the Cold War are whipping up war hysteria in every way, escalating the arms race, and openly stating the admissibility of a limited nuclear war and the first use of nuclear weapons." From the podium, delegates from a number of countries used similar language.

A few of the other American delegates appeared genuinely surprised by the tone of such declarations. Lutheran bishop David Preus of Minneapolis pleaded with the participants for "evenhandedness," saying: "My problem is that I believe this conference is in danger of becoming a political forum heavily tilted against the country I represent and the West in general." But Graham was determined to ignore all that. When asked about the anti-American tenor of the conference, he replied: "I don't know that the conference took that turn."

On the last day, Graham participated in a press conference sponsored by the Russian Orthodox organizers of the gathering. A Soviet reporter asked him about his impressions of Moscow. Graham observed that people were well dressed and dismissed any talk of food shortages. "The meals I have had are among the finest I have ever eaten. In the United States you have to be a millionaire to have caviar, but I have had caviar with almost every meal." When asked by an American television reporter about religious freedom, he marveled at the packed Russian Orthodox churches he was shown. "You never get that in Charlotte, North Carolina." He added that it was "a wonderful thing that in a country that officially professes atheism, so many churches are open."

I had been trying to ask a question for some time, but as Graham was recognizing me the moderator declared that the press conference was over and my microphone went dead. Graham waited for me to reach him as the conference was breaking up. I asked if he had made any inquiries about the fate of the young woman who had been detained after his service in the Baptist church.

"If I were you I would ask some Baptist leader. I didn't even know about that and I won't comment about it."

"You have no comment about it?"

Graham's face tightened. "No, because I don't know that it happened except for your word and that's not good enough for me."

Gene Randall of NBC interjected that several reporters had witnessed the incident.

"I don't know and I would have no comment," Graham persisted, adding: "Some people can be detained for all kinds of reasons, I don't know. We detain people in the United States if we catch them doing something wrong. I have had people coming to my services in the United States and causing some difficulties and they have been taken out by the police."

At the airport as he was taking off, Graham concluded that the church is freer in the Soviet Union than in Britain. "In Great Britain they have a state church. Here, the church is not a state church. It is a free church, not headed officially as the Church of England is headed by the Queen."

What accounted for Graham's performance? One explanation, offered by many commentators, was that he had been manipulated by his hosts, who are experts at whisking the visiting foreign celebrity around in a black limousine, packing his schedule with official meetings, and keeping dissenters away. Up to a point, that was all true. On the eve of Graham's visit, the authorities had attempted to intimidate anyone who might seek to draw his attention to religious persecution. Aside from sending Vasily Barats away for his brief stay in a mental hospital, the police raided the homes of about fifty Baptist families, confiscating their Bibles and placing more than a dozen of them under house arrest. Barats himself gave up trying to contact Graham or other conference delegates directly; he did not know how to reach them.

But that was hardly sufficient explanation. Contacts with people like Barats could have been arranged if there had been any desire on Graham's part to do so. Nor was it a matter of not knowing about the existence of such people and what was happening to them. A Graham aide admitted to me that the preacher's entourage was well aware of the actions that had been taken against believers before and during the trip. Baptist sources had specifically informed members of the Graham party that the woman who had draped the banner from the balcony of the church possibly faced three years of imprisonment.

When pressed to explain why not a single word of support for those who were suffering for their faith had been uttered, Graham aides drifted into a rambling discourse on the need to take a long-term view of what could be accomplished that would have a lasting impact. Then, they let slip the key phrase that was usually reserved for private conversations: "The second coming." It was a term used only half-jokingly, and the serious part was that Graham believed that if he pleased his hosts on this trip he would be invited back to lead a crusade all across the Soviet Union, providing a dramatic cap to his career. The evangelist saw himself spreading the Gospel while he zigzagged through the atheist state, something he eventually acknowledged. "I would like to come back and preach in many places throughout the country if I'm invited and all things work out," he said.

Graham failed to comprehend a vital point: a return trip won at such moral expense would hardly undo the self-inflicted damage or boost his standing in anyone's eyes.

Aside from compromising himself in front of the countless Soviet Protestants who had eagerly awaited his visit and some signal of support and sympathy for their plight, he had failed to win the respect of the officials he tried so hard to please. They milked him to the fullest for his propaganda value, but anytime a Western visitor plays as easily into their hands as Graham did, he is privately scorned by the same officials who so vigorously applaud him in public.

Graham was neither the first nor the last Western visitor to behave in this fashion on Soviet soil. In Stalin's time, such visitors spoke glowingly of the wonders of the Soviet penal system or of what they described as ambitious public-works projects that assured full employment. After U.S. vice-president Henry Wallace stopped in 1944 in the Eastern Siberian region of Kolyma, the location of the most forbidding network of camps in the entire Gulag where 3 million people are believed to have died, he wrote in his book *Soviet Asia Mission* that the gold miners he saw were "big husky young men" who had gone East as "pioneers of the machine age, builders of cities." There is no shortage of other examples of prominent Westerners arriving at similar conclusions after their trips to the Soviet Union.

Those who did so for ideological reasons were easily dismissed and discredited—and their numbers have diminished. However, even today Moscow receives Western visitors who persist in equating progressive thought with uncritical acceptance of Soviet policies. The survival of that breed of Westerner astounds their distinctly more cynical Soviet hosts, whose own allegiance to the system is consciously based on self-interest rather than ideological considerations.

Sasha, an established writer in Moscow, told me about

the time he was assigned to host a West German philosophy professor who was an ardent critic of capitalism. He took him to lunch at the Writers Union dining hall, where the food is good and inexpensive. The professor kept exclaiming how wonderful everything was, without any recognition that he had entered the world of a special elite that bore no relation to how the average Russian lives. When Sasha asked about his reading habits, he explained that he received philosophy journals from East Berlin where he found all the answers he wanted. Sasha's irreverence got the better of him: he rashly asked why, if the professor liked everything so much from the socialist system, he didn't pack his suitcases and move across to East Berlin. "He turned red and declared that he was often asked that question in the West but that this was the first time he had been asked that in Moscow," Sasha recalled. "I realized I had committed a mistake—he only needed to say one word to my boss and my career would be finished here."

But I was less interested in those who kept their eyes shut for ideological reasons than the ease with which other visitors were manipulated or at least outmaneuvered by their Soviet hosts. This applied to conservatives as well as to liberals. A U.S. diplomat who occasionally served as a translator for visiting congressmen told me of his amazement at how often reputed conservative hard-liners merely listened to anti-American harangues and the most outrageous claims about the Soviet system without bothering to reply. In some cases, the visitors knew so little about Soviet affairs that they were incapable of responding to what they were hearing. In others, a bizarre sense that it would be impolite to take anything but mild exception to their hosts' pronouncements appeared to take over—and that it would be downright rude to stray beyond the prescribed itinerary of endless official meetings to seek out other viewpoints and impressions. Intelligent men and women, who anywhere else would insist on meeting with a broad cross section of people before arriving at any conclusions, accepted the unspoken premise that this is impossible in Moscow, never attempting to test its veracity. After their appointed rounds, they returned to the West convinced that they had been exposed to "the Soviet viewpoint."

I was increasingly convinced that the behavior of Western visitors was symptomatic of the broader failure of our societies to develop consistent, long-term policies toward the Soviet Union. It is not just our inability to understand Soviet society, but often a matter of deliberately avoiding anything that contradicts whatever we want to see and believe. Graham's refusal to acknowledge the existence of religious persecution, while an extreme example, illustrated the degree to which self-interest motivates Western perceptions. It is easier to listen only to the sterile discourse of Soviet officials, no different than the already familiar speeches of their leaders, and to return from Moscow with whatever conclusions a visitor is predisposed to find than to confront less predictable impressions from other encounters.

The debate over the advisability and impact of economic sanctions was a case in point. Despite his anti-Soviet rhetoric, Reagan had promised during the 1980 election campaign to lift the partial grain embargo imposed by Jimmy Carter after the Soviet invasion of Afghanistan. His argument was that only American farmers had been hurt by the embargo, not the Soviet Union since Moscow was able to find other suppliers. It was an attractive vote-getting ploy and Soviet officials were only too happy to buttress it with their repeated assertions that the embargo had produced no problems for them. In fact, as the sanctions issue was once again hotly debated in the aftermath of the declaration of martial law in Poland, there was considerable evidence that the embargo had been disruptive, at least in the short run.

According to Western diplomatic analysts in Moscow who monitored the situation, the Carter embargo produced a scramble for alternative suppliers that led to serious bottlenecks in Soviet ports. Shipping plans had to be changed at the last minute, and there were not enough railroad cars to take the arriving grain inland. Those problems occur even in the best of times, but they were dramatically compounded by the embargo. As a result, fodder shortages became more acute, accelerating the recent trend of declining slaughter weights of cattle and lower milk yields per cow as confirmed by official Soviet statistics. In addition, the Soviets had to pay higher prices for much of the grain they eventually purchased elsewhere to make up for what they had been planning to buy from the United States, contributing to the hard-currency crunch that made itself felt in 1981.

None of those consequences was so severe as to cause irreparable damage, and it would have been unrealistic to expect them to force Moscow to reconsider its occupation of Afghanistan. But, if the object was to punish the Soviets and demonstrate American disapproval, as the Carter administration had maintained, then the embargo did initially achieve that more limited goal. For all their protestations that they could do without American grain, the Soviets wanted to keep the United States as a supplier because of its ability to fill large orders, its competitive prices, and the fact that shipping rates out of the Gulf of Mexico were generally cheaper than from other ports. After the embargo, the Soviets were intent on avoiding overdependence on the United States, but they resumed buying substantial amounts of American grain once Reagan gave them the green light.

The embargo undeniably lost much of its effectiveness toward the end, since it was the disruptive factor of surprise that accounted for much of the damage it inflicted. It can be argued that Carter should have anticipated the limitations of its effectiveness when other suppliers were unwilling to join his action, immediately announcing that the embargo was for a fixed period—one year, for example. That would have maximized its impact, dampened expectations that it would force Moscow to reverse itself on Afghanistan, and avoided the appearance of the United States backing away from its condemnation of Soviet policy on this issue. It also might have made it possible for Washington to convince other suppliers to take part. In that sense, Carter's decision to boycott the Moscow Olympics was much more effective: it was a one-time, unambiguous protest action.

But the Reagan administration was not interested in examining the strengths and weaknesses of the embargo; it wanted to believe that the embargo had no effect whatsoever on the Soviet Union and so it saw none. Not surprisingly, the Western Europeans used Reagan's position on grain sales as a counterargument to Washington's pressures that they pull out of the Siberian natural-gas pipeline project, which the Soviet press referred to as "the deal of the century." Why should they back off from their biggest East-West business venture, they asked, when the Americans refused to make any sacrifices in their most important trade with Moscow? The Western Europeans had a point, but they were just as prone as the Americans to see only what they wanted to see when it came to assessing the impact of their actions. France maintained that its signing of a twenty-five-year contract to buy natural gas supplied through the pipeline just one month after the declaration of martial law in Poland in no way weakened its condemnation of Moscow and Warsaw for their actions. But the Soviets themselves hailed the signing as a major political victory.

None of the Western allies was willing to examine the effect of Western actions objectively with a view to producing agreement on a common approach. From the Kremlin's perspective, there was no reason to believe that by taking steps offensive to the West in Afghanistan, Poland, or elsewhere it would suffer any predictable consequences. The Soviets were genuinely surprised and angered by the scope of American reprisals after the invasion of Afghanistan because nothing in the Carter administration's earlier policies had provided any hint that it was capable of such a firm response. Then, with a change in Washington and the change of nothing in Afghanistan itself, the embargo was lifted. Soviet policy-makers could easily conclude that American policy was guided more by domestic political considerations than by their own behavior.

How much leverage would the West really have if it saw fit to use it? Misha, the social scientist, argued that it would not amount to much: "The West cannot provoke bankruptcy here. The possibilities of economic pressures working on the Soviet Union are limited." Perhaps, but Moscow's frantic reaction and loud proclamations that sanctions would hurt only the countries that instituted sanctions instead of the Soviet Union struck me as a betrayal of its own nervousness. The grain embargo had some sting, and if the Western Europeans had abandoned the natural-gas pipeline deal the economic impact would have been enormous. With declining hard-currency earnings from crude oil exports, Moscow was counting on natural gas to fill the gap.

The Soviet Union seeks Western technology transfers, credits, and subsidies not just as a convenience but as an important means of making up for the deficiencies of its economy and keeping pace with the West in high-priority areas. In some fields, like the exploitation of oil and gas reserves, the Soviets have not developed the full range of technology to implement their programs. Their pipes, for example, tend to buckle under the harshest Arctic conditions; high-quality pipes imported from the West do not. Even when the Soviets are capable of developing comparable technology themselves, the inevitable bureaucratic obstacles and general poor performance of Soviet factories often make the importing of Western technology more attractive to economic planners anxious to meet their targets.

In theory, the West could follow policies designed to let Moscow know that it would pay a price for future offensive actions and, conversely, enjoy the benefits of greater economic cooperation if its behavior were more restrained. But after watching the performance of the United States and the Western Europeans in the wake of Afghanistan and Poland, I saw little reason to believe that such policies would be pursued.

The other East-West issue heating up in earnest that spring was the debate over the plans to install American medium-range missiles in Western Europe. In the United States, I had always supported candidates who stressed the need for arms control, and I had neither voted for Reagan nor felt comfortable with his treatment of this vital issue. But my Moscow experience left me skeptical about the alternative policies proposed by the administration's critics.

In May as I was preparing to go to West Germany for a speaking engagement, I asked Lyona, the poet, what I should tell my audience. "Make them understand that disarmament cannot be a striptease by just one side," he said. He explained the dangers of such an action by comparing Soviet behavior abroad with that of a hotel burglar. The burglar goes down the halls checking the doors and, if one is unlocked and the risk of being caught is small, he walks in and takes what he can. If the door is locked, he prefers not to force it open for fear that this may attract attention and possible retaliation.

It was a crude analogy that in the West could easily be

dismissed as right-wing propaganda. But coming from a Russian who is profoundly patriotic if at the same time critical of his own government, I found that it had the ring of simple truth. Many other Russians offered variations on the same theme. These were not the officials who normally met with Western visitors and recited the standard litany of Soviet complaints but the entire range of our friends and acquaintances, from people in established positions to dissidents.

These Russians could not understand why medium-range missiles had caught on as a major issue when American missiles were scheduled for deployment, while the previous massive Soviet deployment of SS-20s had sparked no real debate; why a freeze movement was starting at this particular time; and why prominent Americans like McGeorge Bundy, George Kennan, Robert McNamara, and Gerard Smith were suddenly proposing as they did in the Spring 1982 issue of *Foreign Affairs* that the West renounce the first use of nuclear weapons. The Soviet Union had an overwhelming superiority in conventional forces in Europe but had always had to reckon with the possibility of nuclear retaliation if it used them; if there were neither a conventional nor nuclear deterrent, couldn't people in the West see the door would be unlocked?

On my short excursion to the West, I found that as a rule minds were already made up on these issues. People who endorsed the NATO decision to deploy new missiles welcomed my observations about Kremlin thinking as ammunition for their team, while opponents dismissed what I had to say about Soviet perceptions of the West as irrelevant. I felt distinctly uneasy with how quickly I was categorized in any discussion of this subject. It was a matter of choosing up sides in a domestic political debate, and what relation all this bore to Soviet intentions hardly seemed to matter.

The extensive Soviet media coverage of peace protests in the West was designed to reinforce the Kremlin's contention that the threat to peace originated in Washington, but it produced an unexpected result: a small group of Soviet citizens decided to mount their own peace campaign right in Moscow. Shortly after my return from West Germany, I received a call from Sergei Batovrin, a bearded young artist whom I had met a few months earlier. His soft voice was studiously casual, but there was an undercurrent of urgency in his request that we get together.

Sergei's personal history was unusual because he had spent his boyhood years in the United States. Shortly after he was born in 1957, his father was assigned to the Soviet embassy in Washington and the family lived there and in New York, where his father worked in the Soviet mission to the United Nations, until 1971. Like the children of other Soviet diplomats, Sergei lived in an insulated world, attending Soviet schools and having little direct contact with Americans. He firmly believed in the superior virtues of his native country, which he knew only from the descriptions of his parents and teachers. But his isolation could not be complete; television, radio, and his American surroundings intruded, and Sergei naturally learned to speak fluent English and subconsciously absorbed American culture and its values. In 1968, he witnessed a demonstration against the Soviet invasion of Czechoslovakia in front of the Soviet mission and he found it difficult to brush aside the questions this prompted. "The invasion of Czechoslovakia raised doubts that perhaps everything I imagined about the Soviet Union was not true," he said, recalling the origins of his disenchantment with the Soviet system. "But I was still full of illusions about the Soviet Union until I returned there and encountered reality."

The encounter was a difficult one for a fourteen-year-old boy who had grown up in the United States and had no memory of his native country. In his Soviet school in New York, the teachers had to provide answers for questions that would naturally arise in their pupils' minds and, even if they were rigidly ideological, Sergei had been prone to accept them. But in his new school in Moscow, his questions multiplied and made him immediately suspect. He attempted to raise issues like Czechoslovakia only to be angrily rebuffed by his teachers. His father, who divorced his mother, Luba, shortly after their return, had little patience for his son's disillusionment and growing alienation; his mother tried to comfort him as best she could, but she was experiencing a similar if quieter disenchantment with her homeland. Expelled from school for his "provocative" behavior, Sergei drifted into the hippie milieu. Later, he graduated from night school and briefly enrolled, at his father's insistence, in the Institute of International Relations and the World Economy. The Institute was full of sons and daughters of the Soviet elite preparing for comfortable government careers. Put off by their undisguised cynicism, Sergei dropped out and turned to painting, intent on having as little to do with established Soviet society as possible.

Along with a few friends, Sergei attempted to stage an exhibition of their paintings in 1975, a popular activity of "unofficial" artists that infuriated the authorities. The previous year they had sent in bulldozers to demolish a large outdoor exhibition. Catching wind of Sergei's plans, the KGB detained him and attempted to convince him to call off his exhibition. When he refused, they put him in a mental hospital for nearly three months. Embittered by that experience, Sergei, his wife, Natasha, and his mother, Luba, applied to emigrate in 1976. But his father refused to lend his support to their applications for fear that it would jeopardize his career, only relenting in 1981 when emigration had slowed dramatically. By that time, Sergei had lost hope that they would ever leave.

When I went to their apartment, Sergei was more animated than I ever remembered seeing him. Natasha had recently given birth to their first child, but something else was on Sergei's mind. Both Natasha and Luba watched him anxiously as he explained that he wanted to speak to me about a project he was quietly organizing: the launching of an independent peace group.

Sergei's concept was simple, idealistic—and dangerous. Along with a small group of other artists, physicists, and mathematicians, he had drawn up a preliminary draft of "An Appeal to the Governments and the Public of the U.S.S.R. and U.S.A." calling for the initiation of a "four-sided dialogue" in which Soviet and American citizens, as well as their governments, would participate in discussions about the arms race. "Soviet citizens have only a vague idea and minimum information about the arms race," Sergei said. "They are told America is an aggressive country and nothing more. We want a dialogue between our two countries that will have an informative character." He envisaged the distribution in both East and West of a newsletter to publicize the group's viewpoints and those of others, along with an exhibition of anti-war paintings.

I was skeptical. He sought to reassure me, explaining that there would be an important difference between his group and its counterparts in the West. "We feel this group is very loyal to the Soviet Union. We are not saying anything that goes against the official position of the government and we will not organize any demonstrations." The object, he made clear, was to avoid the dissident label.

Sergei could imagine how the government would view their activities. Although the Kremlin had praised peace groups in the West, it had already revealed its uneasiness about any spillover into the Soviet Union. Marshal Nikolai Ogarkov, the armed forces chief of staff, had called for a struggle against "elements of pacifism," while the weekly *New Times* had complained that people in the West were trying to "provoke in the socialist countries an inverted analogue of the protest movement in the West." Since socialist countries only pursued peaceful policies, it argued, "what is it we should protest against?"

Peace committees, like everything else, are a monopoly of the state in the Soviet Union. The official Soviet Peace Committee is headed by Yuri Zhukov, who had earned a reputation as a neo-Stalinist during a long career at *Pravda* writing particularly vitriolic commentaries denouncing the regime's many "enemies" at home and abroad. It has the express purpose of winning support for Soviet foreign policy, from the invasion of Afghanistan to the deployment of the SS-20s, and routinely turns out thousands of people for rallies applauding the latest government "peace proposals" and denouncing the United States. Even if Sergei's group were created to espouse the exact same positions, it would be viewed as a threat because it had emerged independently.

Another Russian friend had once told me how in his university days a group of his fellow students had been arrested for staging an unauthorized demonstration against American involvement in Vietnam. "As in *Private Chonkin*, all must be authorized," he said, referring to Vladimir Voinovich's magnificent satirical novel *The Life and Extraordinary Adventures of Private Ivan Chonkin*, which describes a local party chairman's fury at a truly spontaneous gathering of villagers when Germany invaded the Soviet Union in 1941. "It's all very logical: if today someone demands on his own initiative an American withdrawal from Vietnam, tomorrow he may decide the Soviets should leave Afghanistan."

Sergei's group, moreover, was not taking all Soviet policy on blind faith. By seeking to establish a free flow of information about disarmament proposals between East and West, it would be implying that citizens should have access to both sides' positions and be free to judge for themselves. "We understand that this will not be welcomed by the government," Sergei said. "But at the same time it has to be careful not to discredit itself with peace groups in the West."

With Natasha and Luba listening intently, he asked me what I thought. I stressed the dangers, saying that there was no guarantee that the government would feel inhibited in retaliating against anyone associated with the group just because it was wooing peace activists in the West. Luba nodded in agreement but added, with concern and pride, that Sergei was still an idealist and that there was no way of convincing him to abandon the idea.

"Would the Western press be interested in this story?" Sergei asked. "We are planning to hold a press conference once we are ready to announce our existence."

I acknowledged that the story would certainly attract attention and agreed to notify other correspondents of the press conference. This would have to be done at the last moment to prevent word from reaching the authorities. But after that, I warned, they would be on their own. The consequences might be severe.

Sergei was not about to reconsider. At a subsequent session with a few of his colleagues, I found the same mixture of idealism, determination, and realistic recognition of the obstacles the group would face. They spoke of making contacts with other independent peace groups in East Germany and Hungary as well as trying to generate support among peace activists in the United States and of soliciting proposals on the arms race from ordinary Soviet citizens. But they realized that they could not expect to attract much popular support. "The Soviet Union is a very special country," an engineer explained. "Even many people who may agree with us won't agree to sign our declaration." He was the one member of the original group of twelve who dropped out at the last minute before the members declared themselves.

That declaration came at a press conference in early June. A day earlier, I had told other members of the press about the group, calling each correspondent outside to make sure my message was not picked up by listening devices. When the time came for the press conference, a motorcade of several correspondents' cars followed my Volvo to Sergei's apartment. Up to that point, I had always parked far away and kept my visits discreet, but now the peace group was going public, and, from their perspective, the more interest the Western press took in them the better.

"The Group for the Establishment of Trust between the U.S.S.R. and the U.S.A." was proclaimed by the eleven founders and their appeal initially carried about forty signatures. Sergei's anti-war posters adorned the wall for the occasion and, as planned, the members expressed their goals in deliberately conciliatory terms. Stressing the independence of the group as opposed to the government control of the official peace movement, mathematician Sergei Rozenoer nonetheless declared: "We are not dissidents. We think our aims and the aims of the Soviet government are one—that is, to preserve peace. So any reprisals that may be applied against us would be a result of a misunderstanding."

In my story about the group, I predicted that its formation "will pose a sticky public-relations problem" for the Soviet leaders: "They know that a harsh crackdown could undermine their efforts to portray themselves as champions of international peace." Other correspondents made similar points in their dispatches, but it did not take long to recognize that this constituted wishful thinking rather than

215

informed analysis. The press conference had caught the authorities by surprise, and in its immediate aftermath they took no action. Sergei and his colleagues kept collecting more signatures on their appeal to the U.S. and Soviet governments and received additional disarmament proposals from others who had heard about their group. The group called for an immediate end to all nuclear testing and publicized its members' phone numbers, inviting anyone from within the country or abroad to call to discuss peace issues. Their phones started ringing, and they claimed that similar groups might be formed in other Soviet cities. But then the retaliation began.

Two members, who, like Sergei, had long-standing applications to emigrate, were suddenly informed that they would be given exit visas if they left immediately; they agreed. Sergei and others were summoned to police stations and warned that their activities were illegal and provocative. Specifically, they were berated for portraying the United States and the Soviet Union as equally responsible for the arms race. Phones were disconnected. Policemen and plainclothesmen staked out their apartments, barring correspondents from visiting them, ostensibly because the peace activists were disseminating "distorted information." For several days at a time, members were kept under house arrest. Three of them were detained when they tried to deliver a letter to the British embassy in support of protests in England against the installation of American missiles.

But the attempts to isolate them were not completely successful. Members of the group or friends and relatives managed to arrange meetings with correspondents and to pass on information on the latest developments, while simultaneously issuing new appeals for peace. They were particularly intent on developing ties with peace groups in the West.

The first major opportunity was the arrival of a large delegation of Scandinavian women to participate in a march sponsored by the official Soviet Peace Committee. Most of the members of Sergei's group were immobilized by the time of their arrival, but they let it be known that they would welcome visits from the Scandinavian activists. They waited in vain: the foreign peace marchers refused even to inquire about the fate of the independent peace group for fear of offending their hosts. They angrily dismissed correspondents' questions about their silence as an attempt by the press to undermine the goodwill their visit was creating between the Soviet people and themselves.

Throughout the spring, Andropov was completing his drive for power that resulted in his winning of Suslov's ideological post in May, signaling his triumph over Chernenko. As Medvedev had predicted, this allowed him to detach himself formally from the KGB and to present himself as Brezhnev's heir apparent. At a diplomatic cocktail party, a Soviet official abandoned his usual fuzziness whenever the leadership issue came up and flatly predicted that Andropov was on the way to the top job. "We consider this a good thing," he said. "You Westerners see him as a man of the KGB, but we see him as a party man. He is intelligent, open to new ideas. If he succeeds Brezhnev, he will be more liberal than the current leadership."

I was surprised by the official's sudden willingness to talk about the succession as if it were imminent but not by his assessment of Andropov. It made sense that the former KGB chief, while distancing himself formally from his policeman's role, would be encouraging the notion that he was more enlightened than his biography suggested. However, I was not prepared for the scope and effect of this campaign. Wherever I went in Moscow, the talk was of Andropov and what kind of a leader he would be. Everybody, including members of the dissident community, appeared to be grasping at rumors and speculation that served to confirm their own hopes that Andropov's rise would mean a change for the better.

There were plenty of stories, conveniently leaked, to buttress what people wanted to believe. Tales of his alleged erudition and taste for the arts were cited as evidence that Andropov was more humane and certainly more intellectually capable than his Politburo colleagues. Andropov had supposedly objected to Soviet military involvement in Afghanistan and counseled caution in Poland, so the stories went, and appreciated the role of scientists and intellectuals, realizing that they must have some access to Western information such as scholarly journals. For Jews, the message was that Andropov was unhappy with the brain drain caused by emigration but that he was willing to promote Jews to high positions in their fields.

All such rumors were unverifiable and unfailingly self-serving, but they produced much of the desired effect. A dissident writer, who led an exceptionally lonely, embittered life, startled me with his assessment of Andropov. "There are two types of people up there. There are those who want to be more humane but cannot, and those who are simply not humane. Andropov is in the first category."

Even Misha abandoned much of his usual cynicism during one long evening we spent together, with the TV as always turned up loud in case there were bugs. Over Georgian brandy, pickles, and cake, the social scientist expounded on Andropov's prospects. He summed up many of the stories I had already heard, alternately offering them with no implicit judgment on their accuracy and abruptly presenting them as his own opinion. Party members, he reported, were saying that Andropov's total lack of experience in agriculture and industrial planning would be beneficial, since he was not tainted by association with Brezhnev's ineffectual policies in those fields. Before he took over the KGB, Andropov had been in charge of the Central Committee department that oversaw Eastern Europe at a time of the start of cautious economic reforms; that record was seen as evidence that Andropov might push similar reforms at home.

Andropov's Eastern European performance could be evaluated in radically different terms, given his role as the Soviet ambassador in Budapest at the time of the bloody Soviet suppression of the Hungarian uprising in 1956 and his voice, as head of the KGB, in the decision to invade Czechoslovakia in 1968. Misha took no sides on that issue. However, he offered one of the most benign interpretations I had heard of Andropov's tenure at the KGB, when he had presided over the systematic campaign to eliminate dissent. "He did not repeat any of the brutal repressions of the past. He only did what any KGB chief would have done in his place."

But in his analysis of Andropov's tactics in his battles with Brezhnev and Chernenko, Misha was once again his old cynical self. As he reconstructed the drama of the past few months, Brezhnev had initially positioned Chernenko well. Many Central Committee members and staffers wanted Chernenko because they believed "he was not very smart and he would be easily manageable." By elevating someone who appeared to be no more than a pale copy of Brezhnev, they could count on retaining their jobs and privileges; no big shake-ups would be likely. Andropov, who "had his own mind" and was smarter, inspired fear. But it was his ability to frighten the apparatchiks that Andropov turned to his advantage. By orchestrating the circus scandals touching on Brezhnev's family and brandishing the corruption weapon, he had reminded everyone of their vulnerability. "They are afraid—he has everything on everyone," Misha said, admiring the effectiveness of the implicit threat that anyone who opposed Andropov had to reckon with possible retaliation in the form of a corruption charge plucked out of the KGB's massive files.

Misha and others did not seem troubled by the contradictory evidence they had presented, portraying Andropov as a relatively liberal politician on the one hand and a ruthless infighter on the other. The latter quality accounted for Andropov's appeal to those Russians, whom I had run into on several occasions, who spoke nostalgically of Stalin, recalling that "then there was order," unlike the untidy drift of the Brezhnev years. Intellectuals and dissidents recoiled at such a portrayal of the Stalinist era, but they too felt frustrated by the present. If the best that could be hoped for was a benevolent despot, they seemed to be saying, then that would be an improvement over the current listless leadership.

The very qualities of Chernenko that made him the favorite of the bureaucrats who had prospered under Brezhnev produced feelings bordering on despair and revulsion among many Russians. They wanted a change, any change, while Chernenko represented, in Misha's words, "another Brezhnev." The idea of a prolongation of the Brezhnev era was disheartening to everybody but the entrenched bureaucrats. When Andropov was elevated to Suslov's post, the common refrain was "Thank God it wasn't Chernenko." Workers tended to be more fatalistic about what would happen after Brezhnev, shrugging off speculation on the subject with the observation that it made no difference who would be next since nothing would fundamentally change. But among those who expressed a preference, the anybody-but-Chernenko sentiment was strong.

That made people receptive to Andropov and to the stories circulating that painted him in a flattering light. But many of my acquaintances began to feel disillusioned from the moment Andropov took over the ideological post. One reason was the man who replaced him as head of the KGB, whom they assumed was Andropov's personal choice. Previously in charge of the notoriously brutal Ukrainian KGB, Vitaly Fedorchuk promised to be every bit as tough as Andropov, if not tougher. It was no accident that Sergei Batovrin's peace movement, which presented him with his first challenge, met with the harsh response it did; from his first days in office, Fedorchuk was determined to complete the task begun by Andropov of eliminating dissent.

At a dinner in Moscow, an academician who had visited the Ukrainian capital of Kiev shortly after Fedorchuk's appointment expressed his astonishment at the atmosphere there. He reported that the local citizenry were afraid even to grumble while waiting in long lines for food, a common practice in Moscow. "People there told me: 'Just you wait. Now that our man has moved to Moscow, pretty soon all of Russia will be the same way.' " As his colleagues listened in gloomy silence, he added, "Andropov may want to play the liberal on top, but Fedorchuk will be keeping everyone in line below."

The leadership struggle and other developments had kept me in Moscow more than I would have liked, and I was eager to begin traveling again. When Alex Beam, the correspondent for McGraw-Hill publications, suggested we take a trip to the Ukraine in early June, I jumped at the opportunity. He wanted to visit the western Ukrainian city of Rovno. There had been unconfirmed reports of an accident that spring at a nuclear power plant nearby, and he was interested in seeing if we could learn anything by talking to people in Rovno. It was a long shot, but that hardly mattered. We were both glad to see something new.

We were almost denied that possibility within half an hour of our arrival. After checking into the Mir (Peace) Hotel, we walked through the quiet streets to the farmers' market, one of the few places where people were congregating on that warm Saturday afternoon. I pulled out my camera and took a couple of shots of customers lined up for cabbage, and we wandered on. At another stall, we paused as a man in his thirties berated an older peasant woman also selling cabbage; in progressively louder terms, he proclaimed that the people from the trans-Carpathian region—where the peasant woman evidently came from— were exploiting Rovno's inhabitants. He must have had several drinks, and he seemed unaware of the scene he was making. A young policeman with a pudgy face and mustache appeared, we assumed, to take care of this tipsy heckler. He motioned for the man but then turned to us, saying we should follow him as well. I asked why. "You'll see," he said.

The three of us were led into the indoor market, a circular concrete structure, past the stalls and into an austere police office down a small corridor. It contained a single desk, a few wooden chairs, and barren walls. Our companion started up immediately on his theme of trans-Carpathian exploitation and, making a logical jump that escaped me, turned abruptly to his family history. His father, he announced, had been a regional party secretary "until he was shot," and someone else in the family was a colonel in the KGB.

"Enough, enough," the policeman warned him. Turning to us, he asked where we were from: "The Baltic republics?"

"I'd like to talk to you guys," our companion interjected as we told the policeman that we were American correspondents based in Moscow. The policeman, who up till then had been stern but not threatening, angrily ordered the heckler out of the room with him, and shut Alex and me in. It was not hard to guess that he delivered a lecture warning him not to wait around for us before sending him on his way.

When the policeman returned alone, we again asked why we were being held, but he offered no explanation. A high-strung, red-haired young man in tight jeans came in and started firing questions at us. We demanded to know who he was, and he identified himself as a police inspector. He, too, provided no answer to our question why we were being held. Instead, he sent us out of the room as he made several phone calls.

Calling us back in, he asked which of us had the camera and demanded the film. "Why?" I asked.

"You were taking pictures of lines."

"There's nothing illegal about that." I launched into a brief discourse on the rights of journalists as spelled out by the Helsinki agreements.

"You can take pictures of museums and monuments, but not of lines. Give me the film."

Two "witnesses" materialized, boys of about twenty, and the inspector started writing out a protocol stating that he was confiscating my film because I had been taking pictures of lines. Realizing that I was not going to get out without surrendering my film, I did so—but only after he promised that it would be returned to me if upon developing and inspection the authorities ruled there was nothing illegal about its contents.

The inspector turned to the witnesses, who were sitting uncomfortably opposite Alex and me. "They take pictures of lines and then they transmit information on the radio that we have lines here."

"That means you don't have lines here?" I asked.

"I'd advise you to return immediately to the Mir Hotel. If you are caught taking pictures of lines again, we'll send you back to Moscow and out of the Soviet Union for good."

He placed the statement he had been writing in front of me, instructing both Alex and me to sign. We refused, saying that we had done nothing wrong. It is a basic rule in such a situation not to sign anything, since any statement could be used against you.

The inspector scowled and his cheeks colored. He ordered the witnesses to sign and handed one of them my film, telling him to break it open. "You can take it back now," he said, holding the exposed film out to me.

I made no motion to take it. "Keep it as a souvenir."

We walked out, glad to be free but with no sense of triumph. The film itself with its two or three snapshots was no great loss, but I felt angry with this reminder that I was subjected to harassment almost every time I traveled. There was also the unsettling sensation of not knowing how far the harassment would go in each of these situations, when the threats would be translated into action. I knew I was supposed to feel that way: the purpose of such treatment was to discourage journalists from traveling on their own without resorting to outright refusals for trips. I had no intention of giving in to such pressures, but it was impossible to shrug them off completely.

After that less-than-promising introduction, we enjoyed Rovno more than we expected. The city itself is distinctly proletarian, with the obligatory five- and nine-story hastily constructed apartment buildings, Lenin statue, Lenin Street, and Peace Avenue. The center of town and outlying streets are slightly perked up by a few colorful parks and flower displays, unusual for Soviet industrial cities and hailed as a great accomplishment by the local authorities. But it was what we saw of Rovno's 192,000 inhabitants—who are overwhelmingly Ukrainian and Russian, with only the occasional Pole left from the interwar years when the city belonged to Poland—that dissolved the sour aftertaste from our encounter with the police.

With the exception of its parks and flowers, Rovno is a typically bland Soviet provincial city, but to young people from neighboring farms it is the big time. Young men swaggered about in jeans bought on the black market for up to $300 a pair, while pretty young women with long blond hair strolled the streets, dropping into meeting places like the Youth Cafe for drink and chatter. In Shevchenko Park, dozens of young men played "blitz," a speeded-up chess game with stopwatches. At night, long lines formed at the town's largest movie theater, next to the Lenin statue. That weekend there was a special treat, a rare showing of an American movie that brought in everyone from miles around. It was a grade-B Hollywood production called *Orca—The Killer Whale*, starring Richard Harris, Charlotte Rampling, and Bo Derek. Leaving the theater after the whale had chomped his way through an entire fishing fleet and countless victims, I overheard a ruddy-faced man reassure his wife: "That's only a fairy tale about whales."

The local authorities also sought to interest young people in more serious matters. As Alex and I strolled through the hilly paths of Shevchenko Park, we came upon an outdoor stage with a banner that proclaimed Lenin's slogan "Art Belongs to the People." Three Komsomol leaders were dutifully spreading the party gospel; one of them, a woman standing on perilously high heels at the edge of the stage, was reading a turgid report on the Ukrainian Komsomol Congress to about twenty people languidly distributed over rows of green benches. A group of four young men rested for a moment on one bench and offered mock applause as

225

they left. Later an airplane pilot urged young people to devote themselves to their work rather than to such dubious activities as listening to "voices," a reference to the Voice of America and other foreign radio stations, or reading "religious materials." No one seemed to be listening. Nearby, policemen were leading away a teenager with a shirt open to his navel, who was thoroughly drunk. His sullen companions looked on as he was shoved into a waiting van; they then returned to the chess tables.

Drinking seemed to be the main form of recreation and it grew heavier as the afternoon and evening wore on. At the Youth Cafe on Peace Avenue, the left section that served only alcohol was packed with males, while the right section that also served cakes and ice cream was quieter and predominantly female. We plunged into the left section, and I struck up a conversation with students from a local teachers' college. They were intrigued by the chance to talk to an American and one of them asked: "Who lives better, the average American or the average Soviet citizen?" There was no hint of irony in his voice, just genuine curiosity.

When I responded the only way I could, he acknowledged that I was probably right but supplied the appropriate explanation. "Americans never went through a war or suffered the losses we did."

Over beers, they ruminated over the choice they faced after graduation: either to teach in a rural school for at least three years, returning to the primitive life they had fled, or to teach in a city school and in all likelihood be obliged to serve a year and a half in the army. "Which would you prefer?" I asked, expecting the first alternative to be the answer.

"Probably to go into the army. No one wants to live in the countryside—life is hard there." Even the possibility of being sent to Afghanistan made no difference. "If you have

226

to go, you have to go. Many of my friends from here have been there. It may be bad, but you do what you are told." Given that attitude, it was not hard to see why the government could continue to fight a war in Afghanistan but could not keep young people on the farm.

Rovno is more Soviet than Ukrainian, with few features in its architecture or general appearance to distinguish it from similar towns in other republics. Because Russians flocked to Rovno as it became a growing industrial center after World War II, many inhabitants have no memories of the interwar years when the city was Polish and bore the name Ròwne. But reminders exist: streets have names like Copernicus and Mickiewicz; another, called September 17, commemorates the day when Soviet troops "reunited the Ukrainian working class" by marching into eastern Poland as arranged by Stalin's secret pact with Hitler. To the distress of Rovno's few remaining Poles, the town's Roman Catholic churches have been converted into movie theaters and a museum. "There is no place to pray," an elderly Polish woman complained. But three Russian Orthodox churches remain open, and they were full on Sunday. Worshippers said that members of the Ukrainian Eastern rite Catholic Church, which was banned by Stalin, pray at the Orthodox churches while preserving their private allegiance to their faith.

Unlike in Vilnius, I rarely used my Polish in Rovno and only with Poles themselves, who welcomed me as a fellow countryman. When I explained my background and the fact that I grew up in the United States, that was brushed aside; in their eyes, I was a Pole, wherever my family emigrated. Even with Ukrainians whom I spoke to in Russian, I was sometimes asked if I was a Pole because they detected a familiar accent. This prompted discussions about Poland, and I found that current attitudes were colored by old prejudices. "An awful nation," a Ukrainian in his sixties said of the Poles, adding for good measure: "But the worst of all are the Jews." However, a Ukrainian woman of about the same age was sympathetic to the efforts of the Poles to liberalize their system. She complained that she had been branded a *kulak*, a rich peasant, when the Soviets took over, losing her small landholding that had assured her of a decent livelihood. "In the Polish days, if you worked hard you lived well, and if you didn't you did not live well," she said. "Now it is just the opposite: the people who live in dachas don't work at all and get everything."

More typical was the attitude expressed by another student, who boasted that the city is better supplied with food than other Russian provincial cities but blamed lengthening lines on the Poles: "We help them—you can't let them starve." At first, he loyally echoed official propaganda that "American imperialism" was to blame for the unrest in Poland. "If it were not for the Soviet Union, America would be in there." But when I suggested that Solidarity was concerned with the general failure of the economy and the corruption of the Polish ruling class, he shifted gears. "We have people like that here, too," he said, referring to the "red bourgeoisie." "In the early days of the Revolution, people were true Communists. Now, they join the party because it makes life comfortable for them."

Such conversations were usually brief and sometimes strained, since KGB agents made little effort to conceal their tailing of us as we wandered the streets. When we were walking down a quiet street of small houses to visit a Polish woman who had invited us for tea, two of our tails played a clumsy game of shadowing us from the other side of the street. As we turned left, one of them tumbled over a hedge he had not noticed, so intent was he on seeing exactly where we were headed. But that was less Keystone Kops than deliberate intimidation: when the tailing was that obvious, its purpose went beyond monitoring our movements; it was a message to everyone around that we were dangerous and it would be safer to stay away from us.

Still, we found people to be friendly, eager for a bit of contact with visitors from a different world. On our second visit to the Youth Cafe, this time to the right section that served sweets along with alcohol and attracted a mostly female crowd, a matronly waitress took a special interest in us. She winked as she went to unlock the door for more customers after closing time. "Decent girls don't come here, but they say they are thirsty so what can I do?"

We watched the procession of mostly young women, some in jeans and T-shirts, others in corduroy pant suits, but only talked briefly with two women at a neighboring table. When the cafe was really closing, our waitress reappeared. "Didn't you meet our girls?" she asked, distressed that we had been left alone. "Are you married?"

"Yes," I laughed.

"That shouldn't stop you from having some fun. It makes the time pass happily."

On our final day, the two students from the teachers' college we had talked to on our first night met us to continue our conversation. They were slightly nervous about being seen with us again, but they eagerly returned to the subject of their future plans, telling us what Rovno meant to them. They said that the chronic Soviet housing shortage meant that upon graduation they would probably have to live in a workers' dormitory or some other temporary accommodations for a long time before they could hope for their own apartments, but that did not bother them. "On the farm you have housing and food, but you work during the day on the collective and at night on your private plot. You make very little and you have nothing to do. Here," said one student, gesturing at the town, "you have everything."

We had not learned anything during our stay about the alleged accident at the nearby nuclear power plant, but neither Alex nor I felt disappointed. Instead, we had seen a slice of Soviet life that demonstrated one of the great strengths of the Soviet system: the ability to convince people that less is more. If an attitude exists that can be described as typically Soviet, it could be defined as the jeans mentality. No one in Rovno I had met, or few people anywhere, questioned why they should have to pay more than a month's salary for a pair of jeans; they were grateful if they had the opportunity to buy them at all. Similarly, the students from the teachers' college did not seriously question why life on the farms where they grew up continued to be so primitive or why their possibilities in Rovno for housing, entertainment, and everything else were as limited as they were; they were just happy to be in Rovno and not in the country. Thus, the system's failures were transformed into personal triumphs.

Christina never complained, but I knew she was nervous every time I left Moscow. She realized that if a provocation was to be staged, it was likely to take place on such trips. Earlier that spring on a trip to Kiev, ABC correspondent Anne Garrels had been attacked by KGB agents who had been tailing her. They grabbed her purse and, when she clung to the strap, they dragged her along the pavement. A Russian friend she was with who tried to protect her was roughed up. That proved to be the first step leading to her departure.

When Anne reported what had happened on the air and talked to other reporters, she was summoned to the Foreign Ministry and warned about spreading "anti-Soviet slander." She also was attacked in the Soviet press. Shortly afterward during an evening downpour, two drunken pedestrians stepped out from in front of a bus directly into the path of her car on Leninsky Prospekt; Anne could not stop in time and one of them was killed. The accident occurred next to an underpass all pedestrians were supposed to use, and witnesses testified that Anne was not to blame for what had happened. But the police kept the investigation open a long time, implicitly threatening that she might be charged with manslaughter. ABC succumbed to the pressure and pulled her out of Moscow.

Precisely because Anne was the only American television correspondent in Moscow who spoke Russian well, was knowledgeable about Soviet affairs, and had a broad range of contacts, the authorities had been eager to get rid of her. With her departure and David Satter's winding up of his tour a few months earlier, they had cause for satisfaction: there were two fewer "problem correspondents" to worry about.

A variety of factors eliminated most correspondents from that category. A lack of language skills ranked at the top of the list, but excessive caution was another. It seemed that the less a correspondent knew about Soviet society, the more prone he was to see himself as constantly threatened by sinister conspiracies. On a Foreign Ministry trip to Lvov, Jim Gallagher of the *Chicago Tribune* asked a wire-service reporter if he would like to accompany him on a visit to a woman who had contacted him in Moscow about a housing problem. The reporter reluctantly agreed, but he grew increasingly nervous when it became apparent they were being followed. "This is exactly the kind of situation I was always warned about," he said, citing his former bureau chief, who upon departing from Moscow after a long tour had boasted that the Foreign Ministry had found no fault with his performance. His warnings to his staff to avoid provocations had been so sweeping as to convince them that practically any departure from a guided Foreign Ministry tour was irresponsible and dangerous.

Some correspondents felt that only official sources should

be cultivated. That was the attitude of the correspondent from a major newspaper who early in my tour had dismissed dissidents as mentally unstable because of the enormous risks they took. Occasionally, such correspondents were rewarded and slipped a piece of real news from the Soviet officials they met with: early word on when the next Central Committee meeting would be held and the main item on the agenda, for example, which amounted to a minor scoop but would become self-evident anyway at a later date. That was a small price to pay to encourage the correspondent to keep coming back, to listen endlessly to discussions of "the Soviet viewpoint" on international issues, which amounted to a rephrasing of what they could have read in *Pravda*, and to avoid encounters with unofficial sources.

All this contributed to the isolation of a majority of the correspondents in a tightly circumscribed world consisting of the foreign community and a group of Soviet contacts made available by the government. Andrei Amalrik, the dissident writer who emigrated to the West in 1976 and later died in a car crash, once explained that no law obliges Western correspondents to lead such an artificial life, largely divorced from the reality of the world around them, but many do so because it is easier. He wrote: "There are clearly two choices: the correspondents can either seek contact of some kind with Russians, and hunt for some sort of information other than the official; or they can fully accept the status to which the Moscow authorities have tied them down with a firm or gentle hand. After seven years of continual contacts with foreign correspondents, I have formed the impression that the majority of them display a readiness to submit to these imposed conditions."

After a year in Moscow, I found no reason to contradict that conclusion. But I felt that the blame had to be shared by the headquarters of major news organizations that not only sent correspondents without proper preparation to Moscow but accepted and even welcomed the most predictable coverage of Soviet affairs. They seemed perfectly content with correspondents who spent their time on the "big stories" such as U.S.–Soviet relations and arms control while rarely if ever going out to do original reporting about Soviet life. Those stories had to be covered, but for the Moscow correspondent this often meant little more than summarizing and quoting speeches by Soviet officials and articles carried on the English-language Tass service. The Soviet authorities were also content with such reporting, even if it was critical of Kremlin policy. It was understood that such reports had to be filed. Similarly, the obligatory major dissident stories raised few eyebrows, since the authorities understood that no reporter could ignore them. What irked them were correspondents like Satter and Garrels who did not stick to the predictable, who tried to make contacts wherever and whenever they could with all kinds of Soviet citizens.

In making such contacts, a correspondent had to trust his instincts and not become paralyzed by fear. There were no set criteria. One new acquaintance I made and had taken an immediate liking to that spring was Boris. The son of a senior party official, he drank too much, knew a lot of shady characters, and irritated me by forgetting appointments and abruptly disappearing from sight, only to reappear badly hung over a few days or weeks later. But I enjoyed his company and my gut feeling was that I could rely on him not to be playing any sort of double game with me.

When Boris offered to introduce me to a black marketeer friend of his to see how that element of Soviet society lives, I agreed without hesitation, although with someone else I might have avoided such an encounter because of its possibilities as a setup. In one respect, the evening was less than

I had hoped for: the black market operator had been on a three-day binge when we went to see him and was incapable of holding a coherent conversation. He clung to his bottle and shouted orders at his girlfriend, who was as bleary-eyed as he was. Boris did not need much urging to keep him company as he continued drinking.

But the apartment spoke for itself. In the heart of old Moscow a short distance from the Kremlin, the black marketeer's modest three rooms in a distinctly unimpressive brown building were crammed full of cassettes and records, radios, cassette recorders, samovars, and icons. The cassettes and records ran from classical to jazz to rock; their street value was from $35 to $140 each. Along with the radios and cassette recorders, they represented an incredible fortune by Soviet standards, without even counting the value of the samovars and icons. As we left, Boris mumbled his apologies about how the visit had turned out, but I told him he was crazy to think I was disappointed.

By contrast to my instinctive trust of Boris, I felt immediately wary of Pavel, a self-proclaimed dissident from a provincial city who one day came to my office and right there detailed his alleged mistreatment by the authorities. I heard him out but offered no encouragement. Still, he contacted me several times in the next few days and insisted we meet again. We did, this time on the street, and he began speaking wildly of committing suicide unless he found a way of getting out of the country. I said I couldn't help him. He offered "to do anything" for me during his travels, which he said took him to various border areas closed to foreigners, adding that he could both report and take pictures. When I explained that my publication insisted on our doing our own reporting and that I could not use anything he might give me, he asked if I could put him in touch with someone at the U.S. embassy who could use his services. "You must know people there," he insisted. I ended the conversation, saying we had nothing more to talk about.

That incident, I suspected, was an indication, like the press reports about me and the harassment during my trips, that I was now at the top of the list of the "problem correspondents." As summer approached, there were other signals. Dima, the translator assigned to my office, suddenly quit after having worked more than a decade for *Newsweek*, saying he had been offered a better job as a book translator. His departure was no great loss because he did not do much work anyway, but I wondered what the real reason was. About the same time, Nick Daniloff of *U.S. News & World Report* called me aside after we were leaving a briefing at the American embassy. He told me that a Russian friend of his had been interrogated by the KGB recently and that my name had come up in the questioning; the agents had wanted to know whether Nick and I were friends. The implication was that Nick's own standing with the authorities could be tarnished if that were true.

I was preparing to leave with Christina and the kids for an early summer vacation in Dubrovnik, Yugoslavia, and looking forward to putting all this out of my mind when a member of the independent peace group called and asked to see me. Like most of his colleagues, he had undergone various interrogations and had been subjected to threats to stop his activities. As we sat at the table of a neighborhood cafe, he spelled out the details and said that my name had also come up in one of his interrogations. The KGB agent who had been in charge of the questioning had told him that he knew of his and the rest of the group's contacts with me, adding in a matter-of-fact tone: "Nagorski will be dealt with soon."

5

SUMMER

I returned from Dubrovnik recharged, refreshed, and re-laxed. My freedom to travel out of the Soviet Union rep-resented a vital difference between my life and the lives of my Soviet friends and the people I wrote about, no matter how involved I liked to think I was in my Soviet surround-ings. I did not suffer any guilt because of that freedom; there were too many reasons not to, even if they smacked of convenient rationalization. It was precisely because of that difference that so much hope is invested in a Western cor-respondent in Moscow.

On the most mundane level, when I traveled abroad I could bring back something unobtainable in the Soviet Union for a friend. It might be as simple an object as a Rubic's Cube, panty hose, or a pure wool scarf that would be much warmer than the scarves of synthetic fabrics available in Moscow; or it might be medicine that could make a differ-ence for someone's health. We were even asked to bring back hotel brochures and postcards, as one friend put it, "for my eyes to see on a picture what they will never really see." But the most valuable prerogative of a foreign correspondent, which accounts for most of the hope he inspires, is his freedom to write about anything he wants. The risks Soviet citizens run just to make contact with a Western reporter underscore the significance of his role. In Moscow, the work of a foreign correspondent has more of an impact than almost anywhere else in the world. What he does or fails to do matters because he directly affects people's lives. That accounts for the persistent sense of anxiety any correspondent feels who develops a network of Soviet contacts and friends; it also accounts for the heightened recognition, which falls just short of a sense of guilt, of his privileged existence.

Upon my return from Yugoslavia, I encountered the denouement of an earlier story that I had reported that reinforced those feelings: the plight of the divided families. Early in the spring, five Soviet citizens with husbands or wives in the West had made the rounds of correspondents to announce the formation of a "Divided Families' Group," warning that they would hold hunger strikes until they were given permission to emigrate. Their inability to join their spouses, they pointed out, directly violated the provisions in the Helsinki Accords on the unification of families. When I first met with them, they exuded youth and vitality, making it hard to imagine the likely consequences if they held fast to their grim pledges.

Some cases were clear-cut, involving Soviet citizens who had married foreign students or visitors and then were denied permission to leave with them; Yuri Balovlenkov, for example, was a former computer programmer who had married a nurse from Baltimore in 1978 who had given birth to a child he had never seen. Other cases were more complex, the result of tortuous emigration ordeals. Tatyana Lozansky had divorced her Jewish husband Edward so that he could emigrate to the United States six years earlier. She was not Jewish and had the added difficulty of being a daughter of a Soviet general, but the authorities had led her to believe that she and her young daughter would be allowed to emigrate. When no permission was forthcoming, she remarried Edward in a proxy ceremony that the Soviet government refused to recognize. She decided to join the hunger strike.

In May and June, the original hunger-strikers, joined by others in similar predicaments, had pushed the government into the same difficult choice it had faced with Sakharov earlier: whether to retreat or risk possible death in the full glare of the international publicity the strike had generated. Other correspondents and I regularly visited the hunger-strikers, while their spouses lobbied for them in the West. On one occasion, I was barred by the police, along with three colleagues, from entering Lozansky's apartment. It was a futile gesture. The press continued to send stories. Photographs of the emaciated young people were flashed around the globe.

The Soviets could hardly maintain that they were standing on principle by refusing the strikers' requests, since many other Soviet citizens married to foreigners had been granted permission to emigrate in the past. But the government, as a way of discouraging such marriages, was deliberately vague as to why some people were allowed to leave and others were not. Anyone marrying a foreigner could never know what his or her chances were.

The same seemingly arbitrary selection process determined the mixed results of the hunger strike. Lozansky, who in terms of Soviet law appeared to have one of the weakest cases, was abruptly allowed to leave after a thirty-two-day fast that reduced her to a mere eighty-eight pounds. When I returned to Moscow, Balovlenkov was starting a second hunger strike, after having fasted even longer than Tatyana the first time. In the end, he fasted for more than a hundred days, with one two-week interruption. His wife was allowed to return for a visit and finally convinced him to stop by telling him the deliberate lie that the authorities had relented; she could not bear to see him die. Of the ten people involved in the hunger strike, six were eventually permitted to go abroad—but Balovlenkov was not among them.

This tactic had the advantage of fracturing the unity of the group, consigning each person's battle to a private struggle. Under the strain, friendships dissolved and bitter recriminations followed. I had witnessed a similar splintering among several writers over a different issue: what attitude to take toward Yevgeny Kozlovsky, the novelist who had been arrested in December and subsequently denounced his own works and apparently talked about other dissident writers during his interrogations. Georgi Vladimov and his wife, Natasha, were enraged to the point of lashing out at friends who refused to condemn Kozlovsky as categorically as they did. Those writers argued that it was unfair to judge Kozlovsky without knowing what pressures he had been subjected to. I watched with sadness as the two factions denounced each other as traitors or tyrants. It also was difficult to stay clear of the fray because I had friends in both camps. As I had first discovered among the Soviet émigré community in California, personal relationships left little room for neutrality.

The other story I came back to was the final act to the Andropov-Chernenko succession battle over an issue I had become familiar with the previous summer: corruption in the Krasnodar region, which includes Sochi. In July, regional party boss Sergei Medunov, who had survived until then thanks to the personal protection of Brezhnev, was ousted. His departure marked the high point of Andropov's anti-corruption drive, which had the real aim of demonstrating that the former KGB chief was unstoppable and that it was dangerous to oppose him. He succeeded by toppling one of Brezhnev's most entrenched allies. No further proof was necessary that Brezhnev no longer had the strength to propel his favorite, Chernenko, into the position of heir apparent.

I was curious about the fate of Sochi's war veterans, who had been responsible for bringing Medunov's crimes to light. From sources in Moscow, I learned that Anatoly Churganov, one of the leaders of the veterans' group who had been arrested before my trip to Sochi, was still in jail and other members of the group continued to be persecuted. Andropov was getting maximum political mileage out of his anti-corruption drive, but he had no more use than Brezhnev for ordinary citizens who tried to protest official wrong-doing. Anti-corruption drives were fine so long as they were orchestrated by the authorities for their particular needs; private initiative in this field was no more welcome than in any other.

The only major uncertainty left in the leadership struggle was when Brezhnev would die, but I wanted to avoid getting stuck in Moscow for the indefinite duration of the death watch. I had come back from vacation determined to travel even more than I had, since each trip offered new insights into Soviet life. I wanted to go to the Central Asian republic of Tajikistan. I had plans to visit Riga, the capital of Latvia, the only Baltic republic I had not been to yet, and to return to Leningrad, which I had only visited once on a brief sight-seeing tour. I had discussed with a worker from Byelorussia the possibility of meeting him in his small village to get a look at rural life. In the coming winter, I hoped to make a long journey through Siberia. I also had other expeditions in mind, so I was impatient to get started.

My first priority was Tajikistan, where I hoped to assess the impact of the war across the border in Afghanistan. I had found it extremely difficult to learn about the Afghanistan conflict in Moscow or on my trips to other European Soviet cities. Whether in Moscow or elsewhere, I was struck by the contrast between the reactions to events in Poland and to those in Afghanistan. Whether sympathetic or antagonistic, people instinctively grasped what the Poles were up to and the fact that the fate of their experiment could have profound implications for their own country and its empire. Poland and the demands of Polish workers evoked visceral responses: people felt either threatened or hopeful. That was not the case with Afghanistan.

When the Kremlin decided to invade in 1979, ordinary citizens had little idea beyond official explanations as to why the action had been taken. Many accepted the government's rationale just as they had swallowed whole the explanation for the previous invasions of Hungary and Czechoslovakia. Dissent was limited to Sakharov's protest, for which he was sent into internal exile, and to a petition by a group of intellectuals from the Baltic states condemning the invasion. But what startled me most was the lack of interest when I questioned friends and acquaintances about the subject.

"Among intellectuals here, Afghanistan is in tenth place as a topic of conversation," an economist observed. "Poland is in first place." A prominent intellectual who had joined in previous protests tried to explain why he had remained silent on Afghanistan but would protest vigorously if his country invaded Poland. "I don't know anything about the situation there [in Afghanistan]. In Poland, I know the situation well."

That may have been an excuse for his silence, but it contained an element of truth. Afghanistan is farther away, both in geographical and in human terms, than Eastern Europe for most ethnic Russians. As an Asian country with an Asian people, it elicited little sympathy. Its recent political history and the Soviet Union's stakes there were in fact unknown to most Soviet citizens: the origins were too complex and the list of characters too long.

Even during the long reign of King Zaher Shah from 1933 to 1973, Afghanistan maintained its formal neutrality but allowed Soviet military and economic advisers. When Muhammad Daud served as prime minister from 1953 to 1963, Soviet involvement grew: Moscow sent large amounts of economic aid along with military assistance and advisers. After Daud was fired by the king in 1963, the United States was encouraged to provide aid to Afghanistan to balance the Soviet involvement. In 1973, Daud staged a coup and abolished the monarchy. But his pro-Soviet advisers gradually grew disenchanted with him once it became obvious that, contrary to expectations, he was intent on limiting Moscow's influence over his regime. As a result, the Kremlin orchestrated another coup in 1978, dumping Daud and replacing him with Nur Muhammad Taraki.

This set off the chain of events culminating in the Soviet invasion. The Taraki government's leftist policies spawned an increasingly effective resistance movement of fundamentalist Muslims, and the regime itself was split into feuding factions. Taraki was deposed and executed by Hafizullah Amin, who in turn was killed when Soviet troops were sent in to install Babrak Karmal as his successor. By that time, Moscow had given up entirely on trying to manage events from afar.

In an effort to justify the invasion to the outside world and to its own people, the Soviet Union maintained that it was merely extending a helping hand to a neighbor that was defending itself against "external counterrevolution." The nightly television news regularly showed visiting delegations from Kabul and Afghan students arriving at Soviet universities thanking Moscow for its assistance. The main outside power intervening in Afghanistan's internal affairs, it was said, was not the Soviet Union but the United States, which was held to blame for the Muslim insurgency. A new joke circulated among cynical Muscovites:

QUESTION: What is the least aggressive country in the world?

ANSWER: Afghanistan.

QUESTION: Why?

ANSWER: Because it does not interfere even in its own internal affairs.

QUESTION: What is the most aggressive country in the world?

ANSWER: The United States.

QUESTION: Why?

ANSWER: Because it interferes in the Soviet Union's internal affairs all over the world.

Moscow claimed it had responded to an Afghan government request for temporary assistance, conveniently disregarding the minor question of why Amin would have invited in the people who then shot him. As the guerrilla war intensified, that "temporary" assistance showed no signs of ending, despite continual assurances in the Soviet press that the situation was rapidly "normalizing." The exact role of Soviet troops was avoided in the press, with most articles mentioning only fighting between Afghan government units and the guerrillas. The Soviet public was kept deliberately in the dark about what their countrymen were doing, and casualties were a closely guarded secret.

Even so, none of this adequately explained the general indifference toward the war. When I recalled the trauma of the Vietnam era in the United States, I found it hard to believe that Soviet citizens could be so oblivious to what their soldiers were doing in Afghanistan simply because there was a virtual news blackout on the subject. I badgered one friend, a Moscow scientist, about this until he attempted to provide an answer. "It is not just the government's policy of deliberately creating a lack of information," he conceded. "People are too concerned with the problems of their own lives: life is too hard here to worry about Afghanistan. Also, the great mass of the Russian people are basically apolitical and frightened of political issues. Finally, the worst reason is that there is a heavy strain of great Russian chauvinism which leads some people to say: 'It's good we've grabbed Afghanistan; now let's grab Iran.' "

Even if he were right, did that mean the government had nothing to worry about? About 100,000 Soviet troops were serving in Afghanistan at any one time and then returning to tell about their experiences. By the most conservative Western estimates, nearly three years of fighting had resulted in about 5,000 dead and another 10,000 wounded, with Afghan guerrillas making far higher claims. While reports persisted that the Soviet Army was burying some of its dead at least temporarily in Afghanistan and sending the wounded off to remote hospitals for recuperation to minimize the psychological impact of their losses back home, burials had taken place within the Soviet Union itself. The fact that the coffins were sealed only heightened the horror stories circulating about what had happened to the victims. According to one account I heard of a burial in the trans-Carpathian region near the Czechoslovak border, an enraged father threatened the members of a burial detail with a crowbar and ordered the opening of his son's coffin. The frightened men obeyed, revealing a totally mutilated corpse. The mother became hysterical and had to be carried away.

Apocryphal or not, such stories indicated that the brutality of the war in Afghanistan had penetrated the consciousness of Soviet citizens. The Soviet press had never described atrocities committed against its own troops and only once during my stay acknowledged the death of a Soviet soldier, but it had on several occasions referred to the mutilation of the bodies of Afghan "patriots" murdered by the guerrillas. A reader of such accounts could easily surmise that the same fate may have awaited Soviet servicemen.

But this realization did not necessarily translate into opposition against the Soviet role. An engineer from Kiev, who disagreed with his government on other issues, summed up the feelings of many of his countrymen. "The Afghans are savages," he said with a shudder. There was not a shred of sympathy for their cause in that angry remark. Sometimes, too, there was willful disbelief. One friend recalled overhearing on a train a woman from Eastern Siberia talking loudly about several boys from her town who had been killed in Afghanistan. A woman from Moscow sitting next to her flatly declared that she did not believe her.

Bits and pieces of information about conditions in Afghanistan did get back to a portion of the population but never anything that formed a complete picture. One officer back from Afghanistan told his friends and relatives in Moscow of brutal methods employed by both sides: the torture of Soviet soldiers captured by the insurgents and Soviet helicopter gunships slaughtering guerrilla units whose only weapons were antiquated rifles. Other soldiers described the Soviet bombing and burning of villages and how even in Kabul they always had to walk in pairs or groups, since assassinations were common. Much of the countryside was completely in the hands of the guerrillas and highly dangerous for any Soviet units. Some Soviet returnees came home with new Japanese radios or other prized foreign items, the result of the barter trade that quickly sprang up when they encountered what to them seemed like fabulously supplied Afghan merchants. Sometimes, they recalled, they even traded their rations away.

But many returning soldiers were reluctant to draw attention to what they had gone through. "No one wants to come home and boast he was in Afghanistan," said one Muscovite. The reasons sounded similar to those of many Vietnam veterans. There may not be any protest movement in the Soviet Union, but few people were convinced that, at best, the Soviet involvement was anything more than the country's necessary but unpleasant duty.

On one of my trips outside of Moscow, I had met a Georgian from Perm, a city in the Urals that is closed to foreigners. The Georgian never revealed why he was living in Perm, but his refusal to discuss his job led me to believe that he was probably in some branch of the military or security services. When I asked him what people in Perm thought about Afghanistan, he became defensive but still provided an answer. "You are a correspondent and you can't ask such questions," he admonished me, adding that he suspected I might be an agent trying to "trap" him. "But no one thinks anything good about Afghanistan."

As usual, Misha, the social scientist, warned me not to jump to hasty conclusions from such encounters. Like many other Russians I talked to, he pointed out that, while enlisted men hated to go to Afghanistan, officers welcomed the opportunity. "It is good for careers and provides them with the combat experience they need," he said. As for the casualties, he claimed that the army deliberately selected a high percentage of rural youths for Afghanistan and tried to avoid sending enlisted men from cities such as Moscow and Leningrad. His voice took on a hardened tone. "The value of life is much lower in the countryside. A soldier dies and people toast him and get drunk." He added that fears of Soviet officials that the war might spark national resent-

ments among Muslims in Central Asian republics like Tajikistan had proven to be unfounded: all was quiet, and
there were no major problems on the home front for Moscow to worry about as it pursued its goals in Afghanistan.
I was about to see for myself whether that was true.

There was one aspect of traveling within the Soviet Union
I never relished: the internal Aeroflot flights. I was not bothered by the discomfort of narrow seats with little leg room
or the cabin service, which usually consisted of a bored
stewardess distributing plastic cups of a fizzy, sweet water,
but by the thoughts I could never quite banish about the
condition of the more essential maintenance services. Planes
on international routes were undoubtedly looked after carefully and those that serviced foreign tourists on such internal
flights as Moscow to Leningrad would be given special attention as well, but I had heard too many reports of crashes
on internal flights that went unacknowledged unless foreigners were among the victims. As Jim Gallagher of the
Chicago Tribune and I buckled in for our 2:30 A.M. flight
to Dushanbe, Tajikistan's capital, my mind registered and
promptly tried to dismiss the fact that we were the only two
foreigners on board.

The other passengers, who looked exhausted but calm,
appeared to have no such thoughts. The Tajiks and Uzbeks,
with their light brown faces and eyes whose shape revealed
their geographical origin in the lands between the major
Asian civilizations and Europe, were returning in all likelihood from profitable business trips to Moscow. It is a common practice for Central Asian merchants to fly into the
Soviet capital loaded with fruit—melons, grapes, peaches—
or flowers. Muscovites are always willing to pay extravagant
prices for both, either to supplement their diet or to honor
the Russian custom of bringing flowers to a hostess, their

children's teachers, and any bureaucrat whose favor is sought. With the proceeds, the merchants easily cover their airfare and pocket a tidy profit besides. This was one form of private enterprise that the authorities rarely cracked down on.

Jim and I also had reason to feel happy to be on our way, whatever my misgivings about the flight. While the post-Helsinki procedures for travel within the Soviet Union had greatly facilitated the work of foreign correspondents, all of us felt a period of uncertainty just before embarking on trips. After filing our travel plans two working days in advance as required, we knew that Yevgeny Petrusevich, the Foreign Ministry official who handled such duties for American correspondents, might call at any moment to inform us that permission had been denied. Given our sensitive destination so close to the Afghanistan border, we had half expected either a last-minute call from Petrusevich, telling us the trip was off because of an "overbooked" hotel, or to be told at the airport that something was wrong with the tickets. None of our fears materialized. Instead, we landed in Dushanbe right on schedule.

Dushanbe has none of the rich history of ancient cities like Samarkand or Bukhara. There are no monuments to past glory, traces of the famed fourteenth-century Mongol conqueror Tamerlane, or old mosques. It was only a village before the Soviet era, and its elevation to the status of capital of the republic after the Revolution brought with it the architecture and city planning of the period. The center features three-story squat, brown buildings, broad avenues, and pleasant parks. A few taller concrete boxy buildings like the Dushanbe Hotel where we stayed provided a touch of more recent Soviet construction, but the city still retained a slightly anachronistic air, making its architectural sterility somehow less noticeable or offensive.

Despite its short history, Dushanbe remains unmistakably Central Asian. A short walk down main streets away from the city center to narrow, unpaved lanes lined with whitewashed mud houses covered by corrugated iron roofs plunges one into the midst of traditional life. Muezzins called the faithful to prayer at neatly maintained mosques with similar whitewashed walls but elaborate wooden roofs, windows, and doors opening on stone courtyards. Bearded Muslim elders clutching walking sticks sat on benches in the shade of the houses, while Tajik girls in colorful printed dresses and boys in regular pants and shirts but wearing the ubiquitous *tubeteyka*, a square embroidered cotton cap, scurried about. Women of all ages were less visible on the streets than men.

The city's main bazaars were a far cry from markets in Russian cities because of the abundance of fresh produce and the mixture of Tajik, Uzbek, and even Korean merchants selling their melons, peaches, and *kimchi*, pickled cabbage. That last group's presence was the result of Stalin's order in 1937 to deport tens of thousands of ethnic Koreans from the Soviet Far East to Central Asia; he was convinced they could not be trusted to remain loyal to Moscow in the looming conflict with neighboring Japan. There was also an abundance of young faces, a reflection of the region's baby boom. Birthrates in Central Asia are more than triple those in the Russian republic, which accounts for the changing demography of the country. About 43 million Soviet citizens are Muslims, comprising 16.7 percent of the population. By the turn of the century, Muslims may number 64 million, pushing their share of the total population to more than 20 percent.

The most striking difference between Dushanbe and its Russian provincial counterparts was a sense of greater personal self-assurance among its people, less fear and trepidation. Outsiders were greeted with traditional hospitality instead of suspicion, especially if they were not Russians. When I was walking through the bazaar, two teenage boys gestured toward my camera and indicated that I should take their picture. I responded in Russian, and one of the teenagers looked me up and down questioningly.

"Where are you from?"

"America."

His face lit up. "Go ahead."

That instinctive trust and openness toward outsiders like Jim and me, coupled with genuine curiosity about the world beyond their borders, made it easy for us to talk to the local inhabitants. Most Tajiks are of peasant stock, a people used to tending sheep and growing cotton, and straightforward in their speech and manners. I was relieved to discover that their Russian was as rough as mine, freeing me of the self-consciousness I sometimes felt with Russians about my frequent grammatical errors. Everyone spoke adequate Russian, but it was clearly a second language.

The subject we had come to explore—the impact of the war in Afghanistan—was raised by one of the first people we met, a twenty-one-year-old Tajik soldier on leave from duty in Mongolia. Without our having even mentioned the war, he pointed out that, unlike one of his brothers, he counted himself lucky that he had escaped service in Afghanistan.

"Mongolia is better—it's less dangerous. Many people from here have died in Afghanistan. Mothers get telegrams that their sons have been killed and their bodies are being returned. From my village, one boy's body came back with his nose and ears cut off." He shook his head slowly. "No one wants war, no one wants to die."

That set the tone for conversations Jim and I had with dozens of draft-age young men, all of whom confirmed that throughout Tajikistan the Afghanistan war was an immediate and emotional issue. Tajiks live on both sides of the border and, because of their proximity and ethnic ties, Moscow had sent a proportionally greater number of them to fight than other Soviet nationalities. In the original invasion, Central Asians were used in large numbers. Later, the Soviet military command realized that this may not have been wise; some of the Muslim recruits apparently demonstrated more sympathy for the Afghans than for their Russian officers, and this led to the formation of a more balanced ethnic mix in the Soviet occupation force. But it was evident from my encounters in Dushanbe that Tajikistan still provided an unusually large percentage of the manpower, especially considering the Tajiks' standing as a small minority within the general Soviet population or even among Soviet Muslims. Tajikistan has 4.2 million inhabitants, with ethnic Tajiks comprising 59 percent of that total and the rest divided among Uzbeks, Russians, and other nationalities.

The Tajiks were kept as much in the dark about the toll of the war as the rest of their countrymen, but they had considerable direct evidence of what it was costing them. We walked to the edge of the Tajik district of mud houses and narrow streets, where one of Dushanbe's four cemeteries spread over a rugged hill with Muslim burial mounds protruding everywhere. A caretaker didn't hesitate to explain that some of the new graves were those of soldiers killed in Afghanistan; he said that one or two bodies a month were received from Afghanistan, always arriving in sealed zinc coffins. "We are not allowed to open them because a leg, nose, or ears are often missing." A young worker claimed that he knew from friends at the city's main hospital that as many as ten bodies a day had been arriving until recently. "Now there are not as many, but they are still coming," he said.

Whatever the real number of casualties, they were deeply

unsettling for the draft-age young men we talked to. Most accepted Moscow's justification for the war but our conversations revealed an underlying mixture of confusion, frustration, and, above all, fear. The Tajiks, in particular, had no illusions about the determination of the *basmachi*, the local term applied to the generations of Central Asian guerrillas who first fought against Russian domination in the nineteenth century, then against the imposition of Soviet rule in the 1920s, and who are now resisting the Soviet occupation of Afghanistan. "The war will take at least ten years—they'll fight to the last man," predicted a seventeen-year-old Tajik who had a brother serving in Afghanistan. Others estimated that the resistance would go on even longer, perhaps even indefinitely.

The Soviet authorities call the *basmachi* "counterrevolutionaries," even attaching the label to them when they had fought czarist Russia. According to that neat historical sleight-of-hand, the Czarist Army was a "civilizing" force that, while it may have represented a reactionary regime, was still more progressive than the feudal Muslim warlords it confronted. Such logic may satisfy Soviet historians seeking to prove that Marxist ideology and Russian imperialist drives, past and present, happily coincide to promote revolutionary ideals, but it is hardly convincing to many Muslims. There is a shared cultural heritage that links the Tajiks and the Afghan resistance fighters that cannot be totally obliterated—and this explains why many Tajiks are not eager to fight. "People here do not like to go to Afghanistan because they are Muslims, too," said a teenager from a village outside of Dushanbe.

Despite Soviet rule, Islam remains strong in Tajikistan. The mullah at one Dushanbe mosque told me that 5,000 worshippers attend Friday services and that "the government does not bother us if we do not bother them." At another mosque, I watched about seventy men dressed in brightly colored turbans or *tubeteykas* gather for one of the five daily prayer services. "Everyone here is a believer," said one of the elderly worshippers. That may be less true of young Tajiks, but even those who considered themselves particularly "modern" in their outlook acknowledged the influence of their Muslim heritage.

"A Tajik proverb is that the foundation of everything is God," a young Communist loyalist told me. When I asked if she believed that, she smiled. "No, I believe the foundation is man—but who created man?"

The Tajiks were not the only ones concerned about the war. Young Russians and members of other nationalities I met were equally nervous about the prospects of serving in Afghanistan. Because they lived in Tajikistan, they felt the same heightened sense of danger that they could be sent across the border. Jim and I spent a long afternoon at Komsomol Lake, a popular cooling-off spot for Dushanbe's residents on steamy summer days, where we met three young Russians whose lives all had been touched by the war. One had a brother serving in Afghanistan. Another had a father engaged in "ideological work" in Kabul. The third was cramming for college entrance examinations in the hope that he would thereby avoid the draft.

All three expressed support for the official Soviet line that this was a "defensive" war. "If we were not there, you Americans would put in missiles to use against us," argued the would-be college student. But he admitted his nervousness over his exams and what would happen if he failed. "I could be dead in two years," he said and took a long swig of his beer. Another of the young men quietly told the story of a friend who had recently lost a brother in Afghanistan. "He, of course, was stunned: he cried for days. It took him some time to accept that this was necessary for his country."

We also met two students at the lake who were in a distinctly cheerier mood: they were Afghans, for whom enrolling along with several hundred of their countrymen in Dushanbe's colleges meant avoiding the draft and the war. A broad-shouldered, muscular eighteen-year-old entering a five-year physical education college was happy to acknowledge his good fortune. "In Afghanistan, there is shooting and killing. Here, it's nice and quiet. I don't intend to go back until it's quiet there, too." But some local residents claimed that their arrival, along with the return of Tajik soldiers completing their tours in Afghanistan, was the reason for an increased flow of *anasha*, marijuana, to Tajikistan.

If that somewhat echoed American experiences during the Vietnam era, so did the signs of the beginning of a generation gap. Older Tajiks did not seem nearly as worried about the war as draft-age men, and they were more inclined to accept Moscow's assurances that the situation was being "normalized." At one mosque, a bearded elder declared: "Now it's quieter than before in Afghanistan." But in Dushanbe even the older generation, both Tajik and Russian, appeared far more aware of the ramifications of the war than Soviet citizens elsewhere. For example, a middle-aged Russian technician conceded that the Soviet occupation had severely damaged U.S.–Soviet relations, an observation that loyal Russians in other parts of the country would never offer. He lowered his voice so his colleagues would not overhear him. "They tell us many things, but we understand that relations started to deteriorate after Afghanistan."

The young people themselves were not united in their outlook. Two Russians we met who were about to be drafted appeared convinced that if they were sent to Afghanistan they would be fighting a noble fight. One Tajik said he would be eager to serve in Afghanistan "to go abroad, to see something new." But he was twenty-two and had already been in the army, so his attitude might have been shaped by the knowledge that he would not be going anyway.

At the bazaar, an eighteen-year-old Muslim declared his admiration for Iranian-style Islamic fundamentalism and the policies of the Ayatollah Khomeini, which he had learned about from monitoring BBC broadcasts. "The Soviet Union stole Afghanistan. It had no right to do that. If I were in Afghanistan, I'd join the *basmachi*." Did his friends share his views? "No, I'm the only one," he disdainfully replied. "Everyone else is a Communist."

The young people we talked to were further split by racial tensions. One group of Russians and a smattering of other "white" nationalities spoke with concern and sensitivity about the war and questioned us intensely about the West, wanting to know everything about pop music and what life was like for their peers in the United States. But when the conversation touched on their relations with Tajiks of their own age, their faces clouded over and their eyes glowered. Fights between the two groups were common, they claimed, and only a week before an outdoor disco party had turned into a brawl in which at least three people were knifed.

It was not hard to believe, since as we walked Dushanbe's streets with them they angrily and loudly described all Tajiks as thieves and a *duratsky narod*, a stupid people. As they assumed a taunting, threatening demeanor that amounted to an open challenge to a fight, they literally brushed shoulders with individual Tajiks passing us from the other direction. They never lowered their voices or slowed the stream of epithets. The quiet, dark streets suddenly seemed charged with electricity. I began to feel extremely uncomfortable and welcomed the first chance to part company with them. I had no desire to find myself in the midst of a racial brawl.

But for all the tensions and divisions, the vast majority

of young men we spoke to, both Tajik and Russian, shared a similar attitude toward Afghanistan. They had bought the government's explanations for the war but wanted to avoid personal involvement, if at all possible. "If we have to go, we will," said a Russian student without enthusiasm. "We are there because the Afghans asked for our help—at least that is what they teach us. I don't know anything else." His voice trailed off, betraying just a hint of a doubt. It was precisely such doubts that led me to suspect that a war without end might gradually erode the loyalty of the young men along the border. Such a development might still have little effect on Moscow's determination to subdue the Afghan rebels, and while there was nothing to indicate that diminished loyalty would foster disobedience, we had found that at least in this corner of the Soviet Union Afghanistan was not an invisible war: it was hitting painfully home.

The Soviet authorities did not appreciate seeing such observations in print, and our meetings and open discussions with young people began to prompt the inevitable efforts at intimidation. When I was changing film at the Dushanbe bazaar, a group of teenage boys crowded around me to ask about my camera and telephoto lens. That expanded into a lively discussion, with the boys eagerly querying me about living conditions in America and other matters that reflected both a high level of curiosity and the fact that many of them had gleaned whatever they could from Soviet publications with an eye to sorting out facts from propaganda. They obviously had other sources of information as well: one boy asked me a question I could not begin to answer about the New York Islanders. As we discussed unemployment in the United States, an older Tajik who had been lingering nearby walked up and addressed me loudly enough for everyone to hear: "So they give you permission to give lectures here."

The warning was clear: we were being observed with

256

disapproval. I did not want to get any of the boys in trouble and indicated that I would go, but one of them dismissed the man with a wave of the hand. "We have many such old people here." His friends nodded and some looked angry at being interrupted, but the warning produced the desired effect. By silent agreement, the group broke up.

At a rooftop canteen where we were having shish kebabs and beer with several Russians just out of high school, an Uzbek in his late twenties insisted on pulling up a chair and joining us. Our conversation revolved around the usual questions about life in the West—music, cars, living standards—with the addition of a brief reference to the draft. One student asked whether what he had heard on a foreign radio station was true: that the United States had no draft. Disbelief showed on everybody's faces when I answered that it was, but the Uzbek appeared genuinely upset. He began trying to discredit anything we said about life in the West to the point that it soon became apparent that he was "on duty," not just spending a night on the town. The young Russians got the hint and decided that it was best to leave.

Our trip was to have included two towns outside of Dushanbe, Nurek and Kurgan Tyube, both of which are listed as open to foreigners. Nurek is the site of a major hydroelectric station and Intourist, the Soviet travel agency, offered an excursion that we took. But when we hired a taxi on our own to take us to Kurgan Tyube, a town south of Dushanbe closer to the Afghanistan border, we never reached our destination.

We drove for more than an hour over a dusty road that took us through bleak, arid terrain. The day was stifling hot and it was a toss-up whether the car was cooler with the windows down or up. We began wondering whether the trip was worth the effort even before we were stopped at a police checkpoint at the outskirts of town. A policeman exchanged a few words in Tajik with our driver and demanded to see written permission to enter Kurgan Tyube. Sounding to myself somewhat like a broken record, I launched into my familiar discourse on the Helsinki Accords, pointing out that correspondents no longer needed to travel with written permission. We had included our travel plans for Kurgan Tyube in our notification to the Foreign Ministry, which was all we were required to do. But as in Rovno such arguments got us nowhere.

The policeman ignored everything I said, his face impassive as he kept repeating his demand for written permission. The existence of the Helsinki Accords was never acknowledged; the rules, as far as he was concerned, were defined right there. I knew what was coming next even before he ordered us to wait in the car. Sitting down on a chair on the side of the road, he laboriously wrote out a protocol, which he presented to us to sign: it was an admission that we had tried to enter Kurgan Tyube without permission. We refused. Two frightened "witnesses" were rounded up; the document was shoved in front of them, and they hastily signed it without reading it. The policeman who had stopped us ordered a colleague to ride back in the taxi with us to make sure that we were deposited in our hotel in Dushanbe. He at least got a free ride, with us picking up the tab for our round-trip to nowhere.

Upon our return, the hotel manager, a short plump Russian woman, was waiting for us in the lobby. She talked with the policeman and summoned us to her office. We had no right to travel on our own instead of with Intourist, she declared. That was nonsense, we replied; correspondents have no obligation to take Intourist tours and we had only taken the one to Nurek because it happened to be convenient. We had presented ourselves to the hotel as regular tourists, she continued. We reminded her that we had filed for our trip as journalists and had given our papers when registering at the hotel, which had "journalist" written all over them.

She shifted gears. Her face took on the solemn expression of a high school principal addressing students caught smoking in the bathroom. "I was not going to bring this up, but I have received many complaints from citizens in this city about your activities." Placing her hand on a hefty stack of papers that were the alleged complaints, she charged us with spreading anti-Soviet propaganda, asking questions about "the Soviet invasion of Afghanistan," and telling young men that the Soviet Union should abolish the draft. My confirmation that the United States had no draft, it appeared, was tantamount to advocating draft resistance.

We denied the charges of spreading anti-Soviet propaganda but freely admitted we had asked people questions about Afghanistan. Asking questions, we pointed out, was what our jobs were all about. Besides, Jim concluded, what business was it of a hotel manager to lecture us on our journalistic responsibilities? Our voices sounded as testy as hers, and the exchange bore as much resemblance to a discussion as Brezhnev's and Reagan's transatlantic pronouncements on arms control.

As we returned to our rooms, I felt weary and discouraged by the persistent harassment, its reemergence on each trip in somewhat different form. But I was satisfied with the results of our reporting in Tajikistan. It had left me with a strengthened conviction that this was exactly the kind of reporting that I wanted to keep doing. We were scheduled to take the next morning's flight back to Moscow, but I had no regrets that we were not staying longer. As on previous expeditions, the possibilities of uninhibited contacts had diminished after the first couple of days. There was little doubt that following our episode on the outskirts of Kurgan Tyube and the confrontation at the hotel, they would have completely disappeared.

The call came on a Friday afternoon, the day after my return from Dushanbe. "Mr. Nagorski, this is Petrusevich. Please come to the Foreign Ministry on Monday at eleven o'clock."
"Whose office should I go to?" I asked, fishing for a hint of what was in store.
"Just come. You will be met."
I had no doubts about the general meaning of such an "invitation": it could only signal the government's intention either to warn me officially or to expel me. Knowing that the pretext might be the Kurgan Tyube incident, I dug out my records of the notification I had given the Foreign Ministry before taking my Tajikistan trip. I had two telexes on file about the trip because we had changed our travel plans once; both included Kurgan Tyube. I called Jim to see if he had been summoned also; he hadn't. That meant that more than Kurgan Tyube would be on the agenda.
Throughout the weekend, I kept wondering what might be in store at the Monday meeting, but I believed expulsion was unlikely. A sudden end of our tour in Moscow was not something I wanted to contemplate seriously, and I assured Christina that there was no cause for alarm. I had never received an official reprimand, I told her, so undoubtedly that was what I could expect on Monday. Tony Barbieri, the *Baltimore Sun* correspondent who had recently received such a warning, and other colleagues assured me that expulsion without a preliminary warning was highly improbable. I was only too happy to agree.
At 10 o'clock on Monday morning, Petrusevich called to suggest that I bring a translator. I neither had one nor needed one, I replied, and he did not press the point. But it

was a worrisome sign indicating that the meeting would be quite formal.

As promised, Petrusevich met me when I arrived promptly an hour later at the press department. A tall, thin man with thinning blond hair, he wore his usual gray suit and looked every bit the junior official anxious for the opportunity to grab the next rung of the ladder. He did not say a word as he led me to the office of a portly superior I had never met, who rose and greeted me with just the right touch of bureaucratic affability to convey the message that he was the bearer of bad tidings. He introduced himself as Yuri Viktorov, deputy director of the press department, and noted apologetically that we had not met before because he did not normally meet journalists himself. That suggested he was the KGB's man in the department since the in-house monitor was unlikely to advertise his presence to outsiders. But he explained that the reason he was handling this meeting was that director Chernyakov was on vacation.

We sat down in two heavy armchairs, with Petrusevich perched on a wooden chair opposite us. "I have a statement to read to you," Viktorov said with a slight grimace, which was meant to indicate that he was merely playing the role of the messenger. He paused and looked down at a paper in his lap. "Your accreditation as *Newsweek*'s correspondent in Moscow has been lifted."

Viktorov stopped, shrugged his shoulders as if to say he was not to blame, and leaned back in his armchair, adding nothing more. I asked him to repeat what he had said to make sure I had caught the exact wording in Russian and had not misunderstood anything, although I knew very well that I had not. He did so.

"What is the reason for this?"

As Viktorov once again ostentatiously looked down at the paper, my mind rushed ahead, anticipating concocted charges of spying or black marketeering—something dramatic and, no matter how groundless, unpleasant to deny.

"Impermissible methods of journalistic activities," Viktorov read.

Now, I was truly puzzled. "What does that mean?"

Viktorov resumed his reading. On my trip to Vologda, I had impersonated the deputy editor of *Krasny Sever* by presenting his calling card as my own. In Rovno, I had presented myself as a "tourist from the Polish People's Republic." Finally, on my most recent trip, I had violated "the existing rules for the movement of foreigners to penetrate into the city of Kurgan Tyube."

I was taken aback, but somewhere in my churning emotions I also felt a trace of relief that the charges were so patently ludicrous. I told Viktorov that all of them were untrue and I wanted to categorically deny them.

Viktorov indicated I could do so, but he turned his palms up in a gesture that left no doubt that my response would not change anything.

For the record, I proceeded. I explained the circumstances of my giving a policeman in Vologda the local deputy editor's card so that he could verify that I was a foreign correspondent on a working visit, which the policeman had initially refused to believe. I recounted how in Rovno I had been asked about my Polish background because I spoke Polish and my Russian had an obvious Polish accent, and how I had explained that I was an American of Polish descent. As for the charge that I had violated travel regulations in Tajikistan, I pulled out my telexes spelling out my plans to go to Kurgan Tyube.

But Viktorov waved away the telexes with the air of someone bored with this childish quibbling over what may or may not have actually happened. "We have other information," he said, indicating the case was closed. My family and I would have a "reasonable amount of time" to pack up and leave, although as of that moment I was no longer an accredited correspondent. He refused to be more specific. As we stood up, he noted that it was unfortunate we had to meet under such circumstances.

The entire session had lasted slightly less than twenty minutes. At 11:23 A.M., just as I was driving home to inform Christina and the children, the English-language service of Tass was transmitting the news of my expulsion, using the exact language Viktorov had read. It concluded: "Soviet citizens and institutions in respect of which Nagorsky [sic] used such methods of collecting information, expressed indignation at his conduct and asked the press department of the Foreign Ministry of the U.S.S.R. to prevent Nagorsky from continuing his activities which are incompatible with the status of foreign journalists."

At 11:30 two officers from the U.S. embassy were summoned to be informed of what had happened. The timing of the Tass item ensured that, unlike several previous cases, there would be no possibility of private negotiations to attempt to have the expulsion order retracted. If the decision had not already been publicized, there would have been an opportunity for Washington to indicate what kind of response there would be if the Soviets insisted on my expulsion. The Soviets had decided that in my case, whatever the American reaction, it would not matter. They wanted me out.

The rest of Monday was so busy it left me little time to indulge or examine my own feelings. There was Christina's shock and dismay, whatever her forebodings had been; Eva's and Sonia's initial stunned disbelief and incomprehension, although they were both old enough to understand why my writing had angered the Soviet authorities; the nonstop phone calls and visits from other correspondents, all of whom were unfailingly supportive and sympathetic, who had to interview me for their stories; my first consultations with my editors in New York, who reacted quickly and gracefully with public and private statements of their complete support for me and rejection of the Soviet charges; and talks with officials at the American embassy, who were preparing their own reports on the case so that Washington could consider its response.

As I reviewed the formal reasons for my expulsion with my editors, other journalists, and the embassy, I realized that I had failed to make a number of points in my refutation of the charges to Viktorov. The articles by *Krasny Sever* deputy editor Shorokhov—whom Viktorov and the Tass account had incorrectly identified as "Shorin"—described David Satter and me as clearly identifiable as foreigners "since they spoke with such a heavy accent, had a foreign camera and clothing." They also mentioned that we introduced ourselves to local citizens "as American journalists." David called from Chicago the same day I was expelled and told Christina something I had completely forgotten: "For Christ's sake, I handed the card of the deputy editor to the policeman, not Andy. So let them charge me with the crime." All that aside, why had it taken from October to August to bring up the charges against me related to this trip?

As for the Kurgan Tyube excursion, why hadn't Jim Gallagher been accused of violating travel regulations if we had done something wrong, since we were both barred from entering the town? The only case for which I had no documentation disproving the charges involved my alleged impersonation of a Polish tourist in Rovno; but I knew from Rovno's residents that the city had not had any visitors from Poland since the birth of Solidarity.

None of this would have made any difference, however.

Viktorov's indifference to my response and the immediate release of the Tass item made that clear. When American Ambassador Arthur Hartman protested the action personally to Yuri Chernyakov, the director of the press department at first maintained that the government could not tolerate correspondents "breaking laws." When Hartman angrily responded that *Newsweek* did not send a correspondent over to break laws, Chernyakov jettisoned the formal charges and argued that the government could not tolerate correspondents spreading "malicious rumors" and "insulting the leadership." At last, he was getting closer to the truth.

From the Kremlin's perspective, those two characterizations could apply to any number of my stories: my reports on attitudes toward Poland in Lithuania and the fears about Afghanistan in Tajikistan, food shortages in Vologda, corruption in Sochi and the privileges of the ruling class such as the special film screenings at Goskino, how Andropov was using the anti-corruption drive to position himself for the succession, and the "Brezhnev's Final Days" cover story. Russian friends and Western diplomats offered their own theories on what had most angered the authorities, but there was little doubt that it was not a single story but a cumulative list of grievances that had resulted in their decision. That decision, I learned from people familiar with the process, must ultimately have been approved by Andropov himself. As the country's chief ideologist at the time, he would have had to sign the order expelling an American correspondent.

In the days that followed, I heard additional explanations for what had happened. The contacts I had, Christina's and my Polish backgrounds, and the fact that Christina spoke Russian well and had her own circle of Russian friends were all mentioned. Lyona, the bearded poet to whom I felt closer than anyone else, offered his analysis. "They obviously were looking you over carefully for a long time, reading everything you filed, and they decided that there was a personal touch to your approach they did not like. You knew too many people and traveled too much." He paused. "Your problem was that you were something of a romantic Pole, who believed that what you did and wrote here could make a difference, that it could have some effect on people in this system. They didn't like that."

Lyona returned to the same theme of his earlier discussions about the Polish situation. "If you made any mistake, it was to underestimate the system's self-defense mechanisms, which have been carefully refined for more than sixty-five years. You ran into the wall of this system and the ceiling came down on you."

Another friend explained that "the frivolous nature" of the formal charges against me was intentional. "It is such nonsense that there is no way to seriously reply." When I asked him why I had never received an official warning, he reminded me of what the KGB agent had told the member of the independent peace group about dealing with me soon, confident that his comment would get back to me. "That was your warning. When you went to Dushanbe, you showed them that you had no intention of changing your behavior. They also knew that an official warning would not work in your case."

As I was leaving my office a couple of days after my Foreign Ministry encounter, a chubby young policeman who was on duty in the guard booth outside called me over. We had never before exchanged more than a nod.

"So you're leaving I hear. Why were you thrown out?"

"Evidently they did not like my stories."

He moved closer as if he were about to share something confidential. "You know, your mistake was that you did not calculate carefully how to work here," he said. I should have followed the example of a correspondent of a major British newspaper who had recently left. "He was here for years. He took *Krokodil* [a Soviet satirical weekly] and wrote his stories from there and never had any trouble. You can find so much critical material in our press. You can even quote the big man's speeches, which are full of criticism, and write an article everyone in the West will be happy with."

He hesitated, but just for a moment. "You had so many Russians coming to see you. I know. Of course it's your business if you meet such people, but you must have written about what they told you and that was not necessary. You could have had equally good material from our press."

Suddenly, he asked, "Will they now allow you to go to other socialist countries?"

"I don't know."

"Well, our Foreign Ministry will of course inform them about you, so it will make things difficult for you." Avuncular again, he added: "But don't be downcast. I'm sure you'll be able to return here as a tourist someday."

I had little hope of that and, knowing just how final my departure would be, I decided to stretch it out as long as seemed safely possible. Since I had lost my accreditation, I could no longer file stories but I wanted time to say good-bye to as many friends as possible and to collect my final impressions. The complex Soviet customs requirements provided a good excuse for not leaving immediately. In addition, Christina and the kids took a shortened planned trip to Poland. Christina had already packed huge amounts of food and clothing to deliver to her family there, including about a dozen pairs of Polish-made shoes, sandals, and slippers available in Moscow stores but impossible to get in her hometown of Czestochowa. The Foreign Ministry, which had immediately canceled our multiple-entry visas, had granted her a single reentry permit that had to be used right away. In all, I stayed in Moscow another two and a half weeks after my Monday morning visit to the Foreign Ministry.

During that period, I was able to observe the broader impact of my expulsion. Aside from being an act directed personally at me, it sent a message to my friends and other Russians about the risks of maintaining contacts with foreign correspondents. The wife of one acquaintance reacted to the news by immediately burning personal letters and every Western magazine in their apartment; she was sure the KGB would be knocking on their door any minute. A close friend, who had taken basic precautions when meeting with us before but never betrayed any fear about our visits to her apartment, looked pale and distressed when I appeared at the door. She disconnected the phone in the hall, closed the door to the living room, and spoke softly in a nervous voice. "You can't be sure of anything now," she said.

Lyona, too, confessed to fears about the implications of our friendship for his future. "I don't think they will use it against me while you are still here and attention in the West is focused on your case. But sometime in the future, when my case has acquired a certain critical mass as yours did, this will appear as one point in the long list of charges against me."

But still people sought me out, even many whom I did not know well or would not have approached myself for fear that such contact might compromise them. Many wrote emotional notes that they affixed to small gifts. "To Andy, one of the victorious in the battle for freedom and justice," one read. A voice I barely recognized on the phone assured me that "it is a great honor to be kicked out of this country." I received gestures of support from both expected and unexpected sources. It was difficult to respond adequately.

Slowly I realized what it was that I would miss most about Moscow: the human bonds forged so strongly because they entailed such risks.

My expulsion also was a warning to other correspondents, a not-so-subtle reminder that they too could suffer the same fate. I assumed good correspondents had not let that prospect affect their behavior before and would not now, just as I assumed that anyone who did practice self-censorship would not admit it. But a West German correspondent, who once had hinted to me that he dabbled in the black market where earnings can be quadrupled by a mere exchange of currency, said, "I have to be careful. I couldn't afford to do the things you did and to be kicked out. I make too much money here."

That correspondent was a member of a minority of journalists who made themselves vulnerable to Soviet blackmail by enriching themselves on the black market. The authorities usually left such reporters alone since they could be trusted never to write anything that would seriously anger the Kremlin. These correspondents were the least likely to be affected by my expulsion; that measure was intended to deepen the fears of honest correspondents who already were reluctant to undertake any reporting that drew them out of the isolation of their foreigners' world.

Two days after my accreditation had been lifted, the State Department announced the expulsion of Melor Sturua, *Izvestia*'s correspondent in Washington. Russian friends who had been feeling depressed about my expulsion suddenly perked up: it was a stronger response than they had anticipated. Washington had picked the best-known Soviet correspondent in the United States, sending a message of its own. But that provided only scant comfort in the midst of our prolonged partings, often over several sessions, with our closest circle of friends. The mood inevitably turned reflective and somber, returning to the nature of the political system they would still have to live with long after I was gone.

The keynote of those final conversations was a pessimism so profound that it could only be understood by people trapped in that system. When I expressed my doubts about the likelihood of an improvement once Brezhnev died, one friend looked at me with a bemused expression. "That is a Western way of looking at the problem. The Russian way is to hope that it won't get worse." A member of the immediate family of a senior Soviet leader who was a household name dismissed the Bolshevik Revolution as an unmitigated disaster for mankind in a single, offhand remark: "To think how much money and resources could have been devoted to improving life rather than to arms if it weren't for 1917."

At a dinner with a professor who had never engaged in public dissent and a younger man who had, it was the professor who was the most distressed by my expulsion. "I somehow feel ashamed by all this, by their behavior, that they could do this."

The dissident shrugged. "Why should you feel ashamed? If you feel ashamed for this, why not feel ashamed for Hungary, Czechoslovakia, and Poland? The list goes on and on, and we could spend our whole lives feeling ashamed."

The professor took a long drag on his cigarette and looked at me. "We grow up in this system and, because we are part of it, we begin to feel shame from the day we are born. It is as if somehow I were responsible for what this country does. But I know there's an increasingly popular logic expressed here even by people who are quite intelligent. It goes like this: there are some things people are not responsible for such as who their parents are and the country in which they are born."

"And the next step in that reasoning," the dissident interjected, "is that because you are not responsible for the system you are born into, it is only normal that you should follow the rules of the system, the rules of the game."

The professor leaned back and nodded; he was no less convinced of his argument about the rationalizations people made despite its predictability. We were back to the question of the degree and nature of the Soviet citizen's acceptance of the system.

The next afternoon, Lyona turned to the same subject unprompted. "The problem here is not just the system but the people. In Poland the system may be bad but you sense that people are striving to overcome it. Here, the people themselves resemble the system."

Perhaps. But that answer didn't explain the countless individual battles against that system that I had witnessed or even the disenchantment and cynicism of a Lyona or a Misha, people completely within the system or hanging on to a place on its periphery. It did not explain the survival of a basic humanity in individuals, whatever has been done in their name.

As I was packing, I received a phone call from Tbilisi, the Georgian capital. "Do you remember me? I met your daughter and you at the airport." I did; we both had been waiting for arriving flights. He had urged me to come to Tbilisi to visit him, and I promised to try to take him up on his offer. "Why haven't you visited us?"

I explained that I was suddenly forced to leave the Soviet Union, making it clear that it was not of my own volition. "Whenever you return to the Soviet Union," he immediately responded, "please be sure to look us up. We will be waiting for you." I thanked him, feeling better than I had since walking out of the Foreign Ministry.

But there was little to encourage me to believe that the system could not continue to prevail over that fragile, yet tenacious humanity or even that widespread disenchantment with the system's failings would be translated into effective pressure for liberalization. Whatever belief was left in the efficacy of such pressures, punctuated by self-sacrifice, belonged to a minuscule, dwindling minority. Pessimism and fatalism had become the prevailing wisdom; it fed on itself and infected everyone. The Solidarity period in Poland had briefly broken through some of that pessimism, showing at least some Soviet citizens that change was possible. That was why Moscow was so intent on suppressing Solidarity. If change were ever to come from within the Soviet system, people first would have to see change work on the edges of that system in Eastern Europe, where the legacy of oppression does not weigh quite as heavily and nationalism fuels the struggle for human rights. Soviet citizens needed a glimmer of hope elsewhere before they could see any hope for themselves, which would be the first step in shedding their fear. But nothing was more frightening for the political elite than the idea that the people could lose that fear and begin questioning their power and privileges.

I found little evidence of hope in my last couple of days in Moscow. Shortly after the order was given to expel me, KGB agents had seized eighty-six of Sergei Batovrin's antiwar paintings that he had planned to exhibit in the apartment of another member of the independent peace group. Batovrin himself was thrown into a mental hospital. When I went to see his wife and mother just before my departure, they reported that he was being held in a ward with the most severely mentally deranged cases and being fed heavy doses of depressant drugs. "Despite all this repression, the members of this group will continue our work for peace," his wife, Natasha, maintained. I could do nothing but wish them luck and wonder to myself how much longer the group could survive.

Galina Barats was in tears when I met her on the street. "I'm sorry I cannot control myself. My husband has disappeared and no one will tell me where he is." Vasily, the former army officer turned Pentecostal activist, had gone to Rovno a few days earlier to visit a small group of fundamentalist Christians there. As he was preparing to leave, KGB agents had beaten him with brass knuckles at the airport and dragged him off in front of numerous witnesses. Galina was convinced he had been taken to another psychiatric hospital and was frantic at the lack of news. All her efforts to contact the authorities in Rovno had met with failure; they denied any knowledge of her husband's whereabouts.

Galina's only hope was to get Western correspondents to write about Vasily, putting the government on notice that his disappearance would not go unnoticed. It was a plea reporters heard often, and it reminded me of a somewhat different encounter a month earlier. A heavyset, middle-aged man in shabby clothes had sought me out to tell his story. He described himself as half Jewish with relatives abroad and claimed that he had been demoted at work and had not been able to get a telephone installed at home because he was considered politically suspect. I prepared myself for the request that I write an article about him, already formulating my explanation of why I could not do so, but he surprised me. "All this may seem quite banal to you. I am no one important and I realize an American publication like yours will not write about me because there are too many other things to write about. But I want to be known—I wanted you to meet me." He looked toward a bus that was approaching, indicating that he would catch it at the last minute to throw off anyone tailing him as a result of our meeting. He added, "People who are not known can disappear in this country without a trace."

Vasily Barats was not unknown—the episode before Billy Graham's arrival had put him briefly in the news and he had met other correspondents—but Galina had not yet managed to convince anyone to write about his recent disappearance. "Help me, I don't know where to turn," she pleaded, unnecessarily apologizing for calling me so close to my departure. She had attempted to contact one of the American news agencies to inform them of what had happened, but the phone was handed to the official Soviet translator because the reporter on duty did not speak Russian. Aghast, she had hung up. I promised to do what I could.

Close friends like Vladimir and Anna Feltsman were the hardest to say good-bye to. During a final evening together, they told us what should have been wonderful news: Anna was pregnant. But Vladimir's joy was tempered by his recognition that their decision to start a family in Moscow rather than abroad as they had originally hoped amounted to a tacit admission of their dashed hopes. He had given us a record of a Chopin concert he had recorded before applying to emigrate, and I had put it on the record player. Vladimir turned to me after a difficult passage. "I'm not sure I could play it that way anymore." At thirty and without an audience since they had asked to leave, he was acutely conscious of time slipping away and his dwindling chances of achieving his aim of relaunching his career in the West.

The invitations from New York, Paris, and London still arrived, but he could not accept them. In June, he had been invited for a concert at Lincoln Center's Avery Fisher Hall, which had been turned into a benefit on his behalf. Vladimir appreciated these and other efforts by artists in the West to pressure the Soviet government to allow him to emigrate—but he was increasingly pessimistic. "The protests are like cannons going off into the air. They make a noise and then drop into the sea somewhere and sink without a trace." As we parted, neither Christina nor I could think of anything to say to contradict him.

With only a few days left, I decided to explore sights I had never seen before. I found myself walking unfamiliar streets. A group of people I passed recommended that I keep walking to reach a market farther away. Following their directions, I came to a narrow path that led down a hill to the market, but I realized that the only way back out was on a special rope tow for pedestrians. I lined up for the rope tow and handed 50 kopecks to the man collecting the fare, but with a sarcastic grin he rejected my coin saying that it was fake. I looked, and in fact it was smaller than the normal 50-kopeck coin. I pulled out a ruble note and gave it to him, which he took but still refused to let me through, claiming that it was also counterfeit. I was now extremely nervous, sensing a setup to compromise me before my departure. Desperately, I looked around for another way out of the market and three men pointed out a different path leading to buildings higher up. I hesitated, wondering if this too might be a provocation. As I vacillated between meekly staying put and trying to escape, I awoke, the emotions the dream had inspired still coursing through my system.

My final days in Moscow when I was officially no longer a correspondent, but still essentially living the life I had led before, brought emotions to the surface that had lain dormant or been suppressed. On a rational level, I knew that the authorities probably would be happy to have me fade quietly from the scene, but I could not completely banish thoughts of a last-minute provocation, some attempt to justify their actions more effectively than they had. The predictable but nonetheless irritating increase in surveillance of me only reinforced my suspicions.

The day after my visit to the Foreign Ministry, Christina

walked over with a Russian couple to my office. When they approached the entrance, a policeman was guarding it instead of standing as he usually did in a guard booth in the parking lot. "Where are you going?" he demanded, blocking their way. Christina, whom he had not recognized at first, turned on him, giving vent to an anger that must have been at the boiling point without her even knowing it. When he realized his mistake, he ordered the Russian couple to show their documents. "Oh, no," Christina said. "You claim to be here to protect us from thieves and you have no right to check the documents of my friends." I opened the door and, seeing what was happening, found myself furiously lecturing him also. He backed off.

On another occasion, I was sharing a bottle of champagne with two Russian friends at a restaurant when a waitress came over. She quietly advised us to lower our voices because two men were making inquiries about us. Any irritation I felt at our watchdogs was more than canceled out by what I was convinced was the genuinely unprompted, unusual act of goodwill by the waitress.

I felt particularly tense during the several days when Christina and the children were in Poland. Although the Foreign Ministry had approved the trip and issued reentry visas, I was anxious for them to return safely; a feeling of uncertainty about what might happen on the border kept me on edge until I saw them waving from the train as they pulled into the station in Moscow. The only event of note during their border crossing had been the behavior of the Soviet customs official. She had asked Christina if she was carrying "any literature," obviously with Solidarity material in mind. Christina, who this time had been especially careful not to have anything that might create problems, told her that she had no Polish publications with her.

"Do you have any fruit?" the woman asked.

"Fruit?"

"Yes, fruit."

"Yes, I have some apples for the children."

The customs inspector demanded that Christina show them to her. She then proceeded to cut two of them into pieces, checking to make sure that they had not been hollowed out and used for smuggling anything subversive.

Getting our household effects through customs in Moscow proved to be a lengthier task. Even under normal circumstances, leaving Moscow with all one's possessions intact can be difficult. Soviet regulations include such provisions as the listing of any book that was published before 1975 and obtaining permission from the Ministry of Culture before it can be taken out. It makes no difference what kind of book it is, where it was published, or that the owner had brought it in with him to Moscow from abroad; without the ministry's approval, it cannot be sent out of the country. Rules governing art and jewelry are even more strict: anything that a foreigner cannot prove he brought with him into the country cannot be shipped out. We had been thoroughly briefed on all this before coming to Moscow and we made sure that we listed and photographed any pictures we brought in, registering them with the Ministry of Culture. But foreigners who did not know of the rules ahead of time or who lost their documentation experienced distressing surprises: they could not get their jewelry or their own collections of art objects, even when obviously of foreign origin, out of the country.

We had tried to anticipate everything, since we had a good idea that the customs officials would not be in a friendly mood when it came time to check our shipment. I had already used other channels to dispatch my complete set of notebooks, which contained everything I had recorded about our daily Moscow experiences. We came armed with long

277

lists of books and paintings bearing the Ministry of Culture's stamp of approval. But from the moment Christina and I arrived at the customs warehouse on the outskirts of Moscow, it was apparent that we were going to be singled out for special attention. As the truck with our belongings pulled up to an unloading dock, Christina overheard an official in a blue shirt instruct a subordinate: "Check them carefully. He's the correspondent who did not conduct himself properly."

For five hours, a team of customs inspectors that varied in size from three to seven people ordered the movers to open up all the boxes and they rummaged through everything—photo albums, slides, clothing, and kitchen utensils. We had no furniture because the Moscow apartment was furnished by *Newsweek*. When they unwrapped our pictures, they found one that was not on the ministry list: it was a cheap sketch of Sonia drawn by a streetside artist in Rome, which we had framed because it was a good likeness. When we explained what it was, the customs inspector looked doubtful and summoned a representative from the Culture Ministry. She questioned us at length as if we were trying to smuggle out a great painting, commenting on the quality of colors. When I offered to show her a photo of Sonia, she reluctantly agreed to allow us to take it.

Going through the pockets of Christina's packed coats, one of the inspectors found loose change amounting to less than a ruble. "It is forbidden to take Soviet currency," he said triumphantly. He kept looking and found a Polish 50-zloty note, the equivalent of about 50 cents. "Foreign currency," he added with satisfaction. I laughed and, once he realized that there was nothing more, the inspector abandoned what had looked like a promising opportunity to charge us with currency smuggling.

Throughout the whole exercise, I helped repack the boxes

but resolutely avoided any discussions with the customs officials that I knew would only lead to argument. I was determined to wait the process out without showing any signs of impatience. But Christina's temperament is different: she could not resist asking why all this was necessary or responding to the chief inspector's unsolicited discourse on the need for foreign correspondents in Moscow to display the proper objectivity "as our correspondents do in America." She fenced with him on and off for several hours, while I stood silently by. As the inspection was drawing to a close and it was clear that they could not come up with anything incriminating, the chief inspector turned to Christina with an appraising air. "You speak Russian much too well for a correspondent's wife who's been here only fourteen months." It was not a compliment but an accusation.

At the airport, the customs check on our baggage was surprisingly perfunctory. The authorities must have realized that they were not going to catch us with anything that might provide them with additional ammunition. My major practical preoccupation was getting our nervous collie cleared and in her cage for the flight, and to ensure that there were no last-minute surprises. Galina Barats and two other Russian friends had come to see us off, despite my advice to them and other friends who had thought of making the trip to the airport not to do so. There was nothing to be gained and considerable risk in associating themselves that closely with us. The news agencies had written stories about Vasily's disappearance, but Galina still had no idea where her husband was. She pressed five carnations into Christina's hands. "Thank you for everything—and I beg you, don't let people over there forget about us here."

The departure itself was a blur of last-minute hugs, waves, and maneuvering ourselves and the children through passport control, where our one-way exit card that we received

279

after I had surrendered my press card was taken away. As we slumped into our seats aboard the Alitalia flight, Christina and I felt overcome by total exhaustion. It was more mental than physical, although we had slept little in the last two weeks. There had been too many tearful embraces and partings, whose pain was sharpened by the knowledge that in most cases there was little chance that we would ever see each other again. We were bound for a world most of our Russian friends would never see and leaving their world that had banished us. Our departure only reminded the Russians we knew, who in their relations with us had sought both friendship and the establishment of contact with that world outside, of their isolation. For those who had once believed that such contacts were destined to steadily increase, my expulsion was only one more piece of evidence that this was more illusion than reality.

Our plane raced down the runway in preparation for the flight to Rome, my next assignment, which I knew I was lucky to get. But I felt no joy at takeoff. My thoughts were in Moscow, on my jumbled impressions and emotions that all amounted to a numb feeling of loss. That sensation was intensified by the more acute distress of our friends. As I looked back at a Moscow already enveloped in the darkness of early evening, one parting remained most vivid in my memory. I was walking a couple we had known well part of the way home after they had already said good-bye to Christina. They both had what were considered good jobs and neither could be described as a dissident, but they moved in Moscow's artistic and literary circles, which had been steadily thinned out by emigration and arrests. The woman was trying not to cry, but her eyes were red when she turned to me. "For you this is an unpleasantness, an interruption of your work here and the rupturing of some friendships. For us, it is yet another permanent loss of a human contact, another in a growing list of losses that isolates us all the more."

Her husband added as we shook hands: "Now you've had a taste of them deciding your fate for you. It happens to us all the time: they decide where you can work, who your friends are, what your future will be. You can now write from first-hand experience what this is all about."

That was the least a correspondent could do, I decided, as he bid such friends and Moscow a reluctant farewell.

Epilogue

Less than a month after our departure, direct dial international telephone service to and from the Soviet Union was cut off for "technical reasons," and the remaining members of the Helsinki group for monitoring compliance with the 1975 agreements formally disbanded. The editor who had predicted that I would be in Moscow for the succession was almost right—and then some: had I been able to complete my tour as originally planned, I would have reported on two leadership changes and just missed a third one. Brezhnev died in November and Andropov took over. The new leader's quick physical collapse gave Chernenko and his supporters the opportunity to regroup and take power when Andropov died in February 1984, in effect giving the Brezhnev era a new lease on life. But Chernenko's tenure was even shorter than Andropov's; his death in March 1985 resulted in the ascension of Mikhail Gorbachev, who had probably been Andropov's original choice as his successor. Those events need no explanation here. Instead, what follows is a rundown on what has happened to some of the people mentioned in this book:

- GALINA BARATS continued to campaign on behalf of her husband, and shortly after our departure she learned that he had been arrested. In March 1983, Vasily was convicted of anti-Soviet agitation and anti-government propaganda and sentenced to five years in a prison camp. According to reports reaching the West in late 1984, he has had two heart attacks since he began serving that sentence. Galina herself disappeared and dissident sources reported in July 1983 that she also had been convicted of anti-Soviet agitation and sentenced to six years in a labor camp and another three years of internal exile.

- BILLY GRAHAM apparently learned nothing from his visit to Moscow, and neither did many of his fellow American clergymen. In June 1984, 266 American church leaders took a two-week tour of the Soviet Union sponsored by the National Council of Churches. The visitors' reactions were similar to Graham's: they professed themselves "impressed" by the number of people they saw attending church services, they proclaimed their commitment to world peace, and they studiously avoided bringing up the issue of persecution of believers for fear of offending their Soviet hosts. The parallels to the Graham visit did not end there: when two believers at a service in Moscow's Baptist church held up a banner proclaiming "This is a persecuted church," plainclothesmen forced them out of the hall, resulting in a scuffle in which several people were knocked to the floor. The American visitors were irritated by the two protesters, not by their treatment. According to *The New York Times* account, tour leader Bruce Rigdon of the McCormick Theological Seminary in Chicago said afterward: "They were asked to leave and they were conducted out by members of the congregation. We believe they are free. I understand that in the United States a situation like this would have been handled by the police." Graham himself ignored a similar protest in a Leningrad Baptist church when he returned for his "second coming" in September 1984, a twelve-day tour of four Soviet cities. He once again declared it was "wonderful" that so many churches were open and praised the extent of religious freedom he found.

• SERGEI BATOVRIN, the peace activist, was released from the psychiatric hospital after one month's confinement, but the harassment of him and other members of the group continued in the form of interrogations, arrests, and efforts to prevent contact between members of the group and Western correspondents or representatives of Western peace movements. In May 1983, Sergei was suddenly told he and his family could emigrate—and it was made clear that if he refused he would face arrest. He now lives in New York, where he continues to lobby for his group's cause, especially for the twenty-eight people affiliated with the group who, as of this writing, are in prison serving sentences ranging from three to seventeen years. Like other political prisoners, they have been increasingly subjected to physical torture. In a letter smuggled out of the labor camp in Kazakhstan where he is being held, group member Aleksandr Shatravka described repeated beatings, prisoners being forced to stand without hats and coats for hours in the cold, and his own sense of desperation that drove him to try to commit suicide by stabbing himself in the side.

Despite such persecution, the peace movement has continued to attract supporters. According to Batovrin, there are now nine groups and about 2,000 people involved. He reported that there have been several attempts to collect signatures on petitions or to hold demonstrations, inevitably resulting in arrests before much could be done. "Our group has had a wide impact on young people," Batovrin told me in November 1984, on a visit to Rome, where he was seeking greater support from Western peace groups. After initially finding many Western peace activists reluctant to help on the ground that human-rights violations are "not so important because the primary cause is peace," Batovrin has been able to mobilize more expressions of concern for the Soviet activists. "Some Western groups now agree that peace and human rights are inseparable, and they are supporting our imprisoned group members," he said. "But you won't see peace rallies in support of Aleksandr Shatravka. For Western peace groups, the ordeal of someone like Shatravka is like an eruption of a volcano on the moon: they can try to imagine it, but they will never understand it."

- VLADIMIR AND ANNA FELTSMAN are still in Moscow, with no sign that the authorities are about to permit them to leave. Their son, Daniel, was born in February 1983. Jewish emigration from the Soviet Union, which peaked at 51,000 in 1979, continues to drop. In 1984, it fell below the 1,000 mark for the first time since 1970. Testifying before the United Nations Human Rights Committee in Geneva in November 1984, Soviet Foreign Ministry official Dmitri Bykov announced that the reunification of Jewish families had been "completed."

- NIKOLAI AND NADEZHDA PANKOV, the two former projectionists at Goskino, the Soviet state film organization, who revealed the information about the moviegoing habits of the Soviet elite, were both committed to a mental hospital in the Moscow region in March 1984. After David Satter wrote in the *Wall Street Journal* about their confinement, they were released in May. In March 1985 they were suddenly allowed to emigrate.

- GEORGI VLADIMOV, the acclaimed author and Amnesty International activist in Moscow, was subjected to more interrogations in the months after our departure. He was told to submit a letter renouncing his "anti-Soviet" activities and naming his contacts; he refused. He wrote a letter to Andropov in January 1983, asking for permission to accept an invitation to teach at a West German university. Although he knew that he would probably not be allowed to return, he said this was for his wife Natasha's sake, who also had been subjected to interrogations. Permission was granted and, after they left, Vladimov was stripped of his citizenship.

• LEONID BORODIN, the Russian nationalist writer whose arrest Vladimov had discussed with me with such concern, was sentenced in May 1983 to ten years in labor camps and five years of internal exile for "anti-Soviet agitation and propaganda."

• ANDREI SAKHAROV staged another hunger strike in May 1984, this time to protest the government's refusal to allow his wife, Yelena Bonner, to seek medical treatment abroad. His fate and that of Bonner, who joined him in the hunger strike, once again became a focus of major international concern. But the outside world never learned how the hunger strike ended, since the Soviet authorities were more effective than on the previous occasion in preventing the Sakharovs from letting friends know what had happened. To cut Sakharov off completely, Bonner herself was reportedly sentenced to five years of internal exile for slandering the Soviet state, thereby also confining her to Gorky. From the Kremlin's perspective, this was an excellent solution. Given the blackout on news of the Sakharovs, they soon dropped out of the headlines in the Western press and protests against their treatment rapidly diminished.

• ROY MEDVEDEV, the iconoclastic Marxist historian who for years had met openly with Western correspondents to discuss political developments in the Soviet Union, was issued an official warning about his "anti-Soviet activities" and "scribblings" in January 1983. In February 1984, after Chernenko succeeded Andropov, policemen were stationed outside his apartment building to bar entry to all foreigners.

• ANATOLY KORYAGIN, the psychiatrist who was arrested for his role in exposing the Soviet practice of confining dissidents to psychiatric hospitals, has been repeatedly beaten in Chistopol Prison, according to reports reaching the West in 1983 and 1984. He also was said to be suffering from severe protein deficiency, caused in part by numerous hunger strikes staged in order to be allowed the family visits he is theoretically entitled to by law. In February 1983, the Soviet Union resigned from the World Psychiatric Association rather than fight the growing pressures for its expulsion because of its misuse of psychiatry for political purposes.

• ALEKSEI NIKITIN, the mine engineer who had protested safety conditions and was diagnosed as sane by Koryagin after he was repeatedly committed to mental institutions, died of stomach cancer in early 1984 at the age of forty-seven. He had been released from his latest confinement in a mental hospital only weeks before his death when the authorities realized the end was near.

• YURI LYUBIMOV, the popular director of Moscow's Taganka Theater that had staged artistically and politically daring productions, now lives in the West. After years of fighting battles with the Soviet authorities about the theater's activities, Lyubimov became increasingly frustrated by their decisions to ban three productions, including further performances of the tribute to balladeer Vladimir Vysotsky after the one show I had seen. While he was in London directing *Crime and Punishment* in September 1983, he publicly demanded that the government give him assurances that the restrictions on the Taganka be lifted before he would return to Moscow. A Soviet embassy official responded by warning him that "the crime had been committed and the punishment will follow." In February 1984, he lost his job at the Taganka and was expelled from the Communist Party. "Their dream was finally realized and they destroyed the theater," he told me in an interview in Florence in April 1984, where he was directing *Rigoletto*.

Lyubimov spoke bitterly of the exiling, emigration, or defection of the Soviet Union's most gifted artists—writers, musicians, dancers—describing it as "a national tragedy, the spiritual impoverishment of the nation." But he expressed guarded hope that the current policies, which amounted to a "gradual and unswerving return to Stalinism," would be reversed. "Even in the party and at the top there are people who understand this is a pernicious policy and that the country is losing prestige and authority," he said. "You cannot construct everything only on tanks, threats, and the methods of force. . . . I am far from alone in this view."

I asked him if that meant he was an optimist. His reply made me feel like I was back in Moscow. "There's the aphorism: a pessimist is a well-informed optimist."

My five seasons in the Soviet Union made me a pessimist— but as defined by that aphorism. The optimist still resides within; he was reinforced by contacts with those cited above and the many friends we left behind in Moscow who cannot be named here.

As the policeman near my office had predicted, my expulsion from Moscow did more than just bar me from continuing my reporting within the Soviet Union itself. In June 1983, I was denied a Polish visa to cover Pope John Paul II's trip to his homeland, despite the fact that I had regularly traveled with the pope on all his foreign trips since coming to Rome. When *Newsweek*'s foreign editor asked for an explanation, Polish government spokesman Jerzy Urban suggested that I should "warm up" my relations with the Russians. Subsequently, I was allowed to visit Poland privately, but not as a journalist.

In the Soviet press, my case has been presented on several occasions as an example of the sinister designs of Western correspondents. The definitive article, reprinted in slightly different form as late as March 1984, was written by political commentator Yuri Kornilov in *Izvestia*'s weekly supplement *Nedelya* a month after my departure from Moscow. It began:

> Do you remember the well-known fable by Krylov about the pig who wangles her way into the Lord's manor? Although she found herself in a luxurious and beautiful place, neither the house nor its inhabitants interested her in the slightest. True to her ways, the pig immediately set off for the back yard to wallow in litter and swim in mud! When she was asked was it not true that the house in which she spent some time was praised for its riches, she grunted in answer:

> > "Well, truly, they speak nonsense,
> > I didn't notice any riches at all:
> > It was only manure and filth;
> > But, it seems, not sparing my snout,
> > I dug up there
> > The whole back yard."

> This story involuntarily comes to mind when leafing through the American magazine *Newsweek* in which A. Nagorski publishes his impressions about the U.S.S.R. [Nagorski] spent more than a year in our country as an

accredited correspondent for *Newsweek*, but when reading his compositions the impression is created that he never saw Moscow and didn't know Soviet life, but instead [he] rehashed absurd fantasies and moldy anti-Soviet "sensations."

Kornilov went on to repeat the charges that I had impersonated both a Soviet journalist and a Polish tourist, adding that I was busy "photographing garbage dumps and conducting anti-Soviet conversations." He concluded with the suggestion that I was lucky to have been only expelled.

Across the ocean they love to cite, in particular, the Helsinki agreements. . . . In them, there is no hint of the right of a journalist to appear with false identification papers to pass himself off as someone else, in short to resort to measures which are judged and prosecuted everywhere, in all countries. Such methods have nothing in common with the free exchange of information or with the maintenance of contacts in the interests of bringing people closer together. The Helsinki Final Act foresees the development of information in the interests of the rapprochement of peoples but not the dissemination of disinformation and slander. . . . Thus, no matter from what side you approach the "Nagorski affair" he looks unattractive, highly unattractive as does the journal he represents.

As I am completing this epilogue, Rome has been blanketed by its first snowfall in fourteen years, reminding me of my one winter in Moscow. I take this as a good omen, perhaps a sign from friends I may never see again. Like them, I would like to believe that the elements will one day see fit to recognize the torment and the courage of the Russian soul.

291